Verse by Verse Commentary on the Book of

1 KINGS

Enduring Word Commentary Series
By David Guzik

The grass withers, the flower fades,
but the word of our God stands forever.
Isaiah 40:8

Commentary on 1 Kings

Copyright ©2018 by David Guzik

Printed in the United States of America
or in the United Kingdom

Print Edition ISBN: 987-1-939466-40-2

Enduring Word

5662 Calle Real #184

Goleta, CA 93117

Electronic Mail: ewm@enduringword.com

Internet Home Page: www.enduringword.com

Contents

1 Kings 1 - Solomon Is Made King

The Books of 1 and 2 Kings were originally joined in one book. We don't know who the human author of this book was; Jewish traditions say it was Jeremiah and it may very well be so. Wiseman gives a good summary of the Books of 1 and 2 Kings: "The narrative covers almost five hundred years from the initiation to the eclipse of their kingship. It is the story of the rise and fall of kingdoms, of high promise and abject failure, of tragedy and yet of hope."

A. Adonijah's bid for the throne.

1. (1-4) King David's weak condition.

Now King David was old, advanced in years; and they put covers on him, but he could not get warm. Therefore his servants said to him, "Let a young woman, a virgin, be sought for our Lord the king, and let her stand before the king, and let her care for him; and let her lie in your bosom, that our Lord the king may be warm." So they sought for a lovely young woman throughout all the territory of Israel, and found Abishag the Shunammite, and brought her to the king. The young woman was very lovely; and she cared for the king, and served him; but the king did not know her.

a. **King David was old, advanced in years**: This was the twilight of a glorious reign. David was now so old that he could not even keep himself warm, much less rule the nation.

i. David was about 70 at this time. He seems even older than his years; but for David, it wasn't just the years - it was the mileage. He seemed to live the lives of four or five men in his lifetime.

b. **Let her lie in your bosom, that our Lord the king may be warm**: This sounds strange - perhaps even immoral - to us, but this was proper of David to allow. This did not bring a moral cloud over the last days of David's life.

i. It was proper because it was *a recognized medical treatment* in the ancient world, mentioned by the ancient Greek doctor Galen. When Josephus described this in his *Antiquities of the Jews*, he said that this was a medical treatment and he called the **servants** of 1 Kings 1:2 "physicians."

ii. It was proper because David almost certainly *made this young woman his concubine*. While it was unwise for David to take more than one wife, it was not at that time illegal or specifically prohibited by God. Later, Adonijah would condemn himself to death by asking for Abishag as a wife. His request would only be so outrageous if Abishag had belonged to David as a concubine.

iii. Therefore they chose someone eligible for marriage or concubinage (**a virgin**), and **a lovely young woman**. "Whose beauty might engage his affections, and refresh his spirits, and invite him to those embraces which might communicate some of her natural heat to him, as was designed" (Poole).

c. **Abishag the Shunammite**: From ancient times, many have wanted to associate this beautiful young woman with the *Shulamite* addressed in the Song of Solomon (Song of Solomon 6:13 and throughout).

i. "According to the theory, as she ministered to David, she became romantically involved with his son Solomon and was later the subject of his love poem." (Dilday)

ii. Yet we must say that this is at best conjecture – and *Shumen* is not the same as *Shulam*. "*Shunem*, the modern Solem, lay eleven kilometers southeast of Nazareth and five kilometers north of Jezreel in Issachar territory, and was visited by Elijah (2 Kings 4:8). There is no need to identify Abishag with the Shulammite of Song of Solomon 6:13" (Wiseman).

d. **She cared for the king**: This scene of David's diminished ability shows that the question of David's successor had to be addressed. King David could not last much longer, and his family history had been marked by treachery and murder. At this point, it was worth wondering if there could be a bloodless transition from David to the next king.

2. (5) Adonijah's presumption.

Then Adonijah the son of Haggith exalted himself, saying, "I will be king"; and he prepared for himself chariots and horsemen, and fifty men to run before him.

a. **Exalted himself**: 2 Samuel 3:2-5 describes the sons of David and lists Adonijah as the fourth son. We know that two of the three sons older than Adonijah were dead (Amnon and Absalom), and we suspect that the other older son (Chileab) either also died or was unfit to rule because he is never mentioned after 2 Samuel 3:3. As the oldest living son of David, by many customs Adonijah would be considered the heir to the throne. But the throne of Israel was not left *only* to the rules of hereditary succession; God determined the next king.

i. Adonijah violated a basic principle in the Scriptures - that we should let God exalt us and not exalt ourselves.

For exaltation comes neither from the east
Nor from the west nor from the south.
But God is the Judge: He puts down one,
And exalts another. (Psalm 75:6-7)

Humble yourselves in the sight of the LORD, *and He will lift you up.* (James 4:10)

b. **He prepared for himself chariots and horsemen, and fifty men to run before him**: Adonijah had a good marketing campaign, and he knew how to present himself as king. He hoped that if he put forth the *image* of a king, he would become king in *reality*.

i. "In effect this was a personal military force designed to anticipate Solomon's claim by a *coup d'etat*. (Out) runners were part of a close royal bodyguard." (Wiseman)

ii. Adonijah was the brother of Absalom, and a look at 2 Samuel 15:1 shows that "He copied the conduct of his brother Absalom in every respect" (Clarke).

3. (6) Adonijah's character.

(And his father had not rebuked him at any time by saying, "Why have you done so?" He was also very good-looking. His mother had borne him after Absalom.)

a. **His father had not rebuked him at any time**: Sadly, David did not do a very good job raising his own sons. David failed to restrain his passions in some areas of his life; his sons showed a much greater inability to restrain their passions. In part, this was because David did not discipline his own sons well.

i. David did not seem to have a very good relationship with his father (1 Samuel 16:11). The godly influence in his life seems to have come more from his mother than from his father. Twice in the Psalms he referred to his mother as a *maidservant* of the LORD (Psalm 86:16 and 116:16). It is likely that David did not have a good example of parenting from his father.

ii. Yet this does not excuse David's deficiencies as a father. He knew how his Heavenly Father treated him - how he was comforted and helped by the correcting rod and staff of his Shepherd (Psalm 23:4). He could have learned how to be a good father from his Father in heaven. Even before it was written, David could have known the counsel of Proverbs 29:17: *Correct your son, and he will give you rest; yes, he will give delight to your soul.*

iii. "David was ever too fond a father, and he smarted for it." (Trapp)

b. **He was also very good-looking**: David was a handsome man and was attracted to beautiful women. It doesn't surprise us that David's children were **very good-looking**. This gave them an unfair and unfortunate advantage.

4. (7-10) Adonijah's banquet.

Then he conferred with Joab the son of Zeruiah and with Abiathar the priest, and they followed and helped Adonijah. But Zadok the priest, Benaiah the son of Jehoiada, Nathan the prophet, Shimei, Rei, and the mighty men who belonged to David were not with Adonijah. And Adonijah sacrificed sheep and oxen and fattened cattle by the stone of Zoheleth, which is by En Rogel; he also invited all his brothers, the king's sons, and all the men of Judah, the king's servants. But he did not invite Nathan the prophet, Benaiah, the mighty men, or Solomon his brother.

a. **They followed and helped Adonijah**: Sadly, Joab (David's chief general) and Abiathar (the high priest of Israel) each supported Adonijah. They did not consult the LORD or David in giving their support to this unworthy son of David.

i. It is sad to see these once trusted associates of David turning against him late in his life. Joab may have sought revenge for David's choice of Amasa over him (2 Samuel 19:13), and because Benaiah now had more authority over military affairs. Abiathar might have been jealous of Zadok the high priest (2 Samuel 8:17). "Professional rivalry had darkened into bitter hate" (Maclaren).

ii. "Joab, the most powerful of Adonijah's supporters, had always been fiercely loyal to David, but not to David's wishes. In supporting Adonijah's pretentions to the throne, Joab was acting characteristically." (Patterson and Austel)

iii. "Joab and Abiathar tarnished a life's devotion and broke sacred bonds, because they thought of themselves rather than of God's will." (Maclaren)

b. **Nathan... Zadok... and the mighty men who belonged to David were not with Adonijah**: Fortunately, there were some prominent people in Israel who did *not* support Adonijah.

c. **Sacrificed sheep and oxen and fattened cattle**: The idea is that Adonijah burned the fat of these animals as a sacrifice to the LORD, and he used the meat to hold a dinner honoring and blessing his supporters.

i. Yet it was important that this was *both* a sacrifice and a feast. "He had not only a splendid feast, but a great sacrifice; and he gave by this a popular colour to his pretensions, by affecting to receive his authority from *God*" (Clarke).

B. Nathan and Bathsheba intercede for Solomon.

1. (11-14) Nathan tells his plan to Bathsheba.

So Nathan spoke to Bathsheba the mother of Solomon, saying, "Have you not heard that Adonijah the son of Haggith has become king, and David our LORD does not know it? Come, please, let me now give you advice, that you may save your own life and the life of your son Solomon. Go immediately to King David and say to him, 'Did you not, my LORD, O king, swear to your maidservant, saying, "Assuredly your son Solomon shall reign after me, and he shall sit on my throne"? Why then has Adonijah become king?' Then, while you are still talking there with the king, I also will come in after you and confirm your words."

a. **And David our LORD does not know it**: This shows both the wrong of Adonijah's attempt to take the throne and how far removed from power David really was. He didn't know what was going on around him in the kingdom.

b. **That you may save your own life and the life of your son Solomon**: Nathan knew that if Adonijah became king, he would immediately kill every potential rival to his throne, including Bathsheba and Solomon.

c. **Your son Solomon shall reign after me**: David made this promise to Bathsheba. The specific promise is not recorded before, but we know from 1 Chronicles 22:5-9 that David did in fact intend for Solomon to succeed him as king.

> i. This was a remarkable display of grace - that a son of the wife David took through adultery and murder in the most infamous scandal of his life should become his heir to the throne.

d. **While you are still talking there with the king, I also will come in after you and confirm your words**: Nathan knew that David was generally indulgent towards his sons and would find it hard to believe that Adonijah would do such a thing. He arranged it so the message would be presented in a convincing way.

2. (15-27) Bathsheba and Nathan tell David of Adonijah's bid for the throne.

So Bathsheba went into the chamber to the king. (Now the king was very old, and Abishag the Shunammite was serving the king.) And Bathsheba bowed and did homage to the king. Then the king said, "What is your wish?" Then she said to him, "My LORD, you swore by the LORD your God to your maidservant, saying, 'Assuredly Solomon your son shall reign after me, and he shall sit on my throne.' So now, look! Adonijah has become king; and now, my LORD the king, you do not know about it. He has sacrificed

oxen and fattened cattle and sheep in abundance, and has invited all the sons of the king, Abiathar the priest, and Joab the commander of the army; but Solomon your servant he has not invited. And as for you, my LORD, O king, the eyes of all Israel are on you, that you should tell them who will sit on the throne of my LORD the king after him. Otherwise it will happen, when my LORD the king rests with his fathers, that I and my son Solomon will be counted as offenders." And just then, while she was still talking with the king, Nathan the prophet also came in. So they told the king, saying, "Here is Nathan the prophet." And when he came in before the king, he bowed down before the king with his face to the ground. And Nathan said, "My LORD, O king, have you said, 'Adonijah shall reign after me, and he shall sit on my throne'? For he has gone down today, and has sacrificed oxen and fattened cattle and sheep in abundance, and has invited all the king's sons, and the commanders of the army, and Abiathar the priest; and look! They are eating and drinking before him; and they say, 'Long live King Adonijah!' But he has not invited me—me your servant—nor Zadok the priest, nor Benaiah the son of Jehoiada, nor your servant Solomon. Has this thing been done by my LORD the king, and you have not told your servant who should sit on the throne of my LORD the king after him?"

a. **Now the king was very old, and Abishag the Shunammite was serving the king**: This is included to remind us of David's limited capabilities as king. He needed the help of Bathsheba and Nathan brought to him in the following verses.

b. **I and my son Solomon will be counted as offenders**: Bathsheba began by telling David the facts about Adonijah's actions. Then she used this tender appeal, reminding David that her life and the life of Solomon were in grave danger if Adonijah became the king.

c. **Nathan the prophet came in**: The last place we saw Nathan was in 2 Samuel 12, where he rebuked his friend David over the scandal with Bathsheba and the murder of Uriah. Yet now, at the end of his days, David received Nathan; the sense is that he remained a trusted friend. David did not treat Nathan as an enemy when he confronted him with a painful truth.

i. "So far was David from hatred of the truth, that he loved Nathan the better for his plain dealing while he lived, gave him free access to his bed-chamber, and now nameth him a commissioner for the declaring of his successor." (Trapp)

d. **Has this thing been done by my LORD the king, and you have not told your servant**: Nathan also stated the facts about Adonijah, and then gave a personal appeal. He asked David - who was his dear and trusted friend – "Is it possible you have chosen Adonijah to be king and have not told me?"

C. Solomon is made king.

1. (28-30) David vows to set things aright for his succession.

Then King David answered and said, "Call Bathsheba to me." So she came into the king's presence and stood before the king. And the king took an oath and said, "As the LORD lives, who has redeemed my life from every distress, just as I swore to you by the LORD God of Israel, saying, 'Assuredly Solomon your son shall be king after me, and he shall sit on my throne in my place,' so I certainly will do this day."

a. **As the LORD lives**: This introduced a solemn oath. David would confirm the previous promise he made to Bathsheba, that her son Solomon would become the next king.

b. **Solomon your son shall be king after me**: David promised to settle the issue *that very day*. He would abdicate the throne and give the crown to Solomon.

2. (31-37) Arrangements are made for the anointing of Solomon as king.

Then Bathsheba bowed with her face to the earth, and paid homage to the king, and said, "Let my LORD King David live forever!" And King David said, "Call to me Zadok the priest, Nathan the prophet, and Benaiah the son of Jehoiada." So they came before the king. The king also said to them, "Take with you the servants of your LORD, and have Solomon my son ride on my own mule, and take him down to Gihon. There let Zadok the priest and Nathan the prophet anoint him king over Israel; and blow the horn, and say, 'Long live King Solomon!' Then you shall come up after him, and he shall come and sit on my throne, and he shall be king in my place. For I have appointed him to be ruler over Israel and Judah." Benaiah the son of Jehoiada answered the king and said, "Amen! May the LORD God of my LORD the king say so too. As the LORD has been with my LORD the king, even so may He be with Solomon, and make his throne greater than the throne of my LORD King David."

a. **Let my LORD King David live forever**: This was a customary expression of thanks and honor. Since David knew that death was near, it must have sounded strange in his ears.

b. **Call to me Zadok the priest, Nathan the prophet, and Benaiah**: These were three prominent leaders in Israel who did *not* support Adonijah as king. David knew who was loyal to him and who was not.

c. **Let Zadok the priest and Nathan the prophet anoint him king**: This is a rare glimpse of all three offices in cooperation – prophet, priest, and king. Each of these offices was gloriously fulfilled in Jesus.

i. David wanted the proclamation of Solomon as successor to be *persuasive*. He had five points to the plan:

- **Ride on my own mule.**
- **Let Zadok the priest and Nathan the prophet anoint him.**
- **Blow the horn.**
- **Say, "Long live King Solomon!"**
- **He shall come and sit on my throne.**

ii. We might say that God is *just* as concerned that we know that we are destined for a throne, that we are His sons, heirs, and will reign with King Jesus.

d. **Amen! May the LORD God of my LORD the king say so too**: Benaiah understood an important principle - that unless the LORD God said "**Amen!**" to the selection of Solomon, he would not stand. Benaiah sensed that this was the LORD's will, and offered the prayer that God would in fact **say so too**.

e. **May He be with Solomon, and make his throne greater than the throne of my LORD King David**: This pious wish of Benaiah had an interesting fulfillment. On a human level, Solomon's reign was indeed **greater than** David's. But on a spiritual, eternal level, it was not.

3. (38-40) Solomon is anointed and proclaimed as king.

So Zadok the priest, Nathan the prophet, Benaiah the son of Jehoiada, the Cherethites, and the Pelethites went down and had Solomon ride on King David's mule, and took him to Gihon. Then Zadok the priest took a horn of oil from the tabernacle and anointed Solomon. And they blew the horn, and all the people said, "Long live King Solomon!" And all the people went up after him; and the people played the flutes and rejoiced with great joy, so that the earth seemed to split with their sound.

a. **And had Solomon ride on King David's mule**: Apparently, this was the Old Testament equivalent to a presidential motorcade.

i. The **mule** was something special in ancient Israel. "Since Hebraic law forbade crossbreeding (Leviticus 19:19), mules had to be imported and were therefore very expensive. So while the common people rode donkeys, the mule was reserved for royalty." (Dilday)

ii. "No subject could use any thing that belonged to the prince, without forfeiting his life. As David offered Solomon to ride on his own mule, this was full evidence that he had appointed him his successor." (Clarke)

iii. **And took him to Gihon**: "Gihon, the site of the anointing, was just outside the city in the Kidron Valley, on the east bank of Ophel. It was at this time Jerusalem's major source of water and was therefore a natural gathering place of the populace" (Patterson and Austel).

b. **A horn of oil from the tabernacle**: Literally, it is *the* **horn of oil**. This was a specific container of oil kept in the tabernacle for special ceremonies of anointing.

c. **The people… rejoiced with great joy, so that the earth seemed to split with their sound**: Though Adonijah put forth his best marketing campaign, he could not win the hearts of the people. They sensed that Solomon was the man, not Adonijah.

D. Solomon's mercy to Adonijah.

1. (41-49) Adonijah hears that Solomon is made king.

Now Adonijah and all the guests who were with him heard it as they finished eating. And when Joab heard the sound of the horn, he said, "Why is the city in such a noisy uproar?" While he was still speaking, there came Jonathan, the son of Abiathar the priest. And Adonijah said to him, "Come in, for you are a prominent man, and bring good news." Then Jonathan answered and said to Adonijah, "No! Our LORD King David has made Solomon king. The king has sent with him Zadok the priest, Nathan the prophet, Benaiah the son of Jehoiada, the Cherethites, and the Pelethites; and they have made him ride on the king's mule. So Zadok the priest and Nathan the prophet have anointed him king at Gihon; and they have gone up from there rejoicing, so that the city is in an uproar. This is the noise that you have heard. Also Solomon sits on the throne of the kingdom. And moreover the king's servants have gone to bless our LORD King David, saying, 'May God make the name of Solomon better than your name, and may He make his throne greater than your throne.' Then the king bowed himself on the bed. Also the king said thus, 'Blessed be the LORD God of Israel, who has given one to sit on my throne this day, while my eyes see it!'" So all the guests who were with Adonijah were afraid, and arose, and each one went his way.

a. **As they finished eating**: The banquet wasn't even over before Solomon was proclaimed king. Bathsheba and Nathan acted quickly and it was rewarded.

i. "Adonijah's feast, as all wicked men's, endeth in horror; for the last dish, is served up astonishment and fearful expectation of just revenge." (Trapp)

b. **So that all the city is in an uproar**: This was very distressing to Adonijah. He had the support of some important, powerful men (those attending his banquet), but now he knew that the heart of the people belonged to Solomon.

c. **Also the king said thus, "Blessed be the LORD God of Israel, who has given one to sit on my throne this day, while my eyes see it!"** This told Adonijah that even King David was completely behind Solomon. There was no hope for his future as king.

d. **All the guests who were with Adonijah were afraid, and arose, and each one went**: They came for a nice dinner, and to support Adonijah. They left quickly as soon as it was clear that he would not and could not be king. Now, it was *dangerous* to say that you supported Adonijah as king.

2. (50-53) Solomon's mercy to Adonijah.

Now Adonijah was afraid of Solomon; so he arose, and went and took hold of the horns of the altar. And it was told Solomon, saying, "Indeed Adonijah is afraid of King Solomon; for look, he has taken hold of the horns of the altar, saying, 'Let King Solomon swear to me today that he will not put his servant to death with the sword.'" Then Solomon said, "If he proves himself a worthy man, not one hair of him shall fall to the earth; but if wickedness is found in him, he shall die." So King Solomon sent them to bring him down from the altar. And he came and fell down before King Solomon; and Solomon said to him, "Go to your house."

a. **Took hold of the horns of the altar**: According to almost universal custom in the ancient world, a religious altar was a place of sanctuary against justice or vengeance. An accused man might find safety if he could flee to an altar before he was apprehended. This is why Adonijah **took hold of the horns of the altar**.

i. It is important to understand that this ancient custom was not used in Israel to protect a guilty man. *But if a man acts with premeditation against his neighbor, to kill him by treachery, you shall take him from My altar, that he may die* (Exodus 21:14).

b. **If he proves himself a worthy man, not one hair of him shall fall to the earth**: Solomon gave Adonijah a limited reprieve. This went against all custom in the ancient world. It was common, even expected, that when a new king assumed the throne, he would execute every potential rival. Solomon not only let a potential rival live, but one who *openly tried to subvert his reign*. This was a large measure of grace and mercy on the part of Solomon, and a good start to his reign.

i. At the same time, Solomon wanted Adonijah to know that if he should show the slightest inclination towards rebellion, he would be killed instantly. Mercy would be withdrawn and justice would be delivered quickly.

c. **He came and fell down before King Solomon**: Adonijah knew he received great mercy from Solomon, and he wanted to show his gratitude for it and his reliance upon Solomon's mercy.

1 Kings 2 - The Securing of Solomon's Throne

A. The final acts of King David.

1. (1-4) David's exhortation to Solomon.

Now the days of David drew near that he should die, and he charged Solomon his son, saying: "I go the way of all the earth; be strong, therefore, and prove yourself a man. And keep the charge of the LORD your God: to walk in His ways, to keep His statutes, His commandments, His judgments, and His testimonies, as it is written in the Law of Moses, that you may prosper in all that you do and wherever you turn; that the LORD may fulfill His word which He spoke concerning me, saying, 'If your sons take heed to their way, to walk before Me in truth with all their heart and with all their soul,' He said, 'you shall not lack a man on the throne of Israel.'

a. **I go the way of all the earth**: David, son of Jesse – Israel's greatest king, apart from the Messiah - recognized that he was but a man and shared the common destiny **of all the earth**. Knowing he would soon pass from this life, David gave a final charge to Solomon.

   i. An expanded account of David's charge to Solomon is in 1 Chronicles 28 and 29. It especially emphasizes Solomon's duty to build the temple.

b. **Be strong, therefore, and prove yourself a man**: Perhaps David sensed some weakness in Solomon. Perhaps he knew Solomon would be tested in far greater ways than before. Whatever the exact reason was, David knew Solomon needed *strength* and *courage* (**prove yourself a man**). Great responsibilities require great strength and courage.

   i. From these words of David we sense that Solomon faced great challenges, whether he knew it or not. "The same expression was used by the Philistines in 1 Samuel 4:9 as they encouraged one another in their battle against what they assumed to be insurmountable odds" (Patterson and Austel).

c. **And keep the charge of the LORD your God**: David also knew that Solomon could not be strong or courageous without obedient fellowship with God. In this place of obedient fellowship, Solomon would **prosper in all that** he did.

d. **That the LORD may fulfill His word which He spoke concerning me**: David had a *general* reason to exhort Solomon to obedience, but he also had a *specific* reason, a specific promise of God. God promised David that as long as his sons walked in obedience, they would keep the throne of Israel.

> i. This was an amazing promise. No matter what the Assyrians or the Egyptians or the Babylonians did, as long as David's sons were *obedient* and followed God with their **heart and with all their soul**, God would establish their kingdom. He would take care of the rest.

> ii. We may envy the sons of David because they had such a promise, but we have a similar promise from God. Jesus said in Matthew 6:33: *But seek first the kingdom of God and His righteousness, and all these things shall be added to you.* God promises that if we put Him first, He will take care of the rest.

2. (5-9) Advice on dealing with friends and enemies.

"Moreover you know also what Joab the son of Zeruiah did to me, and what he did to the two commanders of the armies of Israel, to Abner the son of Ner and Amasa the son of Jether, whom he killed. And he shed the blood of war in peacetime, and put the blood of war on his belt that was around his waist, and on his sandals that were on his feet. Therefore do according to your wisdom, and do not let his gray hair go down to the grave in peace. But show kindness to the sons of Barzillai the Gileadite, and let them be among those who eat at your table, for so they came to me when I fled from Absalom your brother. And see, you have with you Shimei the son of Gera, a Benjamite from Bahurim, who cursed me with a malicious curse in the day when I went to Mahanaim. But he came down to meet me at the Jordan, and I swore to him by the LORD, saying, 'I will not put you to death with the sword.' Now therefore, do not hold him guiltless, for you are a wise man and know what you ought to do to him; but bring his gray hair down to the grave with blood."

a. **Do not let his gray hair go down to the grave in peace**: David wanted Solomon to begin his reign in justice, and to first give justice to **Joab**, who was guilty of the murder of both **Abner**, the general of Israel's army under Saul (2 Samuel 3:27) and **Amasa**, one of David's military commanders (2 Samuel 20:9-10).

> i. Joab is one of the more complex characters of the Old Testament. He was fiercely loyal to David, yet not strongly obedient. He disobeyed David

when he thought it was in David's best interest, and he was cunning and ruthless in furthering his own position.

ii. David didn't mention Joab's killing of Absalom, which David commanded him not to do (2 Samuel 18). Perhaps by this time David recognized that Absalom did in fact have to die for his treason and attempted murder against David.

iii. Many people think that David did not command Joab's execution during his lifetime because Joab knew about the murder of Uriah, the husband of Bathsheba (2 Samuel 11:14-25). The idea is that Joab used this knowledge as blackmail against David. This may be true, but it seems that others knew of David's sin with Bathsheba and against Uriah also (such as Nathan the prophet and servants in David's court). It would seem that Joab's knowledge was only effective as blackmail if no one else knew it.

iv. At the very least, David knew the complexity of Joab's character. He knew the loyalty and sacrifices Joab made for David over the years, and he knew his violence and ruthlessness. "David felt under obligation to Joab, and though David was certainly not lacking in courage, he was not able to cope with the mixture of Joab's loyalty and his misdeeds" (Patterson and Austel).

b. **Show kindness to the sons of Barzillai the Gileadite**: David also wanted Solomon to do justice by these who had helped David in a time of great need.

i. "To *eat at* the king's *table* was the equivalent of having a pension, the beneficiary receiving a regular royal allowance of food and clothing, with a house and land to support him and his family." (Wiseman)

c. **Shimei… bring his gray hair down to the grave with blood**: David vowed that he would not kill the obnoxious rebel Shimei (2 Samuel 16:5-13). It was right for David to keep his vow, but it was also right for him to make sure that Shimei received justice without David breaking his vow.

3. (10-12) David's death.

So David rested with his fathers, and was buried in the City of David. The period that David reigned over Israel was forty years; seven years he reigned in Hebron, and in Jerusalem he reigned thirty-three years. Then Solomon sat on the throne of his father David; and his kingdom was firmly established.

a. **David rested with his fathers**: This phrase will become common throughout 1 and 2 Kings to describe the passing of a king from this world. Truly, David passed from this life to eternal rest and reward.

i. So ended the earthly life of one of the greatest men ever to walk the earth. *So he died in a good old age, full of days and riches and honor.* (1 Chronicles 29:28) "Of his adultery and murder we hear not a word, because he had made a thorough peace with God for those sins in his lifetime" (Trapp).

ii. "He was a shepherd, a soldier, an outlaw, a king, a fugitive, a sinner, a saint, a poet… His experiences were the writing of God on his life, making him into a man after God's own heart." (Redpath)

iii. "In general he lived well, and it is most evident that he died well; and as a king, a general, a poet, a father, and a friend, he has had few *equals*, and no *superior*, from his own time to the present day." (Clarke)

b. **And was buried in the City of David**: The tomb of David was known in the time of Jesus and the apostles, according to Acts 2:29. Afterwards, the Christian writer Jerome speaks of it being known in his time. What is currently known in Jerusalem as David's Tomb is almost certainly *not* the genuine one that was known in ancient times.

i. "According to 2 Kings 11:10, David's weapons were preserved as relics in the sanctuary, while, according to Josephus, other representative treasures of his reign were buried with him in his tomb." (Dilday)

c. **Solomon sat on the throne of his father David; and his kingdom was firmly established**: This is phrased to show that it was a fulfillment of the promise made to David in 2 Samuel 7:12-16. That promise was ultimately fulfilled in Jesus, the Son of David; but it also had a definite and partial fulfillment in Solomon.

i. "With Solomon began, in some senses, the most splendid period in Israel's history. The splendor, however, was largely mental and material. The spiritual is noticeably absent." (Morgan)

B. Solomon secures his throne.

1. (13-18) Adonijah asks Bathsheba to make an appeal on his behalf.

Now Adonijah the son of Haggith came to Bathsheba the mother of Solomon. So she said, "Do you come peaceably?" And he said, "Peaceably." Moreover he said, "I have something to say to you." And she said, "Say it." Then he said, "You know that the kingdom was mine, and all Israel had set their expectations on me, that I should reign. However, the kingdom has been turned over, and has become my brother's; for it was his from the LORD. Now I ask one petition of you; do not deny me." And she said to him, "Say it." Then he said, "Please speak to King Solomon, for he will not refuse you, that he may give me Abishag the Shunammite as wife." So Bathsheba said, "Very well, I will speak for you to the king."

a. **Do you come peaceably**: This was a valid question. Adonijah attempted to succeed David as king over Israel, but was kept from establishing his reign when Nathan and Bathsheba warned King David of Adonijah's attempt. Adonijah had reason to wish revenge on Bathsheba.

b. **You know that the kingdom was mine, and all Israel had set their expectations on me, that I should reign**: Adonijah seemed to suffer from delusions of grandeur. He imagined that there was widespread popular support for him as king. In reality, he only had a handful of influential malcontents to support him, and they quickly deserted him when it was evident that David favored Solomon (1 Kings 1:49).

c. **That he may give me Abishag the Shunammite as wife**: In all likelihood, Abishag was a concubine of David's and therefore legally bound to him. David's death broke that bond, and now Adonijah wanted to take the concubine widow Abishag as wife.

> i. We can surmise that Adonjiah wanted more than Abishag's beauty (1 Kings 1:3-4). In 2 Samuel 16:20-23 Absalom, the brother of Adonijah, asserted his rebellious claim on David's throne by taking David's concubines unto himself. Adonijah wants to *declare* or *build* a claim to Solomon's throne by taking David's widowed concubine as his wife.

> ii. This idea has historical examples. Among the ancient Persians and Arabs, the new king took the harem of the previous king.

2. (19-21) Bathsheba brings the request to Solomon.

Bathsheba therefore went to King Solomon, to speak to him for Adonijah. And the king rose up to meet her and bowed down to her, and sat down on his throne and had a throne set for the king's mother; so she sat at his right hand. Then she said, "I desire one small petition of you; do not refuse me." And the king said to her, "Ask it, my mother, for I will not refuse you." So she said, "Let Abishag the Shunammite be given to Adonijah your brother as wife."

a. **Bathsheba therefore went to King Solomon**: She knew that this was an outrageous request, yet she still agreed to bring it to Solomon. Bathsheba probably believed that it was best that Solomon knew what Adonijah wanted to do.

b. **One small petition**: Bathsheba knew this was not a **small petition** at all. She was at least a little sarcastic, to make the request of Adonijah seem even more offensive to the ears of Solomon.

3. (22-25) Solomon has Adonijah executed for his challenge to the throne.

And King Solomon answered and said to his mother, "Now why do you ask Abishag the Shunammite for Adonijah? Ask for him the kingdom

also—for he is my older brother—for him, and for Abiathar the priest, and for Joab the son of Zeruiah." Then King Solomon swore by the LORD, saying, "May God do so to me, and more also, if Adonijah has not spoken this word against his own life! Now therefore, as the LORD lives, who has confirmed me and set me on the throne of David my father, and who has established a house for me, as He promised, Adonijah shall be put to death today!" So King Solomon sent by the hand of Benaiah the son of Jehoiada; and he struck him down, and he died.

a. **Ask for him the kingdom also**: Solomon understood the situation perfectly. He knew that this was Adonijah's attempt to declare or build a claim to the throne of Israel.

b. **As the LORD lives, who has confirmed me and set me on the throne of David my father**: Solomon was zealous to give justice to Adonijah because he knew that God gave him the throne of Israel.

c. **Adonijah shall be put to death today**: Solomon simply acted according to the "terms of parole" granted to Adonijah in 1 Kings 1:52: *If he proves himself a worthy man, not one hair of him shall fall to the earth; but if wickedness is found in him, he shall die.* Adonijah made a wicked, treasonous request and is executed because of it.

i. We wonder why Adonijah – after hearing the warning Solomon made in 1 Kings 1:52 - would make such an outrageous request. Perhaps he felt that Solomon was too young, too inexperienced, or too timid to do the right thing. He soon found out that Solomon was a wise and decisive leader.

4. (26-27) The exile of Abiathar.

And to Abiathar the priest the king said, "Go to Anathoth, to your own fields, for you are deserving of death; but I will not put you to death at this time, because you carried the ark of the LORD GOD before my father David, and because you were afflicted every time my father was afflicted." So Solomon removed Abiathar from being priest to the LORD, that he might fulfill the word of the LORD which He spoke concerning the house of Eli at Shiloh.

a. **You are deserving of death**: Abiathar deserved death because he supported Adonijah as the next king, in defiance of the will of God and the will of King David (1 Kings 1:7). This was treason against both God and the King of Israel.

b. **I will not put you to death at this time**: Solomon showed mercy and wisdom to Abiathar. Mercy was shown in sparing Abiathar's life in light of his past standing as a chief priest and supporter of David. Wisdom was shown in exiling him and saying, "**I will not put you to death at this time**." Solomon let Abiathar know that he could still be executed.

c. **That he might fulfill the word of the LORD which He spoke concerning the house of Eli at Shiloh**: This refers to the prophecies found in 1 Samuel 2:27-36 and 1 Samuel 3:11-14. In removing Abiathar from the priesthood, Solomon, without direct intention, fulfilled the promise of judgment against the house of Eli, made some 100 years before Solomon took the throne.

5. (28-35) The execution of Joab.

Then news came to Joab, for Joab had defected to Adonijah, though he had not defected to Absalom. So Joab fled to the tabernacle of the LORD, and took hold of the horns of the altar. And King Solomon was told, "Joab has fled to the tabernacle of the LORD; there he is, by the altar." Then Solomon sent Benaiah the son of Jehoiada, saying, "Go, strike him down." So Benaiah went to the tabernacle of the LORD, and said to him, "Thus says the king, 'Come out!'" And he said, "No, but I will die here." And Benaiah brought back word to the king, saying, "Thus said Joab, and thus he answered me." Then the king said to him, "Do as he has said, and strike him down and bury him, that you may take away from me and from the house of my father the innocent blood which Joab shed. So the LORD will return his blood on his head, because he struck down two men more righteous and better than he, and killed them with the sword—Abner the son of Ner, the commander of the army of Israel, and Amasa the son of Jether, the commander of the army of Judah—though my father David did not know it. Their blood shall therefore return upon the head of Joab and upon the head of his descendants forever. But upon David and his descendants, upon his house and his throne, there shall be peace forever from the LORD." So Benaiah the son of Jehoiada went up and struck and killed him; and he was buried in his own house in the wilderness. The king put Benaiah the son of Jehoiada in his place over the army, and the king put Zadok the priest in the place of Abiathar.

a. **And took hold of the horns of the altar**: Joab supported Adonijah in his treasonous attempt to gain David's throne. Now, he imitated Adonijah's attempt to find refuge by taking hold **of the horns of the altar** (as Adonijah did in 1 Kings 1:50-53).

i. "He did not know where to fly except he fled to the horns of an altar, which he had very seldom approached before. As far as we can judge, he had shown little respect to religion during his lifetime. He was a rough man of war, and cared little enough about God, or the tabernacle, or the priests, or the altar; but when he was in danger, he fled to that which he had avoided, and sought to make a refuge of that which he had neglected." (Spurgeon)

ii. "The laying hold upon the literal horns of an altar, which can be handled, availed not Joab. There are many – oh, how many still! – That are hoping to be saved, because they lay hold, as they think, upon the horns of the altar *by sacraments*." (Spurgeon)

b. **Go, strike him down**: Although it was almost a universal custom in the ancient world to find sanctuary at a holy altar, Solomon knew that this ancient custom was not used in Israel to protect a guilty man. *But if a man acts with premeditation against his neighbor, to kill him by treachery, you shall take him from My altar, that he may die* (Exodus 21:14). Since Joab refused to leave, Solomon had him executed right at the altar.

i. "It would have been an insult to justice not to have taken the life of Joab. David was culpable in delaying it so long; but probably the circumstances of his government would not admit of his doing it sooner." (Clarke)

c. **But upon David and his descendants, upon his house and his throne, there shall be peace forever from the LORD**: This was only true as *David's descendants followed the LORD*. Our destiny is not determined by our ancestors, but by our current relationship with God.

i. David reinforced this principle with Solomon earlier in this chapter by reminding him what the LORD promised: *If your sons take heed to their way, to walk before Me in truth with all their heart and with all their soul... 'you shall not lack a man on the throne of Israel* (2 Kings 2:4).

6. (36-46) Solomon settles the past with Shimei.

Then the king sent and called for Shimei, and said to him, "Build yourself a house in Jerusalem and dwell there, and do not go out from there anywhere. For it shall be, on the day you go out and cross the Brook Kidron, know for certain you shall surely die; your blood shall be on your own head." And Shimei said to the king, "The saying is good. As my LORD the king has said, so your servant will do." So Shimei dwelt in Jerusalem many days. Now it happened at the end of three years, that two slaves of Shimei ran away to Achish the son of Maachah, king of Gath. And they told Shimei, saying, "Look, your slaves are in Gath!" So Shimei arose, saddled his donkey, and went to Achish at Gath to seek his slaves. And Shimei went and brought his slaves from Gath. And Solomon was told that Shimei had gone from Jerusalem to Gath and had come back. Then the king sent and called for Shimei, and said to him, "Did I not make you swear by the LORD, and warn you, saying, 'Know for certain that on the day you go out and travel anywhere, you shall surely die'? And you said to me, 'The word I have heard is good.' Why then have you not kept the oath of the LORD and the commandment that I gave you?" The king said moreover to Shimei, "You know, as your heart acknowledges, all the wickedness that you did to my father David; therefore the LORD will return your wickedness on your own head. But King Solomon shall be blessed, and the throne of David shall be established before the LORD forever." So the king commanded Benaiah the

son of Jehoiada; and he went out and struck him down, and he died. Thus the kingdom was established in the hand of Solomon.

a. **Do not go out from there anywhere**: Shimei was associated with the household of the former King Saul, and showed himself as a threat to the House of David (2 Samuel 16:5-8). David instructed Solomon not to allow Shimei to die in peace (1 Kings 2:8). Solomon began dealing with Shimei by placing him under house arrest.

b. **The saying is good**: Shimei knew that Solomon was merciful and generous to him. He not only agreed with the arrangement, he was also grateful for it.

c. **Why then have you not kept the oath of the LORD and the commandment that I gave you**: Solomon extended mercy to Shimei, but Shimei abused it and took advantage of it. It seems to have been mainly a matter of *neglect* or *forgetfulness*, but it was criminal to neglect or forget a royal covenant.

d. **Thus the kingdom was established in the hand of Solomon**: This chapter demonstrates that Solomon's throne was secure at an early date, not like the reign of David or Saul.

i. This initial demonstration of *justice* was important for Solomon to perform. "He seems to think that, while such bad men remained unpunished the nation could not prosper; that it was an act of justice which God required him to perform, in order to the establishment and perpetuity of his throne" (Clarke).

ii. "It is interesting to compare his position now with that of his two predecessors, Saul and David, at the start of their reigns. Both had faced a measure of suspicion or opposition from their own countrymen; both had met this problem with resolute action, coupled with understanding and leniency. Solomon, however, eliminated his potential enemies swiftly and ruthlessly." (Payne)

iii. "Oh that we would be as quick in slaying our arch-rebels, those predominant sins that threaten our precious souls!" (Trapp)

1 Kings 3 - Solomon is Given Great Wisdom

A. God gives Solomon wisdom.

1. (1) Solomon marries an Egyptian princess.

Now Solomon made a treaty with Pharaoh king of Egypt, and married Pharaoh's daughter; then he brought her to the City of David until he had finished building his own house, and the house of the LORD, and the wall all around Jerusalem.

a. **Solomon made a treaty with Pharaoh king of Egypt, and married Pharaoh's daughter**: Marriage to fellow royalty was a common political strategy in the ancient world and continues to the modern age. It was not only because royalty wanted to marry other royalty, but also because conflict between nations was then avoided for the sake of family ties.

   i. This was not Solomon's first marriage. 1 Kings 14:21 tells us that his son Rehoboam came to the throne when he was 41 years old, and 1 Kings 11:42 tells us that Solomon reigned 40 years. This means that Rehoboam was born to his mother, a wife of Solomon named Naamah the Amonitess, before he came to the throne and before he married this daughter of Pharaoh.

   ii. Solomon's multiple marriages, and marriages to foreign women, would cause great disaster in his life. Later in the Book of Nehemiah, Nehemiah was angry and frustrated because the people of Israel married with the pagan nations around them. In rebuking the guilty, Nehemiah remembered Solomon's bad example: *So I contended with them and cursed them, struck some of them and pulled out their hair, and made them swear by God, saying, "You shall not give your daughters as wives to their sons, nor take their daughters for your sons or yourselves. Did not Solomon king of Israel sin by these things? Yet among many nations there was no king like him, who was beloved of his God; and God made him king over all Israel. Nevertheless pagan women caused even him to sin. Should we then hear of your doing all this great evil, transgressing against our God by marrying pagan women?"* (Nehemiah 13:25-27).

iii. The foreign wives made Solomon more than a bad example – they ruined his spiritual life. *But King Solomon loved many foreign women, as well as the daughter of Pharaoh: women of the Moabites, Ammonites, Edomites, Sidonians, and Hittites; from the nations of whom the* LORD *had said to the children of Israel, "You shall not intermarry with them, nor they with you. Surely they will turn away your hearts after their gods." Solomon clung to these in love. And he had seven hundred wives, princesses, and three hundred concubines; and his wives turned away his heart. For it was so, when Solomon was old, that his wives turned his heart after other gods; and his heart was not loyal to the* LORD *his God, as was the heart of his father David* (1 Kings 11:1-4).

iv. 1 Kings 11:4 says this only happened *when Solomon was old*, but the pattern was set with this first marriage to the Egyptian princess. It perhaps made political sense, but not spiritual sense. "Such arranged marriages were a common confirmation of international treaties, but this one was the beginning of Solomon's spiritual downfall" (Wiseman).

v. 2 Samuel 3:3 tells us that David married the daughter of a foreign king: *Maacah, the daughter of Talmai, king of Geshur*. Marrying a foreign woman was not against the Law of Moses – if she became a convert to the God of Israel. What did not ruin David *did* ruin Solomon.

b. **He brought her to the City of David**: Though this was permitted under the Law of Moses, it was not wise or good for Solomon to do this. Later in his life, his foreign wives were the reason his heart turned away from the LORD (1 Kings 11:4).

i. Old legends from Jewish rabbis say that on their wedding night, the Egyptian princess cast a spell on Solomon and put a tapestry over their bed that looked like the night sky with stars and constellations. The spell was intended to make Solomon sleep, and when he did wake, he looked up and thought the stars were still out and it was still night, so he went back to sleep. He slept on past 10:00 in the morning and all Israel was grieved because Solomon kept the keys to the temple under his pillow and they couldn't have the morning sacrifice until he woke up. Finally, his mother Bathsheba roused him from sleep. (Cited in Ginzberg)

2. (2-4) Solomon's great sacrifice.

Meanwhile the people sacrificed at the high places, because there was no house built for the name of the LORD until those days. And Solomon loved the LORD, walking in the statutes of his father David, except that he sacrificed and burned incense at the high places. Now the king went

to Gibeon to sacrifice there, for that was the great high place: Solomon offered a thousand burnt offerings on that altar.

a. **People sacrificed at the high places, because there was no house built for the name of the LORD**: At this time, altars were allowed in Israel at various **high places**, as long as those altars were unto the LORD and not corrupted by idolatry (as commanded in Deuteronomy 16:21). When the temple was built, sacrifice was then centralized at the temple.

b. **Solomon loved the LORD… except that he sacrificed and burned incense at the high places**: There is good and bad in this assessment of Solomon. There is good in that *generally* he walked **in the statutes of his father David**. There is bad in the word "**except**."

> i. At the same time, it seems that God showed mercy to those who violated this law before the temple was built. "Could there be any sin in this, or was it unlawful till after the temple was built? For prophets, judges, the kings which preceded Solomon, and Solomon himself, sacrificed on high places, such as Gibeon, Gilgal, Shiloh, Hebron, Kirath-jearin, etc. But after the temple was erected, it was sinful to offer sacrifices in any other place" (Clarke).

> ii. Solomon *did* love the LORD, yet he also loved foreign wives who eventually helped turn his heart away from the LORD (1 Kings 11:4-10). "The perils of mixed motives and a divided heart are terrible indeed" (Morgan).

c. **Solomon offered a thousand burnt offerings on that altar**: This almost grotesque amount of sacrifice demonstrated both Solomon's great wealth and his heart to use it to glorify God.

> i. This was an important event marking the ceremonial beginning of Solomon's reign. According to 2 Chronicles 1:2-3, the entire leadership of the nation went with Solomon to Gibeon.

d. **Now the king went to Gibeon**: Solomon made these special sacrifices at **Gibeon** because **that was the great high place**. What made it different was that the tabernacle was there, even though the ark of the covenant was in Jerusalem.

> i. The course of the tabernacle and the ark of the covenant in the Promised Land:

> > • Joshua brought the ark and the tabernacle to Shiloh (Joshua 18).
> > • In the days of Eli the ark was captured and the tabernacle wrecked (1 Samuel 4, Psalm 78:60-64, Jeremiah 7:12 and 26:9).
> > • The ark came back to Kiriath-Jearim (1 Samuel 7:1-2).
> > • Saul restored the tabernacle at Nob (1 Samuel 21).
> > • Saul moved the tabernacle to Gibeon (1 Chronicles 16:39-40).

- David brought the ark to Jerusalem and built a temporary tent for it (2 Samuel 6:17, 2 Chronicles 1:4).

ii. There were several reasons to explain why David did not bring the tabernacle from Gibeon to Jerusalem:

- He may have believed if the tabernacle was there, the people would be satisfied with that and they would lose the passion and vision for the temple God wanted built.
- It may be that the tabernacle was only moved when it was absolutely necessary - as when disaster came upon it at Shiloh or Nob.
- David simply focused on building the temple, not continuing the tabernacle.

3. (5-9) God's offer and Solomon's response.

At Gibeon the LORD appeared to Solomon in a dream by night; and God said, "Ask! What shall I give you?" And Solomon said: "You have shown great mercy to Your servant David my father, because he walked before You in truth, in righteousness, and in uprightness of heart with You; You have continued this great kindness for him, and You have given him a son to sit on his throne, as it is this day. Now, O LORD my God, You have made Your servant king instead of my father David, but I am a little child; I do not know how to go out or come in. And Your servant is in the midst of Your people whom You have chosen, a great people, too numerous to be numbered or counted. Therefore give to Your servant an understanding heart to judge Your people, that I may discern between good and evil. For who is able to judge this great people of Yours?"

a. **The LORD appeared to Solomon in a dream**: This remarkable visitation from God happened **in a dream**. This is one of the more significant dreams in the Bible.

b. **Ask! What shall I give you**: This was an amazing promise. God seemed to offer Solomon whatever he wanted. This wasn't only because Solomon sacrificed 1,000 animals; it was because his heart was surrendered to God, and God wanted to work something in Solomon through this offer and his response.

i. The natural reaction to reading this promise of God to Solomon is to wish we had such a promise. We do have them.

- *Ask, and it will be given to you; seek, and you will find; knock, and it will be opened to you.* (Matthew 7:7)
- *If you abide in Me, and My words abide in you, you will ask what you desire, and it shall be done for you.* (John 15:7)
- *Now this is the confidence that we have in Him, that if we ask anything according to His will, He hears us.* (1 John 5:14)

c. **You have shown great mercy**: Before responding to God's offer and asking for something, Solomon remembered God's faithfulness to both David and now to Solomon himself.

d. **But I am a little child**: Solomon was not really the age of a child. He came to God in great humility, especially considering the job in front of him.

> i. "The statement is actually Solomon's poetic way of expressing his inadequacies as he faced the awesome tasks of leadership." (Dilday)

> ii. Solomon didn't have the false humility that said, "I can't do this, so I won't even try." His attitude was, "The job is so much bigger than me; I *must* rely on God."

e. **Give to Your servant an understanding heart**: Solomon asked for more than great *knowledge*; he wanted **understanding**, and he wanted it in his **heart**, not merely in his *head*. Actually, the ancient Hebrew word translated **understanding** is literally, "hearing." Solomon wanted a *hearing heart*, one that would listen to God.

> i. In Ephesians 1:18, the Apostle Paul prayed for Christians, asking that *the eyes of your understanding being enlightened*.

f. **To judge Your people, that I may discern between good and evil**: Solomon already understood that a key component of leadership is wise and just discernment. Many leaders do not have this discernment or the courage to use it.

4. (10-15) God's great promise to Solomon.

The speech pleased the LORD, that Solomon had asked this thing. Then God said to him: "Because you have asked this thing, and have not asked long life for yourself, nor have asked riches for yourself, nor have asked the life of your enemies, but have asked for yourself understanding to discern justice, behold, I have done according to your words; see, I have given you a wise and understanding heart, so that there has not been anyone like you before you, nor shall any like you arise after you. And I have also given you what you have not asked: both riches and honor, so that there shall not be anyone like you among the kings all your days. So if you walk in My ways, to keep My statutes and My commandments, as your father David walked, then I will lengthen your days." Then Solomon awoke; and indeed it had been a dream. And he came to Jerusalem and stood before the ark of the covenant of the LORD, offered up burnt offerings, offered peace offerings, and made a feast for all his servants.

a. **The speech pleased the LORD**: God was pleased by what Solomon *asked for*, in that he knew his great need for wisdom, discernment, and understanding. God was also pleased by what Solomon *did not ask for*, in that he did not ask for riches or fame or power for himself.

i. Solomon's request was *not* bad. We are specifically told that **the speech pleased the LORD**. Yet we can also ask if this was *the best* Solomon could ask for. "Was this the highest gift that he could have asked or received? Surely the deep longings of his father for communion with God were yet better" (Maclaren).

ii. Solomon did his job well, as well or better than anyone. Yet as his falling away in the end showed (1 Kings 11:1-11) there was something lacking in his spiritual life. "There is no sign in his biography that he ever had the deep inward devotion of his father. After the poet-psalmist came the prosaic and keen-sighted shrewd man of affairs" (Maclaren).

b. **I have done according to your words… I have also given you what you have not asked**: God not only answered Solomon's prayer, He also answered it beyond all expectation. Solomon did not ask for **riches and honor** or a long life, but God gave him those also.

i. In Ephesians 3:20, Paul honored God saying, *Now to Him who is able to do exceedingly abundantly above all that we ask or think*. Solomon *experienced* God's ability to do far beyond *all that we ask or think*.

ii. Solomon wisely asked God regarding his character, not his possessions. What we *are* is more important than what we *have*.

c. **Then Solomon awoke**: It was a dream, but it was at the same time also a message from God. God answered Solomon's prayer and made him wise, powerful, rich, and influential. His reign was glorious for Israel.

i. At the same time, his end was tragic. We can fairly say that Solomon *wasted* these gifts God gave him. Though he accomplished much, he could have done much more - and his heart was led away from God in the end (1 Kings 11:4-11).

ii. "Instead of being the *wisest* of men, did he not become more *brutish* than any man? Did he not even lose the *knowledge of his Creator*, and worship the abominations of the Moabites, Zidonians, and [so forth]? And was not such idolatry a proof of the *grossest stupidity?* How few proofs does his life give that the gracious purpose of God was fulfilled in him! He received *much*; but he would have received *much more*, had he been faithful to the grace given. No character in the sacred writings disappoints us more than the character of Solomon." (Clarke)

B. An example of Solomon's great wisdom.

1. (16-22) Two women claim the same child as their own.

Now two women who were harlots came to the king, and stood before him. And one woman said, "O my LORD, this woman and I dwell in the same house; and I gave birth while she was in the house. Then it happened, the

third day after I had given birth, that this woman also gave birth. And we were together; no one was with us in the house, except the two of us in the house. And this woman's son died in the night, because she lay on him. So she arose in the middle of the night and took my son from my side, while your maidservant slept, and laid him in her bosom, and laid her dead child in my bosom. And when I rose in the morning to nurse my son, there he was, dead. But when I had examined him in the morning, indeed, he was not my son whom I had borne." Then the other woman said, "No! But the living one is my son, and the dead one is your son." And the first woman said, "No! But the dead one is your son, and the living one is my son." Thus they spoke before the king.

a. **Two women who were harlots came to the king and stood before him**: This in itself is a remarkable testimony to the goodness and generosity of Solomon. Not many kings would take the time to settle a dispute between two prostitutes.

i. However, some think that these were not **harlots** at all. "Hebrew *zonot*, could equally refer to inn-keepers" (Wiseman).

b. **The dead one is your son, and the living one is my son**: This seemed like an impossible problem to solve. It was surely one prostitute's word against the other, and there was no independent witness to the events (**no one was with us in the house**).

2. (23-27) Solomon's wise solution.

And the king said, "The one says, 'This is my son, who lives, and your son is the dead one'; and the other says, 'No! But your son is the dead one, and my son is the living one.'" Then the king said, "Bring me a sword." So they brought a sword before the king. And the king said, "Divide the living child in two, and give half to one, and half to the other." Then the woman whose son was living spoke to the king, for she yearned with compassion for her son; and she said, "O my LORD, give her the living child, and by no means kill him!" But the other said, "Let him be neither mine nor yours, but divide him." So the king answered and said, "Give the first woman the living child, and by no means kill him; she is his mother."

a. **Bring me a sword**: Solomon's solution to the problem at first looked foolish - even dangerous. The wisdom of his approach was only understood when the matter was settled.

i. In the same way, the works – even the judgments – of God often first seem strange, dangerous, or even foolish. Time shows them to be perfect wisdom.

ii. Trapp on **bring me a sword**: "For what purpose? Thought the standers by; wondering and perhaps laughing within themselves. The actions of wise princes are riddles to vulgar constructions: nor is it for the shallow capacities of the multitude to fathom the deep projects of sovereign authority" (Trapp).

b. **She yearned with compassion for her son**: The true parental relationship was proved by *love*. The true mother would rather have the child *live* without her than to *die* with her. She put the child's welfare above her own.

c. **She is his mother**: Solomon knew that the offer to cut the child in two would reveal the true mother, and he rewarded the mother's love accordingly.

3. (28) Solomon is highly esteemed in the eyes of the people of Israel.

And all Israel heard of the judgment which the king had rendered; and they feared the king, for they saw that the wisdom of God was in him to administer justice.

a. **All Israel heard**: Such a wise decision could not be hidden. The matter was soon known throughout the kingdom.

b. **They feared the king, for they saw that the wisdom of God was in him to administer justice**: The people of Israel saw that Solomon had both the wisdom and the courage to do the right thing as a leader. This made them hesitant to disobey the law of the king.

i. The old Jewish rabbis loved to go beyond the Bible and spin legends about Solomon's wisdom. Ginzberg quotes one, telling of the time when a demon showed Solomon something he had never seen before, a Cainite, whom the demon brought up out of the ground, and Solomon immediately saw that he had two heads. When the Cainite wanted to return again, he could not go back to his dwelling place deep under the earth. So he married and had seven sons, one of whom also had two heads. When the two-headed father died, the two-headed son claimed a double share of the inheritance, but the other six brothers thought he should get only one. The Sanhedrin couldn't decide the case, so Solomon prayed for wisdom and finally poured hot water on one of the heads. When he did, both heads flinched and cried out, and from this Solomon deduced that they were one person, not two, and should have only one share of the inheritance.

1 Kings 4 - Solomon's Administration

A. Solomon's cabinet and governors.

1. (1-6) Solomon's officials.

So King Solomon was king over all Israel. And these were his officials: Azariah the son of Zadok, the priest; Elihoreph and Ahijah, the sons of Shisha, scribes; Jehoshaphat the son of Ahilud, the recorder; Benaiah the son of Jehoiada, over the army; Zadok and Abiathar, the priests; Azariah the son of Nathan, over the officers; Zabud the son of Nathan, a priest and the king's friend; Ahishar, over the household; and Adoniram the son of Abda, over the labor force.

a. **And these were his officials**: Just as the story of the mothers contending over one baby was an example of Solomon's great wisdom, this chapter also shows Solomon's wisdom. The wise way he selected, trained, empowered, and supervised leaders is clearly seen.

    i. *Solomon was a leader of leaders.* No wise leader does it all themselves. They know how to delegate responsibility and authority and get the job done. Solomon's great wisdom enabled him to see the needs to get, train, and employ the right people to meet those needs.

b. **The priest… scribes… the recorder**: Solomon's government was structured much like that in modern nations. He had **officials** who served as ministers or department secretaries over their specific areas of responsibility.

    i. *Solomon's leadership was organized.* He knew that God is a God of design and organization, and that things simply operate better and more efficiently when organized.

    ii. "*Jehoshaphat*, who had served under David (2 Samuel 8:16; 20:24), continued as *recorder*. As such he was more a chief of protocol than a 'remembrancer' or recorder of the past. His status was almost that of a Secretary of State." (Wiseman)

iii. "Since Abiathar had been exiled by Solomon (1 Kings 2:26ff), his inclusion here as a priest seems to be a problem. It must be remembered, however, that while Solomon could only reassign Abiathar's responsibility, he could not take away his title nor his dignity as a priest." (Dilday)

2. (7-19) Solomon's governors.

And Solomon had twelve governors over all Israel, who provided food for the king and his household; each one made provision for one month of the year. These are their names: Ben-Hur, in the mountains of Ephraim; Ben-Deker, in Makaz, Shaalbim, Beth Shemesh, and Elon Beth Hanan; Ben-Hesed, in Arubboth; to him belonged Sochoh and all the land of Hepher; Ben-Abinadab, in all the regions of Dor; he had Taphath the daughter of Solomon as wife; Baana the son of Ahilud, in Taanach, Megiddo, and all Beth Shean, which is beside Zaretan below Jezreel, from Beth Shean to Abel Meholah, as far as the other side of Jokneam; Ben-Geber, in Ramoth Gilead; to him belonged the towns of Jair the son of Manasseh, in Gilead; to him also belonged the region of Argob in Bashan—sixty large cities with walls and bronze gate-bars; Ahinadab the son of Iddo, in Mahanaim; Ahimaaz, in Naphtali; he also took Basemath the daughter of Solomon as wife; Baanah the son of Hushai, in Asher and Aloth; Jehoshaphat the son of Paruah, in Issachar; Shimei the son of Elah, in Benjamin; Geber the son of Uri, in the land of Gilead, in the country of Sihon king of the Amorites, and of Og king of Bashan. He was the only governor who was in the land.

a. **Twelve governors over all Israel**: These men were responsible for taxation in their individual districts. The districts were not strictly separated by tribal borders but often according to **mountains**, **land**, and **region**.

i. *Solomon's leadership was creative.* We can imagine that in the past, **twelve governors** would be apportioned strictly along tribal lines. Solomon knew that the way you did it before wasn't necessarily the best way to do it at the present time. He was willing to try new things.

ii. "The absence of reference to Judah in this list could be explained by 'there was *only one* official in the home-land' (i.e. Judah, RSV) – that is, these twelve districts were additional to Judah, which remained unchanged, some say untaxed." (Wiseman)

b. **Each one made provision for one month of the year**: Taxes were paid in grain and livestock, which were used to support the royal court and the central government. Each governor was responsible for **one month of the year**.

i. *Solomon's leadership was not oppressive.* It doesn't seem too much to do one-twelfth of the work, so each of these governors didn't feel overwhelmed by the burden of raising so much in taxes.

B. The prosperity of Solomon and Israel.

1. (20-21) Peace and prosperity.

Judah and Israel were as numerous as the sand by the sea in multitude, eating and drinking and rejoicing. So Solomon reigned over all kingdoms from the River to the land of the Philistines, as far as the border of Egypt. They brought tribute and served Solomon all the days of his life.

a. **Numerous as the sand by the sea in multitude, eating and drinking and rejoicing**: The reign of Solomon was a golden age for Israel as a kingdom. The population grew robustly and it was a season of great prosperity, allowing plenty of leisure time and pursuit of good pleasures.

b. **So Solomon reigned over all kingdoms from the River to the land of the Philistines, as far as the border of Egypt**: Solomon was not a warrior or a general. This peace was achieved by King David and was enjoyed by King Solomon. It was also assisted - under God's providence - by a season of decline and weakness among Israel's neighbor states.

2. (22-23) Solomon's daily provision.

Now Solomon's provision for one day was thirty kors of fine flour, sixty kors of meal, ten fatted oxen, twenty oxen from the pastures, and one hundred sheep, besides deer, gazelles, roebucks, and fatted fowl.

a. **Ten fatted oxen**: This was an exceptionally large daily meal for one man and shows Solomon clearly had a problem with gluttony (*a small Bible commentator joke - we normally avoided*). This provision was for Solomon's entire household and his royal court.

   i. Some estimate that this much food every day could feed 15,000 to 36,000 people. It supplied considerably more than Solomon's household, large as it was.

   ii. **Fatted oxen** are pen-fed cattle in contrast to open grazing varieties.

b. **Thirty kors of fine flour**: The *kor* equaled 220 liters or about 55 gallons. We can accurately picture 30 55-gallon drums full of **fine flour** being delivered for every day.

c. **One hundred sheep, besides deer, gazelles, roebucks, and fatted fowl**: This list is not meant to stress the idea of opulence and luxury; the stress is on the idea that this daily provision indicated the great prosperity of the kingdom.

   i. "Whether Christianity helps a man to worldly success or not, it helps him to get all the good out of the world that the world can give. It may, or may not, give wealth, but it will make the 'little that a righteous man hath better than the riches of many wicked.'" (Maclaren)

3. (24-28) The political stability of Solomon's kingdom.

For he had dominion over all the region on this side of the River from Tiphsah even to Gaza, namely over all the kings on this side of the River; and he had peace on every side all around him. And Judah and Israel dwelt safely, each man under his vine and his fig tree, from Dan as far as Beersheba, all the days of Solomon. Solomon had forty thousand stalls of horses for his chariots, and twelve thousand horsemen. And these governors, each man in his month, provided food for King Solomon and for all who came to King Solomon's table. There was no lack in their supply. They also brought barley and straw to the proper place, for the horses and steeds, each man according to his charge.

a. **Each man under his vine and his fig tree**: This was a proverbial expression for a time of peace and prosperity in Israel (Isaiah 36:16, Micah 4:4, Zechariah 3:10), indicating safety from both internal and external enemies.

b. **Solomon had forty thousand stalls of horses for his chariots**: The famous stables of Solomon show what a vast cavalry he assembled for Israel. 2 Chronicles 9:25 is a parallel passage and has 4,000 chariots instead of 40,000 – the smaller number seems correct and the larger number is probably due to copyist error.

i. Unfortunately, it also shows that Solomon did not take God's word as seriously as he should. In Deuteronomy 17:16, God spoke specifically to the future kings of Israel: *But he shall not multiply horses for himself.* One may argue if 20 or 100 horses violates the command to *not multiply horses*, certainly **forty thousand stalls of horses** is multiplying horses.

c. **Each man according to his charge**: Spurgeon preached a sermon on this verse, focusing on the idea that we each have a **charge** to fulfill in the Kingdom of God, and we should be diligent to perform it and be expectant in being supplied for this duty.

i. "*In Solomon's court all his officers had a service to carry out*, 'every man according to his charge.' It is exactly so in the kingdom of our Lord Jesus Christ. If we are truly his, he has called us to some work and office, and he wills us to discharge that office diligently. We are not to be gentlemen-at-ease, but men-at-arms; not loiterers, but laborers; not glittering spangles, but burning and shining lights." (Spurgeon)

ii. "Many a servant girl gives her fourpenny-piece to the offering, and if the same proportion were carried out among those who are wealthy, gold would not be so rare a metal in the Lord's treasury. A tithe may be too much for some, but a half might not be enough for another. Let it be, 'Every man according to his charge,' as to measure as well as to matter." (Spurgeon)

iii. Spurgeon concluded the message on a high note: "Everything for Jesus, the glorious Solomon of our hearts, the Beloved of our souls! Life for Jesus! Death for Jesus! Time for Jesus! Eternity for Jesus! Hand and heart for Jesus! Brain and tongue for Jesus! Night and day for Jesus! Sickness or health for Jesus! Honour or dishonor for Jesus! Shame or glory for Jesus! Everything for Jesus, 'Every man according to his charge.' So may it be! Amen."

C. Solomon's wisdom.

1. (29-31) Solomon is famous for his God-given wisdom.

And God gave Solomon wisdom and exceedingly great understanding, and largeness of heart like the sand on the seashore. Thus Solomon's wisdom excelled the wisdom of all the men of the East and all the wisdom of Egypt. For he was wiser than all men—than Ethan the Ezrahite, and Heman, Chalcol, and Darda, the sons of Mahol; and his fame was in all the surrounding nations.

a. **God gave Solomon wisdom and exceedingly great understanding**: In the glory years of Solomon's kingdom, he *used* the great wisdom God gave. Sadly, he did not always use this wisdom, and later fell away from his devotion and worship of God (1 Kings 11:1-11).

b. **His fame was in all the surrounding nations**: Solomon became a prominent and famous man even among kings. In a strong sense, this is the fulfillment of the great promises to an obedient Israel described in Deuteronomy 28.

i. *Now it shall come to pass, if you diligently obey the voice of the LORD your God, to observe carefully all His commandments which I command you today, that the LORD your God will set you high above all nations of the earth.* (Deuteronomy 28:1)

ii. *Then all peoples of the earth shall see that you are called by the name of the LORD, and they shall be afraid of you.* (Deuteronomy 28:10)

iii. In a sense, these blessings came upon Solomon more for *David's* obedience than for his own. David was far more loyal and intimate with God than Solomon; yet God outwardly blessed Solomon more for *David's* sake than He blessed David himself.

c. **He was wiser than all men; than Ethan the Ezrahite, and Heman**: Ethan is the author of Psalm 89 and Heman the author of Psalm 88. The other names are only mentioned in this passage.

2. (32-34) Solomon's broad knowledge of science and nature.

He spoke three thousand proverbs, and his songs were one thousand and five. Also he spoke of trees, from the cedar tree of Lebanon even to the hyssop that springs out of the wall; he spoke also of animals, of birds, of

creeping things, and of fish. And men of all nations, from all the kings of the earth who had heard of his wisdom, came to hear the wisdom of Solomon.

a. **He spoke three thousand proverbs**: Solomon's great wisdom – divinely inspired wisdom in fact – makes up a considerable portion of the Book of Proverbs.

b. **His songs were one thousand and five**: Solomon composed many **songs** but few *psalms* in the sense that David was the *sweet psalmist of Israel* (2 Samuel 23:1). This goes back to Solomon's inferior relationship to God (compared to his father David).

c. **He spoke of trees… also of animals… of creeping things, and of fish**: Solomon's wisdom was not only applied to understanding life and human problems, but also to understanding the world around him. He had a divinely gifted intellect and ability to understand.

i. "Ancient rankings put the cedar tree at the top of the list of plants and hyssop at the lowest level; thus Solomon's botanical interests were all-inclusive." (Dilday)

ii. "While this account reflects Solomon's education as a wise man comparable with those of other contemporary states of his day in literary and scientific attainment, it was no mere rhetoric. The creation of zoological and botanical gardens in the capital city was an achievement boasted by many kings." (Wiseman)

iii. The old rabbis said that even animals brought their disputes to Solomon. A man walked in a field on a hot day with a jug of cool milk when he came upon a serpent dying of thirst. The serpent asked the man for some milk but he refused. Finally, the serpent promised to show the man some hidden treasure if he gave him some milk, and the man agreed. When they went to the place of hidden treasure, the man moved a rock and was about to take the treasure when the serpent pounced upon him and coiled around his neck. The man protested that this was unfair, but the serpent insisted the man would never take his treasure. The man said, "Let's take our case to Solomon" and the serpent agreed. When they went to Solomon the serpent was still coiled around the man's neck. Solomon asked the serpent what he wanted, and the serpent said, "I want to kill this man because the Scriptures command it when they say that I will 'bruise the heel of man.'" Solomon told him to first let go of the man, because the two parties in a trial must have equal standing. When the serpent went to the floor Solomon asked him again what he wanted, and the serpent again said that he wanted to kill the man based on the verse "You shall bruise the heel of the man." Then Solomon turned to the man and said, "To you God's command was to crush the head of the serpent - do it!" And the man crushed the serpent's head (Cited in Ginzberg).

1 Kings 5 - Preparations to Build the Temple

A. Solomon's arrangements with Hiram of Tyre.

1. (1-6) Solomon's message to Hiram of Tyre.

Now Hiram king of Tyre sent his servants to Solomon, because he heard that they had anointed him king in place of his father, for Hiram had always loved David. Then Solomon sent to Hiram, saying: You know how my father David could not build a house for the name of the Lord his God because of the wars which were fought against him on every side, until the Lord put *his foes* under the soles of his feet. But now the Lord my God has given me rest on every side; *there is* neither adversary nor evil occurrence. And behold, I propose to build a house for the name of the Lord my God, as the Lord spoke to my father David, saying, "Your son, whom I will set on your throne in your place, he shall build the house for My name." Now therefore, command that they cut down cedars for me from Lebanon; and my servants will be with your servants, and I will pay you wages for your servants according to whatever you say. For you know *there is* none among us who has skill to cut timber like the Sidonians.

a. **For Hiram had always loved David**: David was a mighty warrior against the enemies of Israel. but he did not regard every neighbor nation as an enemy. David wisely built alliances and friendships with neighbor nations, and the benefit of this also came to Solomon.

i. "Hiram is an abbreviation of Ahiram which means 'Brother of Ram,' or 'My brother is exalted,' or 'Brother of the lofty one'… Archaeologists have discovered a royal sarcophagus in Byblos of Tyre dated about 1200 B.C. inscribed with the king's name, 'Ahiram.' Apparently it belonged to the man in this passage." (Dilday)

ii. **Then Solomon sent to Hiram**: "According to Josephus, copies of such a letter along with Hiram's reply were preserved in both Hebrew and Tyrian archives and were extant in his day (*Antiquities*, 8.2.8)" (Dilday).

b. **You know how my father David could not build a house for the name of the LORD his God**: This means that David told Hiram spiritual things, things that one might think Hiram could not understand or had interest in. In some ways, David spoke to Hiram as if Hiram were already an Israelite.

i. This chapter deals with Solomon's work in obtaining the materials to build the temple. Yet David was so interested in this work that he had already gathered many of the supplies needed to build the temple (2 Chronicles 22:4).

c. **Until the LORD put his foes under the soles of his feet**: "To put *enemies under the feet* was the symbolic act marking conquest. In contemporary art enemies were often depicted as a footstool (as Psalm 110:1)." (Wiseman)

d. **There is neither adversary nor evil occurrence**: The word **adversary** here is literally *Satan*. The Latin Vulgate translates this, "nor a Satan."

e. **I propose to build a house for the name of the LORD my God**: Of course, Solomon did not build a temple for a **name** but for a living God. This is a good example of avoiding direct mention of the name of God in Hebrew writing and speaking. They did this out of reverence to God.

i. Solomon also used this phrase because he wanted to explain that he didn't think the temple would be the house of God in the way pagans thought. "It is to be 'an house for the *name* of the LORD.' That is not the same as 'for the LORD.' Pagan temples might be intended by their builders for the actual residence of the god, but Solomon knew that the heaven of heavens could not contain Him, much less this house which he was about to build" (Maclaren).

f. **Cut down cedars for me from Lebanon**: The cedar trees of Lebanon were legendary for their excellent timber. This means Solomon wanted to build the temple out of the best materials possible.

i. "The Sidonians were noted as timber craftsmen in the ancient world, a fact substantiated on the famous Palmero Stone. Its inscription from 2200 B.C. tells us about timber-carrying ships that sailed from Byblos to Egypt about four hundred years previously. The skill of the Sidonians was expressed in their ability to pick the most suitable trees, know the right time to cut them, fell them with care, and then properly treat the logs." (Dilday)

ii. It also means that Solomon was willing to build this great temple to God with Gentile wood and using Gentile labor. This was a temple to the God of Israel, but it was not only for Israel. Only Jews built the tabernacle, "But the temple is not built without the aid of the Gentile Tyrians. They, together with us, make up the Church of God" (Trapp).

2. (7-12) Hiram's reply to Solomon.

So it was, when Hiram heard the words of Solomon, that he rejoiced greatly and said, "Blessed *be* the LORD this day, for He has given David a wise son over this great people!" Then Hiram sent to Solomon, saying: I have considered *the message* which you sent me, *and* I will do all you desire concerning the cedar and cypress logs. My servants shall bring *them* down from Lebanon to the sea; I will float them in rafts by sea to the place you indicate to me, and will have them broken apart there; then you can take *them* away. And you shall fulfill my desire by giving food for my household. Then Hiram gave Solomon cedar and cypress logs *according to* all his desire. And Solomon gave Hiram twenty thousand kors of wheat *as* food for his household, and twenty kors of pressed oil. Thus Solomon gave to Hiram year by year. So the LORD gave Solomon wisdom, as He had promised him; and there was peace between Hiram and Solomon, and the two of them made a treaty together.

a. **Blessed be the LORD**: We can't say if Hiram was a saved man, but he certainly respected the God of Israel. This was no doubt due to David's godly influence on Hiram.

b. **And you shall fulfill my desire by giving food for my household**: Solomon offered Hiram whatever he wanted as payment for the timber to build the temple (1 Kings 5:6). Hiram did not take unfair advantage, asking only for **food** for his **household**.

i. At the same time, Hiram did expect to be paid. His service and the service of His people were not a gift or a sacrifice. "There are a good many people who get mixed up with religious work, and talk as if it were very near their hearts, who have as sharp an eye to their own advantage as he had. The man who serves God because he gets paid for it, does not serve Him" (Maclaren).

c. **There was peace between Hiram and Solomon**: Solomon, in his God-given wisdom, continued the friendly relationship between Israel and Lebanon.

B. Solomon's labor force.

1. (13-14) The labor force of freemen.

Then King Solomon raised up a labor force out of all Israel; and the labor force was thirty thousand men. And he sent them to Lebanon, ten thousand a month in shifts: they were one month in Lebanon *and* two months at home; Adoniram *was* in charge of the labor force.

a. **The labor force was thirty thousand men**: This huge labor force shows the temple could only be built when Israel could afford the manpower and the materials. It could only be built under the peace and prosperity won by David and enjoyed by Solomon.

b. **Adoniram was in charge of the labor force**: Solomon's wisdom was evident in the way he employed this great workforce. First, he wisely delegated responsibility to men like **Adoniram**. Second, instead of making the Israelites work constantly away from Israel and home, he worked them in shifts.

2. (15-18) The labor force of slaves.

Solomon had seventy thousand who carried burdens, and eighty thousand who quarried *stone* **in the mountains, besides three thousand three hundred from the chiefs of Solomon's deputies, who supervised the people who labored in the work. And the king commanded them to quarry large stones, costly stones,** *and* **hewn stones, to lay the foundation of the temple. So Solomon's builders, Hiram's builders, and the Gebalites quarried** *them;* **and they prepared timber and stones to build the temple.**

a. **Seventy thousand who carried burdens, and eighty thousand who quarried stone**: This seems to describe the number of Canaanite slave laborers that Solomon used.

i. Ginzberg relates some of the legends surrounding the building of the temple. "During the seven years it took to build the Temple, not a single workman died who was employed about it, nor even did a single one fall sick. And as the workmen were sound and robust from first to last, so the perfection of their tools remained unimpaired until the building stood complete. Thus the work suffered no sort of interruption" (Ginzberg).

b. **Besides three thousand three hundred from the chiefs of Solomon's deputies**: This was the middle management team administrating the work of building the temple.

c. **Costly stones**: This is literally *quality stones*, showing that Solomon used high-quality materials even in the foundation where the stones could not be seen.

i. This speaks *to the way we should work for God*. We don't work for appearance only, but also to excel in the deep and hidden things. "I want, dear friends, to urge that all our work for God should be done thoroughly, and especially that part of it which lies lowest, and is least observed of men" (Spurgeon).

ii. This speaks *to the way God works in us*. He works in the deep and hidden things when others are concerned with mere appearances. "We have been the subjects of a great deal of secret, unseen, underground work. The LORD has spent upon us a world of care. My brother, you would not like to unveil those great searchings of heart of which you have been the subject. You have been honored in public; and, if so, you have had many a whipping behind the door lest you should glory in your flesh… All those chastenings, humblings, and searchings of heart have been a private laying of foundations for higher things" (Spurgeon).

iii. This speaks to *the way God builds the church*. He wants to do a work of deep, strong foundations instead of a work a mile wide but an inch deep. "To maintain solid truth you need solid people. Vital godliness is therefore to be aimed at. Twenty thousand people, all merely professing faith, but having no energetic life, may not have grace enough among them to make twenty solid believers. Poor, sickly believers turn the church into an hospital, rather than a camp" (Spurgeon).

d. **The Gebalites quarried them**: "Some suppose that these *Giblites* were the inhabitants of *Biblos*, at the foot of Mount Libanus, northward of Sidon, on the coast of the Mediterranean Sea" (Clarke).

1 Kings 6 - The Construction of the Temple

A. Basic dimensions and structure.

1. (1-6) Basic dimensions of the temple.

And it came to pass in the four hundred and eightieth year after the children of Israel had come out of the land of Egypt, in the fourth year of Solomon's reign over Israel, in the month of Ziv, which *is* the second month, that he began to build the house of the LORD. Now the house which King Solomon built for the LORD, its length *was* sixty cubits, its width twenty, and its height thirty cubits. The vestibule in front of the sanctuary of the house *was* twenty cubits long across the width of the house, *and* the width of *the vestibule extended* ten cubits from the front of the house. And he made for the house windows with beveled frames. Against the wall of the temple he built chambers all around, *against* the walls of the temple, all around the sanctuary and the inner sanctuary. Thus he made side chambers all around it. The lowest chamber *was* five cubits wide, the middle *was* six cubits wide, and the third *was* seven cubits wide; for he made narrow ledges around the outside of the temple, so that *the support beams* would not be fastened into the walls of the temple.

a. **In the four hundred and eightieth year**: This marking point shows just how long Israel lived in the Promised Land without a temple. The tabernacle served the nation well for more than 400 years. The prompting to build the temple was more at the direction and will of God than out of absolute necessity.

i. The date in 1 Kings 6:1 also gives a marking point for the Exodus. As many suppose, the reign of Solomon began in 971 B.C. and ended at 913 B.C. (the temple was begun in 967 B.C.). This means that the Exodus took place in 1447 B.C.

b. **He began to build the house of the LORD**: This was when the actual construction began. Solomon probably started to organize the work right away. There is some evidence that it took three years to prepare timber from Lebanon for use in building. If Solomon began the construction of the temple in the fourth year of his reign, he probably started organizing the construction in the very first year of his reign.

    i. Yet the work was carefully organized and planned even before Solomon became king. 1 Chronicles 28:11-12 tells us, *Then David gave his son Solomon the plans for the vestibule, its houses, its treasuries, its upper chambers, its inner chambers, and the place of the mercy seat; and the plans for all that he had by the Spirit, of the courts of the house of the* LORD, *of all the chambers all around, of the treasuries of the house of God, and of the treasuries for the dedicated things.*

    ii. The writer of 1 Kings never tells us exactly where the temple was built, but the writer of 2 Chronicles tells us that it was built on Mount Moriah (2 Chronicles 3:1), the same place where Abraham went to sacrifice Isaac and Jesus would be crucified (on another part of the hill).

c. **The house which King Solomon built for the** LORD: This chapter describes the building of the temple and its associated areas. There are four main structures described.

- The temple proper (**the house which King Solomon built**), divided into two rooms (the holy place and the most holy place).
- The vestibule or entrance hall on the east side of the temple proper (**the vestibule in front of the sanctuary**). It was thirty feet (10 meters) wide and fifteen feet (5 meters) deep, and the same height as the temple proper.
- The three-storied side chambers (**chambers all around**) which surrounded the temple proper on the north, south, and west sides.
- A large courtyard surrounding the whole structure (the *inner court* mentioned in 1 Kings 6:36).

d. **Its length was sixty cubits, its width twenty, and its height thirty cubits**: Assuming that the ancient cubit was approximately 18 inches (perhaps one-half meter), this means that the temple proper was approximately 90 feet (30 meters) long, 30 feet (10 meters) wide, and 45 feet (15 meters) high. This was not especially large as ancient temples go, but the glory of Israel's temple was not in its size.

    i. Allowing for the outside storage rooms, the vestibule, and the estimated thickness of the walls, the total size of the structure was perhaps 75 cubits long (110 feet, 37 meters) and 50 cubits wide (75 feet, 25 meters).

    ii. The dimensions of the temple also tell us that it was built on the same basic design as the tabernacle, but twice as large. This means that Solomon meant the temple to be a *continuation* of the tabernacle.

e. **He built chambers all around**: These seem to be side rooms adjacent to the temple, yet not structurally part of the temple. The New International Version translates 1 Kings 6:5: *Against the walls of the main hall and inner sanctuary he built a structure around the building, in which there were side rooms.*

2. (7-10) Details of the construction.

And the temple, when it was being built, was built with stone finished at the quarry, so that no hammer or chisel *or* any iron tool was heard in the temple while it was being built. The doorway for the middle story *was* on the right side of the temple. They went up by stairs to the middle *story,* and from the middle to the third. So he built the temple and finished it, and he paneled the temple with beams and boards of cedar. And he built side chambers against the entire temple, each five cubits high; they were attached to the temple with cedar beams.

a. **No hammer or chisel or any iron tool was heard in the temple while it was being built**: The stones used to build the temple were all cut and prepared at another site. The stones were only assembled at the building site of the temple.

i. This speaks to *the way God wants His work done*. The temple had to be built with human labor. God did not and would not send a team of angels to build the temple. Yet Solomon did not want the sound of man's work to dominate the site of the temple. He wanted to communicate, as much as possible, that the temple was of God and not of man.

ii. This speaks to *the way God works in His people*. Often the greatest work in the Kingdom of God happens quietly. Yet the building site of the temple was only quiet because there was a lot of noise and diligent work at the quarry.

iii. This speaks to *God's work in the church*. "But *why* is this so particularly marked? It is not because the temple was a type of the kingdom of God; and the souls of men are to be prepared *here* for *that* place of blessedness? *There*, there is no preaching, exhortations, repentance, tears, cries, nor prayers; the stones must be all squared and fitted here for their place in their New Jerusalem" (Clarke).

b. **He paneled the temple with beams and boards of cedar**: These were some of the finest building materials available. The impression is of a magnificent building.

c. **He built side chambers against the entire temple**: This describes the rooms adjacent to the temple, surrounding it on the north, west, and south sides. These **side chambers** were built in three stories.

B. God's promise and Solomon's building.

1. (11-13) God's promise to Solomon.

Then the word of the LORD came to Solomon, saying: "*Concerning* this temple which you are building, if you walk in My statutes, execute My judgments, keep all My commandments, and walk in them, then I will perform My word with you, which I spoke to your father David. And I will dwell among the children of Israel, and will not forsake My people Israel."

a. **If you walk in My statutes**: This was a conditional promise to Solomon and his descendants. It depended on the obedience of Solomon and his descendants.

b. **I will perform My word with you… And I will dwell among the children of Israel**: God promised an obedient Solomon that he would reign and be blessed, fulfilling the promises God made to David about his reign (2 Samuel 7:5-16). He also promised that His special presence would remain among Israel as a nation.

i. We might say that there was nothing particularly new in this promise. These are essentially the same promises of the Old Covenant made to Israel at Sinai. But this was an important reminder and renewal of previous promises.

c. **And I will dwell among the children of Israel**: God was careful not to say that He would live *in* the temple the way pagans thought their gods lived in temples. He would **dwell among the children of Israel**. The temple was a special place for *man* to meet with God.

2. (14-38) The finished temple.

So Solomon built the temple and finished it. And he built the inside walls of the temple with cedar boards; from the floor of the temple to the ceiling he paneled the inside with wood; and he covered the floor of the temple with planks of cypress. Then he built the twenty-cubit room at the rear of the temple, from floor to ceiling, with cedar boards; he built *it* inside as the inner sanctuary, as the Most Holy *Place*. And in front of it the temple sanctuary was forty cubits *long*. The inside of the temple was cedar, carved with ornamental buds and open flowers. All *was* cedar; there was no stone *to be* seen. And he prepared the inner sanctuary inside the temple, to set the ark of the covenant of the LORD there. The inner sanctuary *was* twenty cubits long, twenty cubits wide, and twenty cubits high. He overlaid it with pure gold, and overlaid the altar of cedar. So Solomon overlaid the inside of the temple with pure gold. He stretched gold chains across the front of the inner sanctuary, and overlaid it with gold. The whole temple he overlaid with gold, until he had finished all the temple; also he overlaid with gold the entire altar that *was* by the inner sanctuary. Inside the inner sanctuary he made two cherubim *of* olive wood, *each* ten cubits high. One wing of the cherub *was* five cubits, and the other wing of the cherub five cubits: ten cubits from the tip of one wing to the tip of the other. And the other cherub *was* ten cubits; both cherubim *were* of the same size and shape. The height of one cherub *was* ten cubits, and so *was* the other cherub. Then he set the cherubim inside the inner room; and they stretched out the wings of the cherubim so that the wing of the one touched *one* wall, and the wing of the other cherub touched the other wall. And their wings touched each other in the middle of the room. Also he overlaid the cherubim with gold. Then he carved all the walls of the temple all around, both the inner and outer *sanctuaries,* with carved figures of cherubim, palm trees, and open flowers. And the floor of the temple he overlaid with gold, both the inner and outer *sanctuaries.* For the entrance of the inner sanctuary he made doors *of* olive wood; the lintel *and* doorposts *were* one-fifth *of the wall.* The two doors *were of* olive wood; and he carved on them figures of cherubim, palm trees, and open flowers, and overlaid *them* with gold; and he spread gold on the cherubim and on the palm trees. So for the door of the sanctuary he also made doorposts *of* olive wood, one-fourth *of the wall.* And the two doors *were of* cypress wood; two panels *comprised* one folding door, and two panels *comprised* the other folding door. Then he carved cherubim, palm trees, and open flowers *on them,* and overlaid *them* with gold applied evenly on the carved work. And he built the inner court with three rows of hewn stone and a row of cedar beams. In the fourth year the foundation of the house of the LORD was laid, in the month of Ziv. And in the eleventh year, in the month of Bul, which is the eighth month, the house was finished in all its details and according to all its plans. So he was seven years in building it.

a. **The inner sanctuary was twenty cubits long, twenty cubits wide, and twenty cubits high**: Special attention was given to the Holy of Holies or Most Holy place. It was a 30-foot (10 meter) cube, completely overlaid with gold. It also had two large sculptures of cherubim (15-foot or 5 meters in height), which were overlaid with gold.

i. There were **gold chains** across the veil separating the Holy Place from the Most Holy Place. "The gold chains, stretched across the front of the inner sanctuary, served to strengthen the concept of the inaccessibility of this Most Holy Place" (Patterson and Austel).

ii. **Two cherubim of olive wood**: These two large sculptures inside the Most Holy Place faced the entrance to this inner room, so as soon as the High Priest entered he saw these giant guardians of the presence of God facing him.

iii. **And the floor of the temple he overlaid with gold**: There was gold everywhere in the temple. The walls were covered with gold (1 Kings 6:20-22), the floor was covered with gold (1 Kings 6:30) and gold was hammered into the carvings on the doors (1 Kings 6:32).

b. **He carved all the walls of the temple all around, both the inner and outer sanctuaries, with carved figures of cherubim, palm trees, and open flowers**: This was after the pattern of the tabernacle, which had woven designs of cherubim on the inner covering.

c. **And he built the inner court**: This **inner court** was the court of the priests where the altar and laver were set and sacrifice was conducted. Outside it was the *great court*, where the people came to pray. Outside it was the *court of the women*, and outside that was the *court of the Gentiles*.

> i. It must always be remembered that under the Old Covenant, the temple was not for the people of Israel. It was only for the priests to meet with God on behalf of the people. The people gathered and worshipped in the outer courtyard.

d. **So he was seven years in building it**: When the temple was finished it was a spectacular building. It was easy for Israel to focus on the temple of God instead of the God of the temple. Yet without continued faithfulness to God, the temple's glory quickly faded. This glorious temple was plundered just five years after the death of Solomon (1 Kings 14:25-27).

1 Kings 7 - Solomon's Palace and the Temple Furnishings

A. The construction of Solomon's palace.

1. (1) Solomon builds his house.

But Solomon took thirteen years to build his own house; so he finished all his house.

a. **But Solomon took thirteen years to build his own house**: 1 Kings 6:38 tells us that Solomon spent 7 years building the temple, but here we learn that he spent 13 years building **his own house**. The temple was glorious, but it seems that Solomon wanted a house that was more glorious than the temple.

i. "It does show the place which his own personal comfort and luxurious tastes had come to occupy in the life of Solomon… It is often by such simple, and unexpected tests, that the deepest facts of a human life are revealed." (Morgan)

ii. We could say that Solomon finished the work of building the temple; the Christian cannot say that the work of spreading the gospel of Jesus Christ is finished.

b. **So he finished all his house**: The following passage describes what a magnificent house Solomon had.

2. (2-12) The splendor of Solomon's palace.

He also built the House of the Forest of Lebanon; its length *was* one hundred cubits, its width fifty cubits, and its height thirty cubits, with four rows of cedar pillars, and cedar beams on the pillars. And *it was* paneled with cedar above the beams that *were* on forty-five pillars, fifteen *to* a row. *There were* windows *with beveled frames in* three rows, and window *was* opposite window *in* three tiers. And all the doorways and doorposts *had* rectangular frames; and window *was* opposite window *in* three tiers. He also made the Hall of Pillars: its length *was* fifty cubits, and its width thirty cubits; and in front of them *was* a portico with pillars, and a canopy *was* in front of them.

Then he made a hall for the throne, the Hall of Judgment, where he might judge; and *it was* paneled with cedar from floor to ceiling. And the house where he dwelt *had* another court inside the hall, of like workmanship. Solomon also made a house like this hall for Pharaoh's daughter, whom he had taken *as wife*. All these *were of* costly stones cut to size, trimmed with saws, inside and out, from the foundation to the eaves, and also on the outside to the great court. The foundation *was of* costly stones, large stones, some ten cubits and some eight cubits. And above *were* costly stones, hewn to size, and cedar wood. The great court *was* enclosed with three rows of hewn stones and a row of cedar beams. So were the inner court of the house of the LORD and the vestibule of the temple.

a. **The House of the Forest of Lebanon**: So much magnificent cedar wood from Lebanon was used to build Solomon's palace that they called it the "**House of the Forest of Lebanon**." Walking in the richly-paneled walls of the palace was like walking in a forest.

i. The **forty-five pillars** set in the House of the Forest of Lebanon also gave the impression of being in a majestic forest.

ii. 1 Kings 10:16-17 mentions 500 gold shields that were hung in the House of the Forest of Lebanon. Isaiah specifically called this building an armory in Isaiah 22:8.

b. **So were the inner court of the house of the LORD**: At the end of the detailed, magnificent description of Solomon's palace, the writer also mentioned that some of the great architectural features of the palace were also used in the **house of the LORD**. We are left with the idea that as great as the temple was, Solomon's palace was better.

i. When one travels in old Europe today, you often come to magnificent cathedrals. These amazing buildings were mostly built hundreds of years ago at great labor and cost to poor people who could never dream of living in such spectacular places. When their most magnificent buildings were churches, it said something about their values. When Solomon made his palace more spectacular than the temple, it said something about his values. Our most magnificent buildings in the modern world – usually given over to business, shopping, or entertainment – say something about our values.

ii. Haggai 1:3-10 speaks powerfully to those who think more about their house than they do the house of God.

B. Huram makes the temple furnishings.

1. (13-14) Huram - half Israeli and the best craftsman around.

Now King Solomon sent and brought Huram from Tyre. He *was* the son of a widow from the tribe of Naphtali, and his father *was* a man of Tyre, a

bronze worker; he was filled with wisdom and understanding and skill in working with all kinds of bronze work. So he came to King Solomon and did all his work.

> a. **Huram from Tyre**: This man was half Israeli and half Gentile, and he was the best craftsman around. Solomon hired him to do **all his work** – that is, the fine artistic work of the palace and especially the temple.

2. (15-51) Huram makes the needed furnishings for the temple basically after the pattern of the tabernacle furnishings.

And he cast two pillars of bronze, each one eighteen cubits high, and a line of twelve cubits measured the circumference of each. Then he made two capitals *of* cast bronze, to set on the tops of the pillars. The height of one capital *was* five cubits, and the height of the other capital *was* five cubits. *He made* a lattice network, with wreaths of chainwork, for the capitals which *were* on top of the pillars: seven chains for one capital and seven for the other capital. So he made the pillars, and two rows of pomegranates above the network all around to cover the capitals that *were* on top; and thus he did for the other capital. The capitals which *were* on top of the pillars in the hall *were* in the shape of lilies, four cubits. The capitals on the two pillars also *had pomegranates* above, by the convex surface which *was* next to the network; and there *were* two hundred such pomegranates in rows on each of the capitals all around. Then he set up the pillars by the vestibule of the temple; he set up the pillar on the right and called its name Jachin, and he set up the pillar on the left and called its name Boaz. The tops of the pillars were in the shape of lilies. So the work of the pillars was finished. And he made the Sea of cast bronze, ten cubits from one brim to the other; *it was* completely round. Its height *was* five cubits, and a line of thirty cubits measured its circumference. Below its brim *were* ornamental buds encircling it all around, ten to a cubit, all the way around the Sea. The ornamental buds *were* cast in two rows when it was cast. It stood on twelve oxen: three looking toward the north, three looking toward the west, three looking toward the south, and three looking toward the east; the Sea *was set* upon them, and all their back parts *pointed* inward. It *was* a handbreadth thick; and its brim was shaped like the brim of a cup, *like* a lily blossom. It contained two thousand baths. He also made ten carts of bronze; four cubits *was* the length of each cart, four cubits its width, and three cubits its height. And this *was* the design of the carts: They had panels, and the panels *were* between frames; on the panels that *were* between the frames *were* lions, oxen, and cherubim. And on the frames *was* a pedestal on top. Below the lions and oxen *were* wreaths of plaited work. Every cart had four bronze wheels and axles of bronze, and its four feet had supports. Under the laver *were* supports of cast *bronze* beside each wreath. Its opening inside the crown at the top *was* one cubit in diameter; and the opening *was* round, shaped *like* a pedestal, one and a half cubits in outside diameter; and also on the opening *were* engravings, but the panels were square, not round. Under the panels *were* the four wheels, and the axles of the wheels *were joined* to the cart. The height of a wheel *was* one and a half cubits. The workmanship of the wheels *was* like the workmanship of a chariot wheel; their axle pins, their rims, their spokes, and their hubs *were* all of cast *bronze*. And *there were* four supports at the four corners of each cart; its supports *were* part of the cart itself. On the top of the cart, at the height of half a cubit, *it was* perfectly round. And on the top of the cart, its flanges and its panels *were* of the same casting. On the plates of its flanges and on its panels he engraved cherubim, lions, and palm trees, wherever there was a clear space on each, with wreaths all around. Thus he made the ten carts. All of them were of the same mold, one measure, *and* one shape. Then he made ten lavers of bronze; each laver contained forty baths, *and* each laver *was* four cubits. On each of the ten carts *was* a laver. And he put five carts on the right side of the house, and five on the left side of the house. He set the Sea on the right side of the house, toward the southeast. Huram made the lavers and the shovels and the bowls. So Huram finished doing all the work that he was to do for King Solomon *for* the house of the LORD: the two pillars, the *two* bowl-shaped capitals that *were* on top of the two pillars; the two networks covering the two bowl-shaped capitals which *were* on top of the pillars; four hundred pomegranates for the two networks (two rows of pomegranates for each network, to cover the two bowl-shaped capitals that *were* on top of the pillars); the ten carts, and ten lavers on the carts; one Sea, and twelve oxen under the Sea; the pots, the shovels, and the bowls. All these articles which Huram made for King Solomon *for* the house of the LORD *were of* burnished bronze. In the plain of Jordan the king had them cast in clay molds, between Succoth and Zaretan. And Solomon did not weigh all the articles, because *there were* so many; the weight of the bronze was not determined. Thus Solomon had all the furnishings made for the house of the LORD: the altar of gold, and the table of gold on which *was* the showbread; the lampstands of pure gold, five on the right *side* and five on the left in front of the inner sanctuary, with the flowers and the lamps and the wick-trimmers of gold; the basins, the trimmers, the bowls, the ladles, and the censers of pure gold; and the hinges of gold, *both* for the doors of the inner room (the Most Holy *Place) and* for the doors of the main hall of the temple. So all the work that King Solomon had done for the house of the LORD was finished; and Solomon brought in the things which his father David had dedicated: the silver and the gold and the furnishings. He put them in the treasuries of the house of the LORD.

a. **He cast two pillars of bronze**: These impressive pillars were actually so noteworthy that they were given names. They were called *Jachin* and *Boaz* (mentioned also in 2 Chronicles 3:17).

> i. "The one on the right was given the name '*Jachin*,' meaning 'He shall establish,' and the one on the left the name '*Boaz*,' meaning 'in strength.'" (Dilday)

> ii. "In practical terms the pillars were to be an ever-present reminder to each successive king of the fact that he was ruling by God's appointment and by his grace, and that in God lay his strength. Just so ought believers today to be ever mindful of God's grace in their lives and of their utter dependence on him." (Patterson and Austel)

> iii. Some believe that the pillars were meant to remind Israel of the twin pillars from the Exodus. The pillar of fire by night and the pillar of cloud by day were constant reminders of the presence of God in the wilderness.

> iv. Every time someone came to the house of the LORD in the days of Solomon they said, "Look! There is *He Shall Establish*. And there is *In Him Is Strength*." This set them in the right frame of mind to worship the LORD. When the crowds gathered at the morning and evening sacrifice to worship the LORD, the Levites led the people standing in front of the temple with these two great, bronze pillars behind them. It was always before them: *He Shall Establish* and *In Him Is Strength*.

> v. One could say that the house of God itself was **Jachin** and **Boaz**. That temple was *established* by God, and built by the *strength* of God. Every time they looked at that temple, they knew that God liked to establish and strengthen things.

> vi. The house of God was a place where people experienced what the pillars were all about. At that house, people were *established* in their relationship with God. At that house, people were given *strength* from the LORD. From this building, it should go out to the whole community: "Come here and get *established*. Come here and receive the *strength* of God."

b. **He made the Sea of cast bronze, ten cubits from one brim to the other**: The huge laver was more than 15 feet (5 meters) across, and was used for the ceremonial washings connected with the temple. In addition, Huram **made ten lavers of bronze; each laver contained forty baths**.

> i. "It was used by priests for cleansing their hands and feet and perhaps also to supply water to the standing basins for the rinsing of offerings (2 Chronicles 4:10)" (Wiseman). Poole believes that perhaps water came out of the bulls that formed the foundation of the Sea.

> ii. "The volume of the Sea was 2,000 baths, generally calculated to be about 11,500 gallons" [43,532 liters] (Patterson and Austel).

c. **The table of gold on which was the showbread**: 2 Chronicles 4:8 says there were 10 tables of showbread. Here, they are described collectively as a unit.

d. **He put them in the treasuries of the house of the LORD**: All these great works of art and articles of great value were placed in the temple. This included the ten carts and the shovels, bowls and other needed utensils for sacrifices.

e. **Solomon brought in the things which his father David had dedicated**: God told David that he could not build the temple, but David still collected furnishings and treasures for the temple that his son Solomon would build (1 Chronicles 29).

1 Kings 8 - The Dedication of the Temple

A. The Ark of the Covenant is brought to the temple.

1. (1-2) All of Israel assembles at Jerusalem.

Now Solomon assembled the elders of Israel and all the heads of the tribes, the chief fathers of the children of Israel, to King Solomon in Jerusalem, that they might bring up the ark of the covenant of the LORD from the City of David, which *is* Zion. Therefore all the men of Israel assembled with King Solomon at the feast in the month of Ethanim, which *is* the seventh month.

a. **Solomon assembled the elders of Israel and all the heads of the tribes, the chief fathers of the children of Israel**: Solomon intended this to be a spectacular opening ceremony for the temple. It was probably on the scale of the large productions in our modern Olympic Games opening ceremonies.

b. **That they might bring up the ark of the covenant of the LORD**: The temple wasn't ready to operate until the ark of the covenant was set in the Most Holy Place. The ark was the most important item in the temple.

c. **Which is the seventh month**: The temple was finished in the eighth month (1 Kings 6:38), but Solomon chose the seventh month for the dedication, eleven months later.

i. "Which time he chose with common respect to his people's convenience, because now they had gathered in all their fruits, and now they were come up to Jerusalem to celebrate the feast of tabernacles." (Poole)

ii. There may have also been another reason. "It has already been observed that Solomon deferred the dedication of the temple to the following year after it was finished, because that year, according to Archbishop Usher, was a *jubilee*" (Clarke).

2. (3-9) The ark of the covenant is set in the Most Holy Place.

So all the elders of Israel came, and the priests took up the ark. Then they brought up the ark of the LORD, the tabernacle of meeting, and all the

holy furnishings that *were* in the tabernacle. The priests and the Levites brought them up. Also King Solomon, and all the congregation of Israel who were assembled with him, *were* with him before the ark, sacrificing sheep and oxen that could not be counted or numbered for multitude. Then the priests brought in the ark of the covenant of the LORD to its place, into the inner sanctuary of the temple, to the Most Holy *Place,* under the wings of the cherubim. For the cherubim spread *their* two wings over the place of the ark, and the cherubim overshadowed the ark and its poles. The poles extended so that the ends of the poles could be seen from the holy *place,* in front of the inner sanctuary; but they could not be seen from outside. And they are there to this day. Nothing *was* in the ark except the two tablets of stone which Moses put there at Horeb, when the LORD made *a covenant* with the children of Israel, when they came out of the land of Egypt.

a. **The priests took up the ark**: Solomon was careful to obey what God commanded about transporting the ark of the covenant, that it was only to be carried by priests. He would not repeat the error of his father David in 2 Samuel 6:1-8.

b. **And all the holy furnishings that were in the tabernacle**: The ark of the covenant was the most important item in the temple, but not the *only* item. They also brought the lampstand, the table of showbread, and the altar of incense from the **tabernacle** into the temple.

> i. "It is generally agreed that there were now *two* tabernacles, one at Gibeon, and the other in the City of David, which one David had constructed as a temporary residence for the ark." (Clarke)

c. **Sacrificing sheep and oxen that could not be counted or numbered for multitude**: Solomon went far beyond custom and expectation in his effort to honor and praise God on this great day.

d. **Nothing was in the ark except the two tablets of stone which Moses put there at Horeb**: At an earlier point in Israel's history, there were three items in the ark of the covenant. Earlier, inside the ark were the golden pot that had the manna (Exodus 16:33), Aaron's rod that budded (Numbers 17:6-11), and the tablets of the covenant (Exodus 25:16). We don't know what happened to the golden pot of manna and Aaron's rod, but they were not in the ark when Solomon set it in the Most Holy Place.

e. **When the LORD made a covenant with the children of Israel, when they came out of the land of Egypt**: The reminder of the deliverance from Egypt is significant, because there was a sense in which this – some 500 years after the Exodus – was the culmination of the deliverance from Egypt. Out of Egypt and into the wilderness Israel (out of necessity) lived in tents - and the dwelling of God was a tent. Now since Solomon built the temple, the structure representing the dwelling of God among Israel was a *building*, a place of permanence and security.

3. (10-13) The glory of God fills the temple.

And it came to pass, when the priests came out of the holy *place*, that the cloud filled the house of the LORD, so that the priests could not continue ministering because of the cloud; for the glory of the LORD filled the house of the LORD. Then Solomon spoke:

"The LORD said He would dwell in the dark cloud.
I have surely built You an exalted house,
And a place for You to dwell in forever."

a. **The cloud filled the house of the LORD**: This was the cloud of glory, seen often in the Old and New Testaments, sometimes called the cloud of *Shekinah* glory. It is hard to *define* the glory of God; we could call it the radiant outshining of His character and presence. Here it was manifested in a cloud.

- This is the cloud that stood by Israel in the wilderness (Exodus 13:21-22).
- This is the cloud of glory that God spoke to Israel from (Exodus 16:10).
- This is the cloud from which God met with Moses and others (Exodus 19:9, 24:15-18, Numbers 11:25, 12:5, 16:42).
- This is the cloud that stood by the door of the Tabernacle (Exodus 33:9-10).
- This is the cloud from which God appeared to the High Priest in the Holy Place inside the veil (Leviticus 16:2).
- This is the cloud of Ezekiel's vision, filling the temple of God with the brightness of His glory (Ezekiel 10:4).
- This is the cloud of glory that overshadowed Mary when she conceived Jesus by the power of the Holy Spirit (Luke 1:35).
- This is the cloud present at the transfiguration of Jesus (Luke 9:34-35).
- This is the cloud of glory that received Jesus into heaven at His ascension (Acts 1:9).
- This is the cloud that will display the glory of Jesus Christ when He returns in triumph to this earth (Luke 21:27, Revelation 1:7).

  i. "There is a parallel to this event in Acts 2:1-4 in which God marks the inception of the church as the temple of the Holy Spirit by making his presence known through the sound of a mighty rushing wind and by filling those present with the Holy Spirit." (Patterson and Austel)

b. **So that the priests could not continue ministering because of the cloud**: The extreme presence of the glory of God made *normal* service impossible. The sense of the presence of God was so intense that the priests felt it was impossible to continue in the building.

i. We know that God is good and that God is love; why should an intense presence of goodness and love make the priests feel they could not continue? Because God is not only goodness and love, He is also *holy* – and the holiness of God made the priests feel that they could no longer stand in His presence.

ii. The intense sense of the presence of our holy God is not a "warm and fuzzy" feeling. Men like Peter (Luke 5:8), Isaiah (Isaiah 6:5), and John (Revelation 1:17) felt *stricken* in the presence of God. This was not because God forced an uncomfortable feeling upon them, but because they simply could not be comfortable sensing the difference between their sinfulness and the holiness of God.

iii. We can also think of the **priests** as those who ministered unto God under the Old Covenant. The New Covenant - the covenant of grace and truth (John 1:17) – offers us a better access to God.

iv. This glory remained at the temple until Israel utterly rejected God in the days of the divided monarchy. The prophet Ezekiel saw the glory depart the temple (Ezekiel 10:18).

c. **I have surely built You an exalted house, and a place for You to dwell in forever**: Solomon rightly sensed that the presence of the cloud meant that God dwelt in the temple in a special way. As long as this did not slip into a superstitious misunderstanding, it was good to recognize a special place to come and meet with God.

i. "Language experts say the poem is incomplete and fragmented, and that it apparently had another opening line in its original form." (Dilday)

4. (14-21) Solomon's speech at the dedication of the temple.

Then the king turned around and blessed the whole assembly of Israel, while all the assembly of Israel was standing. And he said: "Blessed *be* the LORD God of Israel, who spoke with His mouth to my father David, and with His hand has fulfilled *it,* saying, 'Since the day that I brought My people Israel out of Egypt, I have chosen no city from any tribe of Israel *in which* to build a house, that My name might be there; but I chose David to be over My people Israel.' Now it was in the heart of my father David to build a temple for the name of the LORD God of Israel. But the LORD said to my father David, 'Whereas it was in your heart to build a temple for My name, you did well that it was in your heart. Nevertheless you shall not build the temple, but your son who will come from your body, he shall build the temple for My name.' So the LORD has fulfilled His word which He spoke; and I have filled the position of my father David, and sit on the throne of Israel, as the LORD promised; and I have built a temple for the name of the LORD God of Israel. And there I have made a place for the

ark, in which *is* the covenant of the Lord which He made with our fathers, when He brought them out of the land of Egypt."

a. **Who spoke with His mouth to my father David, and with His hand has fulfilled it**: Solomon recognized that the temple was the fulfillment of *God's* plan, more than David's or Solomon's. David and Solomon were human instruments, but the work was God's.

b. **Out of Egypt… out of the land of Egypt**: Solomon pressed the remembrance of the Exodus. Though it happened 500 years before, it was just as important and real for Israel as the day it happened.

B. Solomon's prayer.

1. (22-23) Solomon recognizes the nature and character of God.

Then Solomon stood before the altar of the Lord in the presence of all the assembly of Israel, and spread out his hands toward heaven; and he said: "Lord God of Israel, *there is* no God in heaven above or on earth below like You, who keep *Your* covenant and mercy with Your servants who walk before You with all their hearts.

a. **Stood before the altar of the Lord**: Solomon did not dedicate the temple from *within* the temple. It would be inappropriate for him to do so, because he was a king and not a priest. The Holy Place and Most Holy Place were only for chosen descendants of the High Priest.

b. **And spread out his hands toward heaven**: This was the most common posture of prayer in the Old Testament. Many modern people close their eyes, bow their head, and fold their hands as they pray; but the Old Testament tradition was to spread out the hands toward heaven in a gesture of surrender, openness, and ready reception.

i. "It is worthy of remark concerning this prayer that it is as full and comprehensive as if it were meant to be the summary of all future prayers offered in the temple." (Spurgeon)

ii. "One is struck, moreover, with the fact that the language is far from new, and is full of quotations from the Pentateuch, some of which are almost word for word, while the sense of the whole may be found in those memorable passages in Leviticus and Deuteronomy." (Spurgeon)

c. **There is no God in heaven above or on earth below like You**: Solomon recognized that God was completely unique. The pretended gods of the other nations could not compare to Him in any way.

2. (24-26) Solomon recognizes God as the maker and keeper of promises.

"You have kept what You promised Your servant David my father; You have both spoken with Your mouth and fulfilled *it* with Your hand, as *it is* this day. Therefore, Lord God of Israel, now keep what You promised

Your servant David my father, saying, 'You shall not fail to have a man sit
before Me on the throne of Israel, only if your sons take heed to their way,
that they walk before Me as you have walked before Me.' And now I pray,
O God of Israel, let Your word come true, which You have spoken to Your
servant David my father.

a. **You have kept what You promised**: Solomon first thanked and praised
God for His *past* fulfillment of promises.

b. **Now keep what You promised Your servant David**: Solomon called upon
God to keep the promises that He made. This is the great secret to power
in prayer – to take God's promises to heart in faith, and then to boldly and
reverently call upon Him to fulfill the promises.

i. "God sent the promise on purpose to be used. If I see a Bank of England
note, it is a promise for a certain amount of money, and I take it and use
it. But oh I my friend, do try and use God's promises; nothing pleases
God better than to see his promises put in circulation; he loves to see his
children bring them up to him, and say, 'LORD, do as thou hast said.' And
let me tell you that it glorifies God to use his promises." (Spurgeon)

ii. This kind of prayer *lays hold of* God's promise. Just because God
promises does not mean that we possess. Through believing prayer like
this, God promises and we appropriate. If we don't appropriate in faith,
God's promise is left unclaimed.

3. (27-30) Solomon asks God to dwell in this place and honor those who seek
Him here.

"But will God indeed dwell on the earth? Behold, heaven and the heaven
of heavens cannot contain You. How much less this temple which I have
built! Yet regard the prayer of Your servant and his supplication, O LORD
my God, and listen to the cry and the prayer which Your servant is praying
before You today: that Your eyes may be open toward this temple night
and day, toward the place of which You said, 'My name shall be there,' that
You may hear the prayer which Your servant makes toward this place. And
may You hear the supplication of Your servant and of Your people Israel,
when they pray toward this place. Hear in heaven Your dwelling place; and
when You hear, forgive.

a. **How much less this temple which I have built**: We are glad that Solomon
said this. From his statement in 1 Kings 8:12-13, we might have thought that
he drifted towards a superstitious idea that God actually *lived* in the temple to
the exclusion of other places. It was important to recognize that though God
had a *special* presence in the temple, He was far too great to be restricted to
the temple.

b. **May You hear the supplication of Your servant and of Your people Israel, when they pray toward this place**: Solomon asked God to incline His ear towards the king and the people when they prayed toward the temple. For this reason, many observant Jews still pray facing the direction of the site of the temple in Jerusalem.

c. **When You hear, forgive**: Solomon knew that the most important thing Israel needed was *forgiveness*. This was the greatest answer to prayer Israel could expect from God.

4. (31-32) Hear when Your people take an oath at the temple.

"When anyone sins against his neighbor, and is forced to take an oath, and comes *and* takes an oath before Your altar in this temple, then hear in heaven, and act, and judge Your servants, condemning the wicked, bringing his way on his head, and justifying the righteous by giving him according to his righteousness.

a. **And comes and takes an oath before Your altar in this temple**: The temple grounds were used as a place to verify and authorize oaths. When a dispute came down to one word against another, Solomon asked that the temple would be a place to properly swear by.

b. **Hear in heaven, and act, and judge Your servants**: Solomon asked the God who can see what man can't – who knows the hidden heart of man – to enforce from heaven the oaths made at the temple.

i. The old Puritan commentator John Trapp could not resist mentioning a fulfillment of this principle in his own day: "Anne Averies, who, forswearing herself, A.D. 1575, February 11, at a shop of Wood Street in London, praying God she might sink where she stood if she had not paid for the wares she took, fell down presently speechless, and with horrible stink died."

5. (33-34) Hear when Your people are defeated.

"When Your people Israel are defeated before an enemy because they have sinned against You, and when they turn back to You and confess Your name, and pray and make supplication to You in this temple, then hear in heaven, and forgive the sin of Your people Israel, and bring them back to the land which You gave to their fathers.

a. **When Your people Israel are defeated before an enemy**: Many times in their history, Israel suffered defeat and could only cry out to God. It was even worse when the defeat was because they had **sinned against** the LORD Himself.

b. **When they turn back to You and confess Your name, and pray and make supplication to You in the temple, then hear in heaven**: Solomon asked God to hear the prayers of a defeated, yet humble and penitent Israel. God answered this prayer of Solomon, and He forgives and restores His defeated people when they come in humble repentance.

6. (35-40) Hear in times of plague and famine.

"When the heavens are shut up and there is no rain because they have sinned against You, when they pray toward this place and confess Your name, and turn from their sin because You afflict them, then hear in heaven, and forgive the sin of Your servants, Your people Israel, that You may teach them the good way in which they should walk; and send rain on Your land which You have given to Your people as an inheritance. When there is famine in the land, pestilence *or* blight *or* mildew, locusts *or* grasshoppers; when their enemy besieges them in the land of their cities; whatever plague or whatever sickness *there is*; whatever prayer, whatever supplication is made by anyone, *or* by all Your people Israel, when each one knows the plague of his own heart, and spreads out his hands toward this temple: then hear in heaven Your dwelling place, and forgive, and act, and give to everyone according to all his ways, whose heart You know (for You alone know the hearts of all the sons of men), that they may fear You all the days that they live in the land which You gave to our fathers.

a. **When the heavens are shut up and there is no rain**: Drought was a constant threat for the agriculturally-based economy of Israel. If there was no rain, there was no food.

b. **When they pray toward this place and confess Your name, and turn from their sin because You afflict them, then hear in heaven**: Solomon doesn't take it for granted that God would forgive and hear His repentant people. God's good response to our repentance comes from His *grace*, not from *justice*.

c. **When each one knows the plague of his own heart**: Solomon recognized that some plagues are easily seen, but other plagues come from our own heart. Many are cursed by a plague that no one else can see, but lives in their **own heart**. Solomon asks God to answer such a plague-stricken man when he humbly pleads at the temple.

i. A man did not have to be sinless or righteous to have his prayer answered at the temple. He could be a guilty man, stricken by **the plague of his own heart**, and still find a gracious God when He came in humble repentance.

ii. "A great many men think they know the plague of other people's hearts, and there is a great deal of talk in the world about this family, and that person, and the other. I pray you let the scandals of the hour alone, and think of your own evils." (Spurgeon)

7. (41-43) Hear when a foreigner prays.

"Moreover, concerning a foreigner, who *is* not of Your people Israel, but has come from a far country for Your name's sake (for they will hear of

Your great name and Your strong hand and Your outstretched arm), when he comes and prays toward this temple, hear in heaven Your dwelling place, and do according to all for which the foreigner calls to You, that all peoples of the earth may know Your name and fear You, as *do* Your people Israel, and that they may know that this temple which I have built is called by Your name.

> a. **Moreover, concerning a foreigner**: The temple was in Israel, but it was always intended to be a house of prayer for *all* nations (Isaiah 56:7). God wanted the court of the Gentiles to be a place where the nations could come and pray.
>
> > i. The violation of this principle made Jesus angry. When He came to the temple and found the outer courts – the only place where the Gentile nations could come and pray – more like a swap meet than a house of prayer, He drove out the moneychangers and the merchants (Matthew 21:13).
>
> b. **Hear in heaven Your dwelling place, and do according to all for which the foreigner calls to You, that all peoples of the earth may know Your name and fear You**: Solomon asked God to hear the prayer of the foreigner out of a *missionary* impulse. He knew that when God mercifully answered the prayers of foreigners, it drew those from other nations to the God of all nations.

8. (44-53) Hear when Israel goes out to battle and prays from captivity.

"When Your people go out to battle against their enemy, wherever You send them, and when they pray to the LORD toward the city which You have chosen and the temple which I have built for Your name, then hear in heaven their prayer and their supplication, and maintain their cause. When they sin against You (for *there is* no one who does not sin), and You become angry with them and deliver them to the enemy, and they take them captive to the land of the enemy, far or near; *yet* when they come to themselves in the land where they were carried captive, and repent, and make supplication to You in the land of those who took them captive, saying, 'We have sinned and done wrong, we have committed wickedness'; and *when* they return to You with all their heart and with all their soul in the land of their enemies who led them away captive, and pray to You toward their land which You gave to their fathers, the city which You have chosen and the temple which I have built for Your name: then hear in heaven Your dwelling place their prayer and their supplication, and maintain their cause, and forgive Your people who have sinned against You, and all their transgressions which they have transgressed against You; and grant them compassion before those who took them captive, that they may have compassion on them (for they *are* Your people and Your

inheritance, whom You brought out of Egypt, out of the iron furnace), that Your eyes may be open to the supplication of Your servant and the supplication of Your people Israel, to listen to them whenever they call to You. For You separated them from among all the peoples of the earth *to be* Your inheritance, as You spoke by Your servant Moses, when You brought our fathers out of Egypt, O Lord God."

a. **When Your people go out to battle against their enemy, wherever You send them**: Solomon prayed with the idea that God should answer the prayers for victory made in foreign lands towards the temple, but only when they battle as God *sent* them. This was not a blanket request for blessing on every military adventure.

b. **When they sin against You (for there is no one who does not sin)**: This is a succinct Old Testament statement of the principle most clearly stated in Romans 3:23: *for all have sinned and fall short of the glory of God.*

c. **When they come to themselves in the land where they were carried captive**: Solomon also asked God to hear Israel's prayer from captivity in a foreign land. This recognized that the God of the Temple could answer prayers made away from the temple.

C. Solomon blesses the people.

1. (54-61) Solomon blesses the people of Israel.

And so it was, when Solomon had finished praying all this prayer and supplication to the Lord, that he arose from before the altar of the Lord, from kneeling on his knees with his hands spread up to heaven. Then he stood and blessed all the assembly of Israel with a loud voice, saying: "Blessed *be* the Lord, who has given rest to His people Israel, according to all that He promised. There has not failed one word of all His good promise, which He promised through His servant Moses. May the Lord our God be with us, as He was with our fathers. May He not leave us nor forsake us, that He may incline our hearts to Himself, to walk in all His ways, and to keep His commandments and His statutes and His judgments, which He commanded our fathers. And may these words of mine, with which I have made supplication before the Lord, be near the Lord our God day and night, that He may maintain the cause of His servant and the cause of His people Israel, as each day may require, that all the peoples of the earth may know that the Lord *is* God; *there is* no other. Let your heart therefore be loyal to the Lord our God, to walk in His statutes and keep His commandments, as at this day."

a. **He arose from before the altar of the Lord, from kneeling on his knees with his hands spread up to heaven**: 1 Kings 8:22 tells us that Solomon began this prayer standing, but some time before he finished, he fell to his knees in reverence to God.

> i. Ezra prayed on his knees (Ezra 9:5), the Psalmist called us to kneel (Psalm 95:6), Daniel prayed on his knees (Daniel 6:10), people came to Jesus kneeling (Matthew 17:14, Matthew 20:20, Mark 1:40), Stephen prayed on his knees (Acts 7:60), Peter prayed on his knees (Acts 9:40), Paul prayed on his knees (Acts 20:36, Ephesians 3:14), and other early Christians prayed on their knees (Acts 21:5). Most importantly, Jesus prayed on His knees (Luke 22:41). The Bible has enough prayer *not* on the knees to show us that it isn't required, but it also has enough prayer *on* the knees to show us that it is good.

b. **There has not failed one word of all His good promise, which He promised through His servant Moses**: Since Solomon prayed often appealing to God's promises, it makes sense that he praised God for the *past* fulfillment of His promises. Knowing this gave Solomon confidence in prayer.

c. **May the LORD our God be with us, as He was with our fathers**: God promised to be with Israel, but Solomon knew it was important to ask God to fulfill His promise. He comes pleading the promises of God.

d. **That all the peoples of the earth may know that the LORD is God**: Solomon again shows the often-neglected missionary impulse God wanted in Israel. Blessing to Israel wasn't meant to end with Israel; God wanted to bless the world *through* Israel.

2. (62-66) The feast of dedication for the temple.

Then the king and all Israel with him offered sacrifices before the LORD. And Solomon offered a sacrifice of peace offerings, which he offered to the LORD, twenty-two thousand bulls and one hundred and twenty thousand sheep. So the king and all the children of Israel dedicated the house of the LORD. On the same day the king consecrated the middle of the court that *was* in front of the house of the LORD; for there he offered burnt offerings, grain offerings, and the fat of the peace offerings, because the bronze altar that *was* before the LORD *was* too small to receive the burnt offerings, the grain offerings, and the fat of the peace offerings. At that time Solomon held a feast, and all Israel with him, a great assembly from the entrance of Hamath to the Brook of Egypt, before the LORD our God, seven days and seven *more* days—fourteen days. On the eighth day he sent the people away; and they blessed the king, and went to their tents joyful and glad of heart for all the good that the LORD had done for His servant David, and for Israel His people.

a. **He offered to the LORD, twenty-two thousand bulls and one hundred and twenty thousand sheep**: This was a staggering - almost grotesque - amount of sacrifice. Each animal was ritually sacrificed and a portion was dedicated to the LORD, and the remainder was given to the priests and the people. It was enough to feed a vast multitude for two weeks.

i. It was such a great amount of sacrifice that they specially consecrated the area in front of the temple to receive sacrifices, because **the bronze altar that was before the LORD was too small to receive the burnt offerings**.

b. **At that time Solomon held a feast, and all Israel with him**: From the time of year and the length of this **feast**, we understand that this was the Feast of Tabernacles, extended beyond its normal seven days on this special occasion.

i. "The Feast of Booths was in itself a grand occasion for rejoicing and for an enhanced spirit of community among all Israelites. The dedication of the temple made this occasion all the more joyful and memorable, and the time of the celebration was suitably extended." (Patterson and Austel)

c. **For all the good that the LORD had done for His servant David, and for Israel His people**: This account of the dedication of the temple ends where the story of the temple began – with David, not Solomon. The writer remembers that it was David's heart and vision that started the work of the temple (2 Samuel 7:1-3 and following).

i. "How happy must these people have been, and how prosperous, had their king continued to walk uprightly before God! But alas! the king fell, and the nation followed his example." (Clarke)

1 Kings 9 - God's Warning to Solomon

A. God appears to Solomon again.

1. (1-5) God confirms the answer to Solomon's prayer.

And it came to pass, when Solomon had finished building the house of the LORD and the king's house, and all Solomon's desire which he wanted to do, that the LORD appeared to Solomon the second time, as He had appeared to him at Gibeon. And the LORD said to him: "I have heard your prayer and your supplication that you have made before Me; I have consecrated this house which you have built to put My name there forever, and My eyes and My heart will be there perpetually. Now if you walk before Me as your father David walked, in integrity of heart and in uprightness, to do according to all that I have commanded you, *and* if you keep My statutes and My judgments, then I will establish the throne of your kingdom over Israel forever, as I promised David your father, saying, 'You shall not fail to have a man on the throne of Israel.'"

a. **When Solomon had finished building the house of the LORD and the King's house**: This was some 24 years after Solomon came to the throne. The temple and the palace work at Jerusalem were finished. Now Solomon had to deal with life *after* completing his greatest accomplishment.

i. "It was the hour when the accomplishment of work means the relaxation of effort. That is always a perilous hour, and the greater the work done the graver the peril. A life which has been full of activity, when that activity ceases, demands some new interest, and will find it, either high or low, noble or ignoble." (Morgan)

ii. John Trapp on the words, **all Solomon's desire**: "The word signifieth such a desire as a young man hath after his mistress, or a bridegroom toward his bride; which showeth that Solomon took too much content in his buildings and furniture, passed over his affections too much unto them, and here began his fall."

b. **The LORD appeared to Solomon the second time**: God was good to give Solomon a special appearance at the beginning of his reign (1 Kings 3:5-9). It was even better of God to grant a unique appearance **to Solomon the second time**.

i. "Brethren, we want renewed appearances, fresh manifestations, new visitations from on high; and I commend to those of you who are getting on in life, that while you thank God for the past, and look back with joy to his visits to you in your early days, you now seek and ask for a second visitation of the Most High." (Spurgeon)

ii. "We do not need to be converted again; yet we do want that again over our heads the windows of heaven should be opened, that again a Pentecost should be given, and that we should renew our youth like the eagles, to run without weariness, and walk without fainting. The Lord fulfill to everyone of his people to-night his blessing upon Solomon!" (Spurgeon)

c. **I have heard your prayer**: The great prayer of Solomon in 1 Kings 8 meant nothing unless God **heard** the prayer. The true measure of our prayer is if God in heaven *answers* the prayer.

i. "Have you never known what it is to leave off prayer when you are in the middle of it, and say, "I am heard: I am heard"? Have you not felt that you needed not to cry any longer, for you had gained your suit, and must rather begin to praise than continue to pray? When a man goes to a bank with a cheque, and he gets the money, he does not stand loafing about the counter: he goes off about his business. And oftentimes before God, he that is prepared to be a long time in prayer if it should be necessary, feels that he must be brief in petition and long in thanksgiving." (Spurgeon)

ii. This answer seems to have come many years after the actual dedication of the temple. Yet God also gave Solomon an immediate answer of approval at the time of dedication, when the sacrifices were consumed with fire from heaven (2 Chronicles 7:1-7).

d. **I have consecrated this house which you have built**: The building was Solomon's work, done in the power and inspiration of the LORD. The *consecration* of the building was God's work. Solomon could build a building, but only God could hallow it.

i. "Man builds; God hallows. This co-operation between man and God pervades all life. Man performs the outward and mechanical; God the inward and spiritual… We must be careful to do our part with reverence and godly fear, remembering that God must work in realms we cannot touch, and to issues we cannot reach, before our poor exertions can avail." (Meyer)

e. **Now if you walk before Me as your father David walked… then I will establish the throne of your kingdom over Israel forever**: God's answer to Solomon's previous prayer had a great *condition*. If Solomon walked before God in obedience and faithfulness, he could expect blessing on his reign and the reign of his descendants, and the dynasty of David would endure forever.

i. God did not demand perfect obedience from Solomon. David certainly did not walk perfectly before the LORD, and God told Solomon to **walk before Me as your father David walked**. This was not out of reach for Solomon.

2. (6-9) God warns Solomon.

"But **if you or your sons at all turn from following Me, and do not keep My commandments** *and* **My statutes which I have set before you, but go and serve other gods and worship them, then I will cut off Israel from the land which I have given them; and this house which I have consecrated for My name I will cast out of My sight. Israel will be a proverb and a byword among all peoples. And** *as for* **this house,** *which* **is exalted, everyone who passes by it will be astonished and will hiss, and say, 'Why has the LORD done thus to this land and to this house?' Then they will answer, 'Because they forsook the LORD their God, who brought their fathers out of the land of Egypt, and have embraced other gods, and worshiped them and served them; therefore the LORD has brought all this calamity on them.'"**

a. **But if you or your sons at all turn from following Me… then I will cut off Israel from the land**: The positive promise of 1 Kings 9:1-5 was followed by a negative promise. If Solomon or his descendants were to **turn from following** the LORD, God promised to correct a disobedient Israel.

b. **And this house which I have consecrated for My name I will cast out of My sight**: God answered Solomon's prayer in 1 Kings 8, but it was not an unqualified promise to bless the temple in *any* circumstance. God blessed the temple and filled it with the glory of His presence, but he would cast it out of His sight if the kings of Israel forsook the LORD.

i. With such a glorious temple, Israel would be tempted to forsake the God of the temple and make an idol of the temple of God. Here the LORD made them know that He could never bless this error.

c. **Israel will become a proverb… everyone who passes by it will be astonished and will hiss**: Under the Old Covenant, God promised to use Israel to exalt Himself among the nations one way or another. If Israel obeyed, He would bless them so much that others had to recognize the hand of God upon Israel. If Israel disobeyed, He would chastise them so severely that the nations would **be astonished** at the hard work of God among His disobedient people, and they would know that **the LORD has brought all this calamity on them**.

    i. The Living Bible has a vivid wording of 1 Kings 9:7: "Israel will become a joke to the nations and an example and proverb of sudden disaster."

B. The ways and means of Solomon's great building projects.

1. (10-14) Lumber and gold from King Hiram of Tyre.

Now it happened at the end of twenty years, when Solomon had built the two houses, the house of the LORD and the king's house (Hiram the king of Tyre had supplied Solomon with cedar and cypress and gold, as much as he desired), *that* King Solomon then gave Hiram twenty cities in the land of Galilee. Then Hiram went from Tyre to see the cities which Solomon had given him, but they did not please him. So he said, "What *kind of* cities *are* these which you have given me, my brother?" And he called them the land of Cabul, as they are to this day. Then Hiram sent the king one hundred and twenty talents of gold.

    a. **Hiram the king of Tyre had supplied Solomon with cedar and cypress and gold**: Tyre – the prominent city in the land just north of Israel (modern Lebanon) – was noted for its fine wood.

    b. **King Solomon then gave Hiram twenty cities in the land of Galilee**: This was not good. Hiram was indeed a friend to both David and Solomon, but the land of Israel was given to Israel by divine decree. Trading Israel's land for a glorious temple and palace was not a good deal.

        i. However, the transaction may be described here to show that Solomon was a shrewd dealer and got the better of Hiram in these arrangements. It seems that Solomon gave Hiram some fairly insignificant settlements and received a large amount of gold in return.

        ii. "To pay for the *gold* Solomon mortgaged *twenty* 'settlements' (rather than *towns*, for *irim* is used of any group of habitations from a hamlet to a metropolis)." (Wiseman)

        iii. "It is clear that Hiram considered the cities to be worthless, and taunted Solomon for giving him 'good-for-nothing' towns. Hiram nicknamed the cities *Kabul*, which literally means 'good-for-nothing.' Even though he was displeased with the trade, Hiram went ahead with it in good humor and sent Solomon 120 talents of gold" (Dilday). A talent is calculated to be about 70 pounds of gold. Dilday estimated the value of this gold at more than $50 million (something close to $161 million at 2015 prices).

    c. **But they did not please him**: We don't know exactly why Hiram was displeased with these cities. Perhaps he was displeased with his compromise, knowing that Solomon did something his father David never would.

2. (15-24) Slave labor from remnant Canaanite peoples.

And this *is* the reason for the labor force which King Solomon raised: to build the house of the LORD, his own house, the Millo, the wall of Jerusalem, Hazor, Megiddo, and Gezer. (Pharaoh king of Egypt had gone up and taken Gezer and burned it with fire, had killed the Canaanites who dwelt in the city, and had given it *as* a dowry to his daughter, Solomon's wife.) And Solomon built Gezer, Lower Beth Horon, Baalath, and Tadmor in the wilderness, in the land *of Judah*, all the storage cities that Solomon had, cities for his chariots and cities for his cavalry, and whatever Solomon desired to build in Jerusalem, in Lebanon, and in all the land of his dominion. All the people *who were* left of the Amorites, Hittites, Perizzites, Hivites, and Jebusites, who *were* not of the children of Israel—that is, their descendants who were left in the land after them, whom the children of Israel had not been able to destroy completely—from these Solomon raised forced labor, as it is to this day. But of the children of Israel Solomon made no forced laborers, because they *were* men of war and his servants: his officers, his captains, commanders of his chariots, and his cavalry. Others *were* chiefs of the officials who *were* over Solomon's work: five hundred and fifty, who ruled over the people who did the work. But Pharaoh's daughter came up from the City of David to her house which *Solomon* had built for her. Then he built the Millo.

a. **This is the reason for the labor force which King Solomon raised**: Solomon raised this massive labor force to complete massive building projects. Archaeology is a witness to the ambitious and successful building projects of Solomon.

b. **He built the Millo**: The Hebrew term *millo* is probably a name for a prominent fortress near the temple and the palace. However, it is possible that it describes architectural terracing and buttressing along the northeastern slope of the east hill of Jerusalem, the city of David.

c. **Hazor, Megiddo, and Gezer**: These were three prominently fortified cities in the days of Solomon. "Recent work has demonstrated that these three cities had certain characteristics in common with regard particularly to their fortifications attributable to the Solomonic era… Most distinctive are the gate complexes, which are identical in plan and virtually of the same dimensions in all three cities." (Patterson and Austel)

i. "Hazor was strategically placed in the north (c. three miles north of the Sea of Galilee), being situated at the juncture of the two major highways approaching from the north. It became Israel's chief bulwark against northern invaders until it was destroyed in the eighth century by Tiglath-pileser III." (Patterson and Austel)

ii. "Megiddo was the great fortress that controlled on the major passes from the Plain of Sharon on the coast into the Valley of Jezreel through the Carmel range. It figures in prophecy as the staging area for the last great battle (Armageddon) in which Christ will defeat the forces of the Antichrist." (Patterson and Austel)

iii. "Gezer, on the road from Joppa to Jerusalem, had been a powerful Canaanite city. Though it was included in the tribal territory of Ephraim, it was not occupied by the Israelites until the time of Solomon. Then it was given to Solomon as a wedding gift by Pharaoh to his daughter." (Patterson and Austel)

d. **All the people who were left of the Amorites, Hittites, Perizzites, Hivites, and Jebusites… from these Solomon raised forced labor, as it is to this day**: This was another apparent compromise by Solomon. God strictly commanded that the remnants of these tribes be driven out of the land, not used as slave laborers in Israel. Solomon didn't make Israelites forced laborers, but used them to oversee the remnants of the Canaanite tribes.

3. (25-28) Financing from naval expeditions that brought back gold.

Now three times a year Solomon offered burnt offerings and peace offerings on the altar which he had built for the LORD, and he burned incense with them *on the altar* that *was* before the LORD. So he finished the temple. King Solomon also built a fleet of ships at Ezion Geber, which *is* near Elath on the shore of the Red Sea, in the land of Edom. Then Hiram sent his servants with the fleet, seamen who knew the sea, to work with the servants of Solomon. And they went to Ophir, and acquired four hundred and twenty talents of gold from there, and brought *it* to King Solomon.

a. **Three times a year Solomon offered burnt offerings and peace offerings on the altar which he had built for the LORD, and he burned incense**: It is possible that this was another transgression by Solomon. It may be that he took upon himself the exclusive duties of a priest, offering burnt offerings and incense. However, as is the case in some other passages, this may refer to Solomon initiating such sacrifice and ceremony properly through a priest.

b. **They went to Ophir, and acquired four hundred and twenty talents of gold from there**: It is hard to say with certainty where the land of **Ophir** was. Some suggest it was in southern Arabia or the eastern coast of Africa. This shows the great enterprise and industriousness of Solomon's administration.

i. "No man knows certainly, to this day, where this *Ophir* was situated. There were two places of this name; one somewhere in India, beyond the Ganges, and another in Arabia, near the country of the Sabaeans, mentioned by Job 22:24." (Clarke)

1 Kings 10 - The Queen of Sheba Visits Solomon

A. The Queen's visit.

1. (1) The Queen of Sheba arrives at Jerusalem.

Now when the Queen of Sheba heard of the fame of Solomon concerning the name of the LORD, she came to test him with hard questions.

a. **The Queen of Sheba**: Sheba (also known as *Sabea*) was where modern-day Yemen is today (Southern Arabia). We know from geography this was a wealthy kingdom with much gold, spices, and precious woods. History also tells us that they were known to have queens as well as kings.

i. This was a long trip – up to about 1,500 miles (2,400 kilometers). She probably came as part of a trade delegation (1 Kings 10:2-5), but there is no doubt that she was highly motivated to see Solomon and his kingdom.

b. **When the Queen of Sheba heard of the fame of Solomon concerning the name of the LORD, she came to test him**: She came to Solomon and Israel at their material zenith. The great prosperity, splendor, and wisdom of Solomon's kingdom were internationally famous.

2. (2-5) What the Queen of Sheba saw.

She came to Jerusalem with a very great retinue, with camels that bore spices, very much gold, and precious stones; and when she came to Solomon, she spoke with him about all that was in her heart. So Solomon answered all her questions; there was nothing so difficult for the king that he could not explain *it* to her. And when the Queen of Sheba had seen all the wisdom of Solomon, the house that he had built, the food on his table, the seating of his servants, the service of his waiters and their apparel, his cupbearers, and his entryway by which he went up to the house of the LORD, there was no more spirit in her.

a. **She came to Jerusalem with a very great retinue**: This queen traveled in the manner of queens, with a large royal procession, heavily laden with gifts and goods for trade.

b. **When she came to Solomon, she spoke with him about all that was in her heart**: Solomon's kingdom was famous not only for its material prosperity, but also for his great wisdom. The Queen of Sheba had great - and seemingly difficult - questions, and **Solomon answered all her questions**.

i. "The hard questions were not just riddles, but included difficult diplomatic and ethical questions... The test was not an academic exercise but to see if he would be a trustworthy business party and a reliable ally capable of giving help." (Wiseman)

c. **When the Queen of Sheba had seen all the wisdom of Solomon, the house that he had built, the food on his table... there was no more spirit in her**: This Queen was obviously familiar with the world of royal splendor and luxury. Yet she was completely overwhelmed by the wisdom of Solomon and the glory of his kingdom.

i. "What happened to the Queen of Sheba is a natural and not an uncommon effect which will be produced in a delicate sensible mind at the sight of rare and extraordinary productions of art." (Clarke)

3. (6-9) How the Queen of Sheba reacted.

Then she said to the king: "It was a true report which I heard in my own land about your words and your wisdom. However I did not believe the words until I came and saw with my own eyes; and indeed the half was not told me. Your wisdom and prosperity exceed the fame of which I heard. Happy *are* your men and happy *are* these your servants, who stand continually before you *and* hear your wisdom! Blessed be the Lord your God, who delighted in you, setting you on the throne of Israel! Because the Lord has loved Israel forever, therefore He made you king, to do justice and righteousness."

a. **Indeed the half was not told me**: The Queen of Sheba heard wonderful things about Solomon and his kingdom, but upon seeing it with her own eyes she realized it was far greater than she had heard.

b. **Happy are your men and happy are these your servants**: It is a joyful thing to serve a great, wise, and rich king. If it was a happy thing to serve Solomon, it is a much happier thing to serve Jesus.

c. **Blessed be the Lord your God, who delighted in you**: This is an example of what God wanted to do for Israel under the promises of the Old Covenant. God promised Israel that if they obeyed under the Old Covenant, He would bless them so tremendously that the world would notice and give glory to the Lord God of Israel.

i. *Now it shall come to pass, if you diligently obey the voice of the Lord your God, to observe carefully all His commandments which I command you today, that the Lord your God will set you high above all nations of the earth... Then all peoples of the earth shall see that you are called by the name of the* LORD, *and they shall be afraid of you.* (Deuteronomy 28:1, 10)

ii. God wanted to reach the nations through an obedient and blessed Israel. If Israel did not obey, then God would speak to the nations through a thoroughly disciplined Israel.

d. **Blessed be the** LORD **your God**: It is fair to ask if this was a true confession of faith, expressing allegiance to the God of Israel. Taken in their context, these may not be more than the queen's response to the astonishing blessing evident in Solomon's Jerusalem.

i. "Her statement about the blessings of the Lord on Israel and Solomon in verse 9 were no more than a polite reference to Solomon's God... There is no record that she accepted Solomon's God, who was so majestically edified by the temple." (Dilday)

ii. "*Praise to the* LORD implies recognition of Israel's national God and need not necessarily be an expression of personal faith." (Wiseman)

iii. If we take the Queen of Sheba as an example of a *seeker*, we see that Solomon impressed her with his wealth and splendor, and also impressed her personally. But she returned home without an evident expression of faith in the God of Israel. This shows that impressing seekers with facilities and programs and organization and professionalism isn't enough.

iv. Regardless of the result of her search, we can admire her seeking.

- She came from a great distance.
- She came with gifts to offer.
- She came to question and to learn.
- She came and saw the riches of the king.
- She came for an extended period.
- She came telling all that was on her heart.

v. Jesus used the Queen of Sheba as an example of a seeker: *The queen of the South will rise up in the judgment with this generation and condemn it, for she came from the ends of the earth to hear the wisdom of Solomon; and indeed a greater than Solomon is here* (Matthew 12:42). If the Queen of Sheba sought Solomon and the splendor of his kingdom so diligently, *how much more* should people today seek Jesus and the glory of His Kingdom. The Queen of Sheba will certainly also rise up in judgment against *this* generation.

e. **Because the** LORD **has loved Israel forever, therefore He made you king**: This statement is especially meaningful because Solomon was not necessarily the most logical successor of his father David. There were several sons of David born before Solomon.

i. "It was God's special act to make him king rather than his elder brother." (Poole)

4. (10-13) An exchange of gifts.

Then she gave the king one hundred and twenty talents of gold, spices in great quantity, and precious stones. There never again came such abundance of spices as the Queen of Sheba gave to King Solomon. Also, the ships of Hiram, which brought gold from Ophir, brought great *quantities* of almug wood and precious stones from Ophir. And the king made steps of the almug wood for the house of the LORD and for the king's house, also harps and stringed instruments for singers. There never again came such almug wood, nor has the like been seen to this day. Now King Solomon gave the Queen of Sheba all she desired, whatever she asked, besides what Solomon had given her according to the royal generosity. So she turned and went to her own country, she and her servants.

a. **There never again came such abundance of spices as the Queen of Sheba gave to King Solomon**: She came from a region rich in spices and skilled in the processing of spices.

b. **Solomon had given her according to the royal generosity**: To give according to the **royal generosity** means to give a lot. This description of Solomon's measure of generosity to the Queen of Sheba also describes the measure of God's generosity towards us.

i. According to tradition – fanciful stories, perhaps – the Queen of Sheba wanted a son by Solomon, and he obliged her. Her child was named Menilek, and he became the ancestor of all subsequent Ethiopian monarchs.

B. Solomon's great wealth.

1. (14-15) Solomon's yearly income.

The weight of gold that came to Solomon yearly was six hundred and sixty-six talents of gold, besides *that* from the traveling merchants, from the income of traders, from all the kings of Arabia, and from the governors of the country.

a. **Six hundred and sixty-six talents of gold**: This was a vast amount of gold, which came to Solomon **yearly**. One commentator estimated the value of the 666 talents of gold at $281,318,400. According to the value of gold in 2015, it would be just under $1 billion dollars. This speaks not only to the great wealth of Solomon, but it also makes him the only other person in the Bible associated with the number 666.

i. The other Biblical connection to 666 is the end-times world dictator and opponent of God and His people often known as the Antichrist

(Revelation 13:18). In fact, the Revelation passage specifically says that the number 666 is *the number of a man*, and the *man* may be Solomon.

ii. This isn't to say that Solomon was the Antichrist or that the coming Antichrist will be some strange reincarnation of Solomon. But it may indicate that the Antichrist may not be someone purely evil from the very beginning. Instead, he may be like Solomon – a good man corrupted.

b. **Besides that from the traveling merchants**: Solomon received *more* than 666 talents of gold a year. The 666 talents was just his beginning salary.

i. The writer of 1 Kings gives us a warning signal here. He assumes that we know of the instructions for future kings of Israel in Deuteronomy 17:14-20. He assumes we know verse 17 of that passage, which says: *nor shall he greatly multiply silver and gold for himself.* God blessed Solomon with great riches, but Solomon allowed that blessing to turn into a danger because he disobediently multiplied silver and gold for himself.

2. (16-27) Examples of Solomon's wealth and prosperity.

And King Solomon made two hundred large shields *of* hammered gold; six hundred *shekels* of gold went into each shield. He also *made* three hundred shields *of* hammered gold; three minas of gold went into each shield. The king put them in the House of the Forest of Lebanon. Moreover the king made a great throne of ivory, and overlaid it with pure gold. The throne had six steps, and the top of the throne *was* round at the back; *there were* armrests on either side of the place of the seat, and two lions stood beside the armrests. Twelve lions stood there, one on each side of the six steps; nothing like *this* had been made for any *other* kingdom. All King Solomon's drinking vessels *were* gold, and all the vessels of the House of the Forest of Lebanon *were* pure gold. Not *one was* silver, for this was accounted as nothing in the days of Solomon. For the king had merchant ships at sea with the fleet of Hiram. Once every three years the merchant ships came bringing gold, silver, ivory, apes, and monkeys. So King Solomon surpassed all the kings of the earth in riches and wisdom. Now all the earth sought the presence of Solomon to hear his wisdom, which God had put in his heart. Each man brought his present: articles of silver and gold, garments, armor, spices, horses, and mules, at a set rate year by year. And Solomon gathered chariots and horsemen; he had one thousand four hundred chariots and twelve thousand horsemen, whom he stationed in the chariot cities and with the king in Jerusalem. The king made silver *as common* in Jerusalem as stones, and he made cedar trees as abundant as the sycamores which *are* in the lowland.

a. **Two hundred large shields of hammered gold… three hundred shields of hammered gold**: These shields made beautiful displays in the House of the Forest of Lebanon, but they were of no use in battle. Gold was too heavy and too soft to be used as a metal for effective shields. This shows Solomon had the *image* of a warrior king, but without the *substance*.

i. According to Dilday, each large shield was worth about $120,000 ($250,000 at 2015 values). The smaller shields were worth $30,000 ($57,000 at 2015 values). $33 million was invested in gold ceremonial shields.

b. **Not one was silver, for this was accounted as nothing in the days of Solomon**: This was a statement of wealth. If taken seriously, it shows the tremendous abundance of Solomon's kingdom. Truly, **King Solomon surpassed all the kings of the earth in riches and wisdom**, and the promises of Deuteronomy 28:1-14 were fulfilled in his reign: *The LORD will open to you His good treasure, the heavens, to give the rain to your land in its season, and to bless all the work of your hand. You shall lend to many nations, but you shall not borrow* (Deuteronomy 28:12).

c. **Now all the earth sought the presence of Solomon to hear his wisdom, which God had put in his heart**: This was another fulfillment of the promises of Deuteronomy 28: *And the LORD will make you the head and not the tail; you shall be above only, and not be beneath, if you heed the commandments of the LORD your God* (Deuteronomy 28:13).

d. **Solomon gathered chariots and horsemen; he had one thousand four hundred chariots and twelve thousand horsemen**: In comparison to the reign of David, there were few military conflicts during the reign of Solomon, yet he still saw the importance of a strong defense. Perhaps there were few military conflicts *because* Solomon had a strong defense.

i. Remains of Solomon's fortress and stables at Megiddo can be seen today.

e. **The king made silver as common in Jerusalem as stones**: When we think of Solomon's great wealth, we also consider that he originally did not set his heart upon riches. He deliberately asked for wisdom to lead the people of God *instead* of riches or fame. God promised to *also* give Solomon riches and fame, and God fulfilled His promise.

i. We also consider that Solomon gave an eloquent testimony to the vanity of riches as the preacher in the Book of Ecclesiastes. He powerfully showed that there was no ultimate satisfaction through materialism. We don't have to be as rich as Solomon to learn the same lesson.

3. (28-29) Solomon's interest in horses.

Also Solomon had horses imported from Egypt and Keveh; the king's merchants bought them in Keveh at the *current* price. Now a chariot that was imported from Egypt cost six hundred *shekels* of silver, and a horse one hundred and fifty; and thus, through their agents, they exported *them* to all the kings of the Hittites and the kings of Syria.

a. **Solomon had horses imported from Egypt and Keveh**: At the end of this great description of Solomon's wealth and splendor, we have the sound of this dark note. This was in direct disobedience to Deuteronomy 17:16, which said to the Kings of Israel: *But he shall not multiply horses for himself, nor cause the people to return to Egypt to multiply horses, for the LORD has said to you, "You shall not return that way again."*

b. **Thus, through their agents, they exported them to all the kings of the Hittites and the kings of Syria**: This may explain why Solomon broke such an obvious commandment. Perhaps the importation of horses from Egypt began as trading as an agent on behalf of other kings. From this, perhaps Solomon could say, "I'm importing horses from Egypt, but I am not doing it for myself. I'm not breaking God's command." Many examples of gross disobedience begin as clever rationalizations.

1 Kings 11 - Solomon's Decline and Death

A. Solomon's apostasy.

1. (1-3) Solomon's unlawful marriages.

But King Solomon loved many foreign women, as well as the daughter of Pharaoh: women of the Moabites, Ammonites, Edomites, Sidonians, *and* Hittites—from the nations of whom the LORD had said to the children of Israel, "You shall not intermarry with them, nor they with you. Surely they will turn away your hearts after their gods." Solomon clung to these in love. And he had seven hundred wives, princesses, and three hundred concubines; and his wives turned away his heart.

a. **Solomon loved many foreign women**: There are two obvious problems here. First, that he loved **foreign** women who worshipped other gods and brought pagan influences to Israel. Second, that he loved **many** women, rejecting God's plan from the beginning for one man and one woman to become one flesh in marriage (Matthew 19:4-6, Genesis 2:23-24).

b. **Nations of whom the LORD had said to the children of Israel, "You shall not intermarry with them"**: God gave a general warning to all Israel to not intermarry with these nations, because **surely they will turn away your hearts after their gods**. For all Solomon's great wisdom, he did not have the wisdom to apply this simple command to his own life.

i. Solomon probably did what many of us do. He somehow thought that he would be the exception, that he would escape the consequences of this sin, despite seeing how it affected others. Solomon learned – or should have learned – that he was not the exception to this rule.

c. **Solomon clung to these in love**: At this point, Solomon wanted romance and sensual fulfillment more than he wanted the LORD. For all his wisdom, he was snared by the power of romantic and sensual love. He did not seriously consider that it is possible to be romantically and sensually attracted to people we have no moral or righteous reason to be attracted to. Once under the power of this attraction, he **clung to these in love** instead of giving them up to the LORD.

d. **He had seven hundred wives, princesses, and three hundred concubines**: This is an almost unbelievable number of marriage partners. His wives were considered **princesses**, but his **concubines** were legal partners without the same standing as wives. All said, Solomon had far more marriage partners than any man could possibly give attention to – sexual attention or other attention.

> i. In this sense a concubine was a legal mistress. Many prominent men in the Old Testament had concubines. Examples include Abraham (Genesis 25:6), Jacob (Genesis 35:22), Caleb (1 Chronicles 2:46), Saul (2 Samuel 3:7), David (2 Samuel 5:13), and Rehoboam (2 Chronicles 11:21). Significantly, the Bible *never* shows this kind of family life blessed by God.

> ii. We can say that Solomon had so many marriage partners because he followed the bad example of his father David, who had many wives and concubines himself (2 Samuel 5:13-16).

> iii. We can say that Solomon had so many marriage partners because of his own sexual lust. This is a profound and sobering example of the principle that if one wife is not enough to satisfy a man, then 1,000 wives will not be enough. When a man is unsatisfied with the woman God gave to him, the problem is with him, not with his wife. 1,000 women cannot satisfy the lust of man. Solomon should have listened to Proverbs 27:20: *Hell and Destruction are never full; so the eyes of man are never satisfied.*

> iv. We can say that Solomon had so many marriage partners because of his lust for power and prestige. In those days a large harem was a status symbol. It said to the world, "Look how many wives and children I can support. Look how many women I have authority over." Solomon's desire for worldly prestige led him to these ungodly marriages.

> v. "Partly for his lust, which being indulged, becomes infinite and unsatiable; and partly from his pride, accounting this a point of honour and magnificence." (Poole)

e. **And his wives turned away his heart**: Of course they did. Based upon the Song of Solomon, we can say that at the first Solomon seemed to know what true love was with one woman. Yet his subsequent history shows us that it is possible to be in that place *and depart from it*. It is not true to say that "love will keep us together." Solomon shows us that we can know true love and depart from it. It is better said that the blessing and power of God upon our obedience will keep us together.

> i. We don't know when Solomon added his second wife. When he did, it was easy for him to rationalize it - after all, the greatest King of Israel, his father David, had several wives and concubines. Yet once he followed

his father David into this departure from God's plan from the beginning (Matthew 19:4-6 and Genesis 2:23-24), it was easy to keep adding wives.

ii. As he added wives, he broke the specific commandment God gave to the future kings of Israel in Deuteronomy 17:17: *Neither shall he multiply wives for himself, lest his heart turn away.* Solomon *did* multiply wives for himself (by any account 1,000 marriage partners is multiplication), and it *did* turn away his heart.

iii. "It would have been useless to argue with Solomon for the claims of idols. He could at once, by his wisdom, have annihilated all infidel arguments, and have established the existence and unity of God. But, step by step, he was led by silken cords, a captive, to the worship of other gods." (Meyer)

iv. "The whole story of King Solomon is full of the most solemn value. His was a life full of promise, but it ended in failure and gloom, because his heart turned from loyalty to God, in response to the seductions of his sensual nature." (Morgan)

2. (4-8) Solomon's wives turn him away from God.

For it was so, when Solomon was old, that his wives turned his heart after other gods; and his heart was not loyal to the LORD his God, as *was* the heart of his father David. For Solomon went after Ashtoreth the goddess of the Sidonians, and after Milcom the abomination of the Ammonites. Solomon did evil in the sight of the LORD, and did not fully follow the LORD, as *did* his father David. Then Solomon built a high place for Chemosh the abomination of Moab, on the hill that *is* east of Jerusalem, and for Molech the abomination of the people of Ammon. And he did likewise for all his foreign wives, who burned incense and sacrificed to their gods.

a. **When Solomon was old, that his wives turned his heart after other gods**: Age did not make Solomon wiser. He seemed to be wiser in his youth, and old age hardened the sinful tendencies that were present in his younger days. Age and experience should make us more godly and wise, but they do not *automatically* do so.

b. **His heart was not loyal to the LORD his God**: Solomon is a contrast to those who *did* fully follow the LORD. This phrase is used in a *positive* sense of three men in the Old Testament: Joshua and Caleb (Numbers 32:11-12, Deuteronomy 1:36, Joshua 14:8-9, 14), and here of David. Solomon was conspicuous as someone who did *not* wholly follow the LORD.

c. **As was the heart of his father David**: Solomon had more than one wife and David had more than one wife (fifteen, according to 1 Chronicles 3:1-9). David spiritually survived this failing and Solomon did not survive it.

i. From what we know of the world beyond from the story of Jesus in Luke 16:19-31, we can say that David was not yet in heaven, but in a place of blessing and comfort known as Abraham's bosom. If it were possible for someone in Abraham's bosom to see life on the earth and be sorry, David was very sorry when he saw Solomon and his sin. David no doubt hoped that his children would be better than he, and find more victory in the areas of life that troubled him. Sadly, David's sons found *less* victory in controlling the lust of the flesh, and especially sexual lust.

ii. Yet David's sin did not turn his heart away from the LORD. It is possible for a particular sin in one person to be a hindrance that they would do better without, while in another person that sin is the cause of ruin. David's lack of romantic and sexual restraint *hindered* him; it *destroyed* Solomon. This is one reason why we must be so careful with the sin of stumbling another brother or sister (Romans 14, 1 Corinthians 8).

d. **For Solomon went after Ashtoreth the goddess of the Sidonians... after Milcom... Solomon built a high place for Chemosh... and for Molech**: This seems almost unbelievable. We might not accept it unless the Scriptures clearly stated it. This man of great heritage, wisdom, and blessing turns to the most depraved gods of the pagan nations.

i. Probably Solomon did not see this as a *denial* of the Lord GOD of Israel. In his mind, he probably thought that he still honored the LORD, he simply *added* the honor of these other gods to his honor of the LORD. But this is never acceptable to God. He demands to be the *only* God in our life.

ii. This is a tragic example of the power of the lust of the flesh. Because of lust, Solomon found himself in a place where he *never* thought he would find himself. He found himself burning incense at the altars of depraved pagan gods. He found himself at the altar of *child sacrifice* unto the god Molech. This is the power of lust - it can capture us in a spell, in a fog of spiritual confusion until we do things we *never* thought we would do.

iii. The reader should carefully consider: If this was the case with the *wisest man who ever lived*, then what hope do you have apart from constant dependence upon Jesus Christ? Let the example of Solomon drive you to greater dependence upon and abiding with Jesus.

iv. "'Ashtoreth' is a deliberate distortion of Ashtart, the Canaanite fertility goddess. The revocalization is based on the word for 'shame'." (Patteson and Austel)

3. (9-13) God announces His judgment.

So the LORD became angry with Solomon, because his heart had turned from the LORD God of Israel, who had appeared to him twice, and had

commanded him concerning this thing, that he should not go after other gods; but he did not keep what the LORD had commanded. Therefore the LORD said to Solomon, "Because you have done this, and have not kept My covenant and My statutes, which I have commanded you, I will surely tear the kingdom away from you and give it to your servant. Nevertheless I will not do it in your days, for the sake of your father David; I will tear it out of the hand of your son. However I will not tear away the whole kingdom; I will give one tribe to your son for the sake of my servant David, and for the sake of Jerusalem which I have chosen."

a. **So the LORD became angry with Solomon**: God had special reason to be displeased with Solomon - He **had appeared to him twice**, and Solomon still went after other gods. Solomon's sin was base ingratitude and a waste of great spiritual privilege.

i. We sometimes think that great spiritual experiences will keep us from sin and will keep us faithful to God. This was not the case with the wisest man who ever lived, and it will not be the case with us also.

b. **I will surely tear the kingdom away from you and give it to your servant**: God promised the entire kingdom of Israel to the descendants of David forever, if they only remained obedient. David reminded Solomon of this promise shortly before his death (1 Kings 2:4). Yet *they could not remain faithful even one generation*.

i. Solomon's kingdom was an outstanding example of wealth, military power, and prestige. Yet the true security of Israel did not rest in any of those things. It rested in the blessing of God and in the obedience and faithfulness of their king.

c. **I will not do it in your days, for the sake of your father David; I will tear it out of the hand of your son**: For the sake of David, God delayed this judgment until after Solomon's generation. But the disobedience that brought the judgment came in the first generation.

d. **However I will not tear away the whole kingdom; I will give one tribe to your son for the sake of my servant David**: Even in this great judgment, God must mingle undeserved mercy with deserved judgment. God announces that the kingdom will be divided, and part of it will be loyal to the descendants of David and part of it will be under a different dynasty.

i. Many other passages in the Old Testament (such as 2 Chronicles 11:12) tell us that the southern kingdom was made up of *two* tribes, Judah and Benjamin. Several times in this chapter the southern kingdom is referred to as **one tribe**. This is because either Benjamin is swallowed up in Judah, or the idea was **one tribe** *in addition* to Judah.

B. Two foreign adversaries of Solomon.

1. (14-22) Hadad the Edomite.

Now the L**ORD** **raised up an adversary against Solomon, Hadad the Edomite; he** *was* **a descendant of the king in Edom. For it happened, when David was in Edom, and Joab the commander of the army had gone up to bury the slain, after he had killed every male in Edom (because for six months Joab remained there with all Israel, until he had cut down every male in Edom), that Hadad fled to go to Egypt, he and certain Edomites of his father's servants with him. Hadad** *was* **still a little child. Then they arose from Midian and came to Paran; and they took men with them from Paran and came to Egypt, to Pharaoh king of Egypt, who gave him a house, apportioned food for him, and gave him land. And Hadad found great favor in the sight of Pharaoh, so that he gave him as wife the sister of his own wife, that is, the sister of Queen Tahpenes. Then the sister of Tahpenes bore him Genubath his son, whom Tahpenes weaned in Pharaoh's house. And Genubath was in Pharaoh's household among the sons of Pharaoh. So when Hadad heard in Egypt that David rested with his fathers, and that Joab the commander of the army was dead, Hadad said to Pharaoh, "Let me depart, that I may go to my own country." Then Pharaoh said to him, "But what have you lacked with me, that suddenly you seek to go to your own country?" So he answered, "Nothing, but do let me go anyway."**

> a. **Now the** L**ORD** **raised up an adversary against Solomon, Hadad the Edomite**: Solomon's reign was glorious, but God did not allow it to be completely without problems. He **raised up** adversaries like Hadad against Solomon.

>> i. "When he sent to Hiram to assist him in the building of the temple of the Lord, he could say, *There was no Satan* [1 Kings 5:4]… but now that he had turned away from God three *satans* rise up against him at once, *Hadad, Rezon*, and *Jeroboam*." (Clarke)

> b. **He was a descendant of the king in Edom**: Hadad sought to avenge his conquered people. He found refuge and support in Egypt.

> c. **Let me depart, that I may go to my own country**: We are not told specifically how Hadad troubled or was an adversary to Solomon, only that he returned to bother Solomon with the permission of Pharaoh.

2. (23-25) Rezon, from the north country.

And God raised up *another* **adversary against him, Rezon the son of Eliadah, who had fled from his lord, Hadadezer king of Zobah. So he gathered men to him and became captain over a band** *of raiders,* **when David killed those** *of Zobah.* **And they went to Damascus and dwelt there, and reigned in Damascus. He was an adversary of Israel all the days of**

Solomon (besides the trouble that Hadad *caused*); and he abhorred Israel, and reigned over Syria.

C. Jeroboam - A special adversary.

1. (26-28) Jeroboam, the servant of Solomon.

Then Solomon's servant, Jeroboam the son of Nebat, an Ephraimite from Zereda, whose mother's name *was* Zeruah, a widow, also rebelled against the king. And this *is* what caused him to rebel against the king: Solomon had built the Millo *and* repaired the damages to the City of David his father. The man Jeroboam *was* a mighty man of valor; and Solomon, seeing that the young man was industrious, made him the officer over all the labor force of the house of Joseph.

a. **Jeroboam the son of Nebat, an Ephraimite**: Jeroboam was different from the two previously mentioned adversaries of Solomon, because he was a fellow Israelite.

b. **This is what caused him to rebel against the king: Solomon had built the Millo and repaired the damages to the City of David**: It is not immediately apparent why these construction projects **caused him to rebel** against Solomon. Jewish traditions say he opposed the oppressive use of forced labor in these building projects. Since he was **the officer over all the labor force**, this tradition makes some sense.

i. According to Dilday, the name **Jeroboam** means, "may the people be great." He perhaps was a populist leader.

ii. "Though only presenting the people's petition, it is nevertheless probable that Jeroboam was not idle, but like an artful politician, busy behind the scenes, till the coveted crown became his." (Knapp)

c. **Jeroboam was a mighty man of valor**: This made him a more dangerous adversary of Solomon.

2. (29-36) The prophet Ahijah speaks to Jeroboam.

Now it happened at that time, when Jeroboam went out of Jerusalem, that the prophet Ahijah the Shilonite met him on the way; and he had clothed himself with a new garment, and the two *were* alone in the field. Then Ahijah took hold of the new garment that *was* on him, and tore it *into* twelve pieces. And he said to Jeroboam, "Take for yourself ten pieces, for thus says the LORD, the God of Israel: 'Behold, I will tear the kingdom out of the hand of Solomon and will give ten tribes to you (but he shall have one tribe for the sake of My servant David, and for the sake of Jerusalem, the city which I have chosen out of all the tribes of Israel), because they have forsaken Me, and worshiped Ashtoreth the goddess of the Sidonians, Chemosh the god of the Moabites, and Milcom the god of the people of

Ammon, and have not walked in My ways to do *what is* right in My eyes and *keep* My statutes and My judgments, as *did* his father David. However I will not take the whole kingdom out of his hand, because I have made him ruler all the days of his life for the sake of My servant David, whom I chose because he kept My commandments and My statutes. But I will take the kingdom out of his son's hand and give it to you—ten tribes. And to his son I will give one tribe, that My servant David may always have a lamp before Me in Jerusalem, the city which I have chosen for Myself, to put My name there.

a. **Take for yourself ten pieces**: In this acted-out prophecy, Ahijah showed Jeroboam that he would lead ten tribes of a divided Israel after the death of Solomon.

i. "It was indeed a shock for Rehoboam and the tribe of Judah to be reduced overnight from the most powerful tribe in an illustrious and world-renowned kingdom to a small state that was soon stripped of what wealth it had left." (Patterson and Austel)

b. **Because they have forsaken Me**: God promised to divide Israel and put ten of the twelve tribes under Jeroboam as judgment for the sin and idolatry of Solomon. God would still keep **one tribe** under the house of David, in faithfulness to His promise to David.

i. This is the first we hear of the divided kingdom, which became Israel's history for hundreds of years after the death of Solomon. At this first description we would expect that the **ten tribes** under Jeroboam would be larger, greater, and more enduring than the **one tribe** left unto the House of David. As it worked out, just the opposite happened because the **ten tribes** forsook the LORD, while the **one tribe** was more obedient.

3. (37-40) Jeroboam's great opportunity.

So I will take you, and you shall reign over all your heart desires, and you shall be king over Israel. Then it shall be, if you heed all that I command you, walk in My ways, and do *what is* right in My sight, to keep My statutes and My commandments, as My servant David did, then I will be with you and build for you an enduring house, as I built for David, and will give Israel to you. And I will afflict the descendants of David because of this, but not forever.'" Solomon therefore sought to kill Jeroboam. But Jeroboam arose and fled to Egypt, to Shishak king of Egypt, and was in Egypt until the death of Solomon.

a. **I will take you, and you shall reign over all your heart desires, and you shall be king over Israel**: God ordained the division of Israel and the reign of Jeroboam. He did this as a judgment – a great judgment – upon Solomon for his embrace of idolatry.

b. **Then I will be with you and build for you an enduring house**: This was an amazing offer. God promised to make a lasting dynasty for Jeroboam, *if* he would **do what is right** in the sight of the LORD. An obedient Jeroboam had the opportunity to establish a parallel dynasty to the House of David.

> i. Both Jeroboam and David were appointed by God to follow after disobedient kings. David waited upon the LORD to make the throne clear, and God blessed his reign. Jeroboam did not wait on the LORD but made his own way to the throne, and God did not bless his reign.

c. **Solomon therefore sought to kill Jeroboam**: This is another startling evidence of Solomon's decline. God specifically said this would happen *after* the death of Solomon, and *in judgment* of Solomon's apostasy. Solomon didn't want to hear it, so he **sought to kill Jeroboam**. Solomon thought he could defeat God's will in this, but he was unsuccessful. God's word through Ahijah proved true.

4. (41-43) Solomon's death.

Now the rest of the acts of Solomon, all that he did, and his wisdom, *are* they not written in the book of the acts of Solomon? And the period that Solomon reigned in Jerusalem over all Israel *was* forty years. Then Solomon rested with his fathers, and was buried in the City of David his father. And Rehoboam his son reigned in his place.

a. **The period that Solomon reigned in Jerusalem over all Israel was forty years**: Many commentators believe that Solomon began his reign when he was about 20 years old. This means that Solomon did not live a particularly long life. This means that the promise made in 1 Kings 3:14 was not fulfilled to Solomon, because of his disobedience.

> i. *So if you walk in My ways, to keep My statutes and My commandments, as your father David walked, then I will lengthen your days.* (1 Kings 3:14)

> ii. "When we consider the excess in which he lived, and the criminal passions which he must have indulged among his thousand wives, and their idolatrous and impure worship, this life was as long as could be reasonably expected." (Clarke)

b. **Then Solomon rested with his fathers**: This does not necessarily mean that Solomon died a saved man. It is a familiar phrase used in 1 and 2 Kings (used 25 times) and was used of such wicked kings as Ahab (1 Kings 22:40). It simply means that Solomon passed to the world beyond. We cannot say with certainty that he is in heaven.

> i. The last look at the life of Solomon in 1 Kings leads us to believe that *he died in apostasy*. There is no hopeful or cheerful end to the story in this account. "If he did repent, yet the silence of the Scriptures about it in this history was not without wise reasons; as, among others, that his eternal

condition being thus far left doubtful, his example might have the greater influence for the terror and caution of future offenders" (Poole).

ii. However, it may be that Solomon was shown special mercy for the sake of David his father (as in 2 Samuel 7:14-15, if that promise also applies to Solomon as well as the Messiah). Some also believe that Solomon wrote the Book of Ecclesiastes at the very end of his life as a renunciation of his fall into vanity.

iii. "And surely it had been better for Solomon to have been buried alive, than thus to have miscarried in his old age, and to the great dishonour of God, and offence of his people Israel." (Trapp)

1 Kings 12 - Rehoboam and Jeroboam

A. Rehoboam and the division of Israel.

1. (1-5) The elders of Israel offer Rehoboam the throne of Israel.

And Rehoboam went to Shechem, for all Israel had gone to Shechem to make him king. So it happened, when Jeroboam the son of Nebat heard *it* (he was still in Egypt, for he had fled from the presence of King Solomon and had been dwelling in Egypt), that they sent and called him. Then Jeroboam and the whole assembly of Israel came and spoke to Rehoboam, saying, "Your father made our yoke heavy; now therefore, lighten the burdensome service of your father, and his heavy yoke which he put on us, and we will serve you." So he said to them, "Depart *for* three days, then come back to me." And the people departed.

a. **Rehoboam went to Shechem, for all Israel had gone to Shechem to make him king**: This was a logical continuation of the Davidic dynasty. Solomon succeeded David, and now **Rehoboam**, the son of Solomon, was assumed to be the next king.

i. Rehoboam was the only son of Solomon that we know by name. Solomon had 1,000 wives and concubines, yet we read of *one son* he had to bear up his name, and he was a fool. This demonstrates that sin is a bad way of building up a family.

ii. "It is difficult to believe that he had no other sons; yet it is a fact that Rehoboam is the only one mentioned (1 Chronicles 3:10)." (Knapp)

iii. **Shechem** was a city with a rich history. Abraham worshipped there (Genesis 12:6). Jacob built an altar and purchased land there (Genesis 33:18-20). Joseph was buried there (Joshua 24:32). It was also the geographical center of the northern tribes. All in all, it showed that Rehoboam was in a position of weakness, having to meet the ten northern tribes on *their* territory, instead of demanding that representatives come to Jerusalem.

b. **When Jeroboam the son of Nebat heard it**: Jeroboam was mentioned previously in 1 Kings 11:26-40. God told him through a prophet that he would rule over a portion of a divided Israel. Naturally, Jeroboam was interested in Solomon's successor. He was specifically part of the group of elders that addressed Rehoboam.

c. **Your father made our yoke heavy; now therefore, lighten the burdensome service of your father**: Solomon was a great king, but he *took* a lot from the people. The people of Israel wanted relief from the heavy taxation and forced service of Solomon's reign, and they offered allegiance to Rehoboam if he agreed to this.

> i. God warned Israel about this in 1 Samuel 8:10-19, when through Samuel He spoke of what a king would *take* from Israel. After the warning, the people still wanted a king, and now they knew what it was like to be ruled by a *taking* king.

> ii. Sadly, the elders of Israel made no *spiritual* demand or request on Rehoboam. Seemingly, the gross idolatry and apostasy of Solomon didn't bother them at all.

2. (6-7) The counsel from Rehoboam's older advisors.

Then King Rehoboam consulted the elders who stood before his father Solomon while he still lived, and he said, "How do you advise *me* to answer these people?" And they spoke to him, saying, "If you will be a servant to these people today, and serve them, and answer them, and speak good words to them, then they will be your servants forever."

a. **Rehoboam consulted the elders who stood before his father Solomon while he still lived**: Wisely, Rehoboam asked the counsel of these older, experienced men. They seemed to advise Solomon well, so it was fitting that Rehoboam asked for their advice.

b. **If you will be a servant to these people today... then they will be your servants forever**: The elders knew that Rehoboam was not Solomon, and could not expect the same from the people that Solomon did. Rehoboam had to relate to the people based on who *he* was, not on who his father was. If he showed kindness and a servant's heart to the people, they would love and serve him forever. This was good advice.

3. (8-11) The counsel from Rehoboam's younger advisors.

But he rejected the advice which the elders had given him, and consulted the young men who had grown up with him, who stood before him. And he said to them, "What advice do you give? How should we answer this people who have spoken to me, saying, 'Lighten the yoke which your father put on us'?" Then the young men who had grown up with him spoke to him, saying, "Thus you should speak to this people who have spoken to you,

saying, 'Your father made our yoke heavy, but you make *it* lighter on us'—thus you shall say to them: '**My little *finger* shall be thicker than my father's waist! And now, whereas my father put a heavy yoke on you, I will add to your yoke; my father chastised you with whips, but I will chastise you with scourges!'"**

a. **But he rejected the advice which the elders had given him, and consulted the young men**: Before Rehoboam ever consulted with the younger men, **he rejected the advice** of the elders.

 i. This is a common phenomenon today - what some call *advice shopping*. The idea is that you keep asking different people for advice until you find someone who will tell you what you want to hear. This is an unwise and ungodly way to get counsel. It is better to have a few trusted counselors you will listen to even when they tell you what you don't want to hear.

b. **And consulted the young men who had grown up with him**: These men were much more likely to tell Rehoboam what he already thought. By turning to those likely to think just as he did, it shows that Rehoboam only asked for advice for the sake of appearances

 i. Their unwise advice shows the wisdom of seeking counsel from those *outside* our immediate situation and context. Sometimes an outsider can see things more clearly than those who share our same experiences.

c. **And now, whereas my father put a heavy yoke on you, I will add to your yoke**: The younger men offered the opposite advice to the elders. They suggested an adversarial approach, one that would make Rehoboam more feared than Solomon was.

 i. Solomon asked a lot of Israel, in both taxes and service. Yet we don't have the impression that Israel followed Solomon out of fear, but out of a sense of shared vision and purpose. They believed in what Solomon wanted to do, and were willing to sacrifice to accomplish it. Rehoboam did not appeal to any sense of shared vision and purpose – he simply wanted the people to follow his orders out of the fear of a tyrant.

 ii. "With a dozen rash words, Rehoboam, the bungling dictator, opened the door for four hundred years of strife, weakness, and, eventually, the destruction of the entire nation." (Dilday)

4. (12-15) Rehoboam answers Jeroboam and the elders of Israel harshly.

So Jeroboam and all the people came to Rehoboam the third day, as the king had directed, saying, "Come back to me the third day." Then the king answered the people roughly, and rejected the advice which the elders had given him; and he spoke to them according to the advice of the young men, saying, "My father made your yoke heavy, but I will add to your yoke; my father chastised you with whips, but I will chastise you with scourges!" So

the king did not listen to the people; for the turn *of events* was from the LORD, that He might fulfill His word, which the LORD had spoken by Ahijah the Shilonite to Jeroboam the son of Nebat.

a. **So the king did not listen to the people**: In this case, Rehoboam clearly should have listened to the people. This is not to say that a leader should always lead by popular vote, but a leader needs the wisdom to know when what the people want is actually best for them.

i. Rehoboam was a fool. Ironically, his father Solomon worried about losing all he worked for under a foolish successor: *Then I hated all my labor in which I had toiled under the sun, because I must leave it to the man who will come after me. And who knows whether he will be wise or a fool? Yet he will rule over all my labor in which I toiled and in which I have shown myself wise under the sun. This also is vanity* (Ecclesiastes 2:18-19).

b. **For the turn of events was from the LORD**: God managed this whole series of events, but He did not *make* Rehoboam take this unwise and sinful action. God simply left Rehoboam alone and allowed him to make the critical errors his sinful heart *wanted* to make.

i. "Notice also, dear friends, that God is in events which are produced by the sin and the stupidity of men. This breaking up of the kingdom of Solomon into two parts was the result of Solomon's sin and Rehoboam's folly; yet God was in it: "This thing is from me, saith the Lord." God had nothing to do with the sin or the folly, but in some way which we can never explain, in a mysterious way in which we are to believe without hesitation, God was in it all." (Spurgeon)

5. (16-19) Rehoboam is rejected as king over the ten northern tribes.

Now when all Israel saw that the king did not listen to them, the people answered the king, saying: "What share have we in David? *We have* no inheritance in the son of Jesse. To your tents, O Israel! Now, see to your own house, O David!" So Israel departed to their tents. But Rehoboam reigned over the children of Israel who dwelt in the cities of Judah. Then King Rehoboam sent Adoram, who *was* in charge of the revenue; but all Israel stoned him with stones, and he died. Therefore King Rehoboam mounted his chariot in haste to flee to Jerusalem. So Israel has been in rebellion against the house of David to this day.

a. **What share have we in David**: Rehoboam's foolishness made Israel reject not only Rehoboam, but also the entire dynasty of David. They rejected the descendants of Israel's greatest king.

b. **King Rehoboam sent Adoram, who was in charge of the revenue; but all Israel stoned him with stones**: Apparently, Rehoboam did not take the rebellions seriously until this happened. When his chief tax collector was murdered, he knew that the ten tribes were serious about their rebellion.

i. Adoram was the wrong man for Rehoboam to send. He was famous for his harsh policy of forced labor (1 Kings 4:6 and 5:14). Rehoboam probably sent Adoram because he wanted to make good on his promise to punish those who opposed him. His tough-guy policy didn't work.

c. **So Israel has been in rebellion against the house of David to this day**: From this point on in the history of Israel, the name "Israel" referred to the ten northern tribes and the name "Judah" referred to the southern tribes of Benjamin and Judah.

i. There was a long-standing tension between the ten northern tribes and the combined group of Judah and Benjamin. There were two earlier rebellions along this line of potential division in the days after Absalom's rebellion (2 Samuel 19:40-43), which developed into the rebellion of Sheba (2 Samuel 20:1-2).

ii. "Rehoboam ought to have been thankful that God's love to David had left him even two tribes." (Knapp)

6. (20-24) Rehoboam attempts to re-unify the nation by force.

Now it came to pass when all Israel heard that Jeroboam had come back, they sent for him and called him to the congregation, and made him king over all Israel. There was none who followed the house of David, but the tribe of Judah only. And when Rehoboam came to Jerusalem, he assembled all the house of Judah with the tribe of Benjamin, one hundred and eighty thousand chosen *men* who were warriors, to fight against the house of Israel, that he might restore the kingdom to Rehoboam the son of Solomon. But the word of God came to Shemaiah the man of God, saying, "Speak to Rehoboam the son of Solomon, king of Judah, to all the house of Judah and Benjamin, and to the rest of the people, saying, 'Thus says the LORD: "You shall not go up nor fight against your brethren the children of Israel. Let every man return to his house, for this thing is from Me." Therefore they obeyed the word of the LORD, and turned back, according to the word of the LORD.

a. **When all Israel heard that Jeroboam had come back, they sent for him and called him to the congregation, and made him king**: Thus, the prophecy of Ahijah in 1 Kings 11:29-39 was fulfilled. At the time the prophecy was made, it seemed unlikely - but God's word through His prophet was fulfilled.

i. This King Jeroboam is sometimes called Jeroboam I to distinguish him from a later king of Israel also named Jeroboam, usually known as Jeroboam II (2 Kings 14:23-29).

b. **To fight against the house of Israel, that he might restore the kingdom to Rehoboam**: Rehoboam intended to make war against the seceding tribes of Israel, but God spoke through a prophet and stopped him. To his credit – or perhaps due to a lack of courage – Rehoboam listened to God's word through **Shemaiah the man of God**.

> i. "Here is one Shemaiah, – some of you never heard of him before, perhaps you will never hear of him again; he appears once in this history, and then he vanishes; he comes, and he goes, – only fancy this one man constraining to peace a hundred and eighty thousand chosen men, warriors ready to fight against the house of Israel, by giving to them in very plain, unpolished words, the simple command of God… Why have we not such power? Peradventure, brethren, we do not always speak in the name of the Lord, or speak God's Word as God's Word. If we are simply tellers out of our own thoughts, why should men mind us?" (Spurgeon)

B. Jeroboam's idolatry.

1. (25) Jeroboam's new capital – Shechem.

Then Jeroboam built Shechem in the mountains of Ephraim, and dwelt there. Also he went out from there and built Penuel.

a. **Then Jeroboam built Shechem in the mountains of Ephraim**: Jeroboam needed a capital city because Jerusalem was in the territory of Judah and Benjamin. The city of **Schechem** became the capital city of the northern kingdom of Israel.

b. **He went out from there and built Penuel**: It seems that Jeroboam's reign began with energy and opportunity. He had a significant promise from God through the prophet Ahijah: that *if you heed all that I command you, walk in My ways, and do what is right in My sight, to keep My statutes and My commandments, as My servant David did, then I will be with you and build for you an enduring house, as I built for David, and will give Israel to you* (1 Kings 11:38).

2. (26-29) Jeroboam makes a religion to serve the state.

And Jeroboam said in his heart, "Now the kingdom may return to the house of David: If these people go up to offer sacrifices in the house of the LORD at Jerusalem, then the heart of this people will turn back to their lord, Rehoboam king of Judah, and they will kill me and go back to Rehoboam king of Judah." Therefore the king asked advice, made two calves of gold, and said to the people, "It is too much for you to go up to Jerusalem. Here are your gods, O Israel, which brought you up from the land of Egypt!" And he set up one in Bethel, and the other he put in Dan.

a. **If these people go up to offer sacrifices in the house of the LORD at Jerusalem, then the heart of this people will turn back to their lord,**

Rehoboam: The fact of the divided kingdom did not mean that the northern tribes were exempt from their covenant obligations. They were under the Law of Moses as much as the southern tribes, but Jeroboam feared the *political* implications of yearly trips down to the capital city of the southern kingdom of Judah.

b. **They will kill me and go back to Rehoboam king of Judah**: Jeroboam seems to forget or ignore the promise God made to him through the prophet Ahijah recorded in 1 Kings 11. Jeroboam could best secure his throne by radical obedience to God, not by leading the ten northern tribes into idolatry.

c. **Therefore the king asked advice**: There was no point in asking advice for this evil purpose. Jeroboam wanted advice on how to do a bad thing in the best way.

   i. Jeroboam was even more foolish than it first appears. "It literally says, 'Therefore the king took counsel of *himself*'" (Dilday). "The phrase discovers the fountain of his error, that he did not consult with God, who had given him the kingdom; as in all reason, and justice, and gratitude he should have done" (Poole).

d. **It is too much for you to go up to Jerusalem. Here are your gods, O Israel, which brought you up from the land of Egypt**: Jeroboam appealed to their natural desire for *convenience*. Men will usually take the easy way out when they can; therefore, it was thought to be good if an idol in Bethel or Dan could replace the trip all the way to Jerusalem.

   i. Jeroboam became an example of a political leader who shapes religion for his own purpose. The issue of *true* religion was unimportant to Jeroboam; he was interested in *useful* religion.

   ii. **Here are your gods, O Israel**: Jeroboam repeated the same words of Aaron about 500 years before his time (Exodus 32:4).

   iii. It is possible – perhaps even likely – that Jeroboam intended the gold calves to represent the God of Israel. This wasn't the introduction of a *new* god, but a perversion of the proper worship of the true God. "Men are willing to worship God if they are allowed to have a ritual and symbols which they have themselves devised" (Spurgeon).

3. (30-33) The establishment of Jeroboam's religion.

Now this thing became a sin, for the people went *to worship* before the one as far as Dan. He made shrines on the high places, and made priests from every class of people, who were not of the sons of Levi. Jeroboam ordained a feast on the fifteenth day of the eighth month, like the feast that *was* in Judah, and offered sacrifices on the altar. So he did at Bethel, sacrificing to the calves that he had made. And at Bethel he installed the priests of the high places which he had made. So he made offerings on the altar which he

had made at Bethel on the fifteenth day of the eighth month, in the month which he had devised in his own heart. And he ordained a feast for the children of Israel, and offered sacrifices on the altar and burned incense.

a. **Now this thing became a sin**: It was a sin when Jeroboam suggested it, but it was *more* of a sin when the people followed it. The people were so attracted to the religion of Jeroboam that they went **as far as Dan** (at the far north of Israel) to worship at the shrine of the golden calf there.

b. **He made shrines on the high places**: Jeroboam made more places of worship than the main centers at Bethel and Dan. These **high places** were even more convenient for the people.

c. **Made priests from every class of people, who were not of the sons of Levi**: Jeroboam rejected the commandments of God regarding the priesthood of Israel, and established a priesthood of his own liking.

   i. The legitimate priests and Levites who lived in the northern ten tribes did not like this. They, along with others who *set their hearts to seek the LORD God of Israel*, moved from the northern kingdom of Israel to the southern kingdom of Judah during this period (2 Chronicles 11:13-16). Spiritually speaking, Israel was struck twice – by the ungodly religion of Jeroboam and by the departure of the godly and faithful. There were few godly people left in the northern kingdom.

   ii. "He felt he could afford to let priests and worshippers whose standards were higher abandon their possessions and go south to Judah (cf. 2 Chronicles 11:13ff.)." (Payne)

   iii. "Viewed even as a stroke of policy, this ejection of the Lord's priests and Levites was a blunder. They went over in a body, almost, to Jeroboam's rival, and thereby 'strengthened the kingdom of Judah.'" (Knapp)

d. **In the month which he had devised in his own heart**: This is a good summary of Jeroboam's religion - it was **devised in his own heart**. Jeroboam is an example of those who create their own religion according to their own taste.

   i. For the most part, the world embraces the religion of Jeroboam. Not necessarily his particular expression of golden calves and high places, but a religion created according to taste. In the book *Habits of the Heart*, Robert Bellah and his colleagues interviewed a young nurse named Sheila Larson, whom they described as representing many Americans' experience and views on religion. Speaking about her own faith and how it operated in her life she said, "I believe in God. I'm not a religious fanatic. I can't remember the last time I went to church. My faith has carried me a long way. It is 'Sheilaism.' Just my own little voice." This "pick-and-choose-as-I-go-along-according-to-my-inner-voice" approach is the modern version of Jeroboam's religion – and in opposition to the *revealed* religion of the Bible.

ii. Therefore, it was natural that Jeroboam served as his own priest (**and offered sacrifices on the altar and burned incense**). "Jeroboam probably performed the functions of high priest himself, that he might in his own person condense the civil and ecclesiastical power" (Clarke).

1 Kings 13 - The Man of God from Judah

A. A prophecy from a man of God.

1. (1-2) The coming destruction of the altar in Bethel.

And behold, a man of God went from Judah to Bethel by the word of the LORD, and Jeroboam stood by the altar to burn incense. Then he cried out against the altar by the word of the LORD, and said, "O altar, altar! Thus says the LORD: 'Behold, a child, Josiah by name, shall be born to the house of David; and on you he shall sacrifice the priests of the high places who burn incense on you, and men's bones shall be burned on you.'"

a. **A man of God went from Judah to Bethel**: Apparently, there were no qualified messengers within the northern kingdom of Israel. This is a sad commentary on the spiritual state of Jeroboam's kingdom.

i. This anonymous **man of God** was used in an important way. He demonstrates that one does not need to be famous to be significantly used by God.

b. **Behold, a child, Josiah by name, shall be born to the house of David; and on you he shall sacrifice the priests of the high places who burn incense on you**: This is a remarkable prophecy that would be precisely fulfilled 340 years later. 2 Kings 23:15 documents the fulfillment of this prophecy in the days of Josiah, King of Judah: *Moreover the altar that was at Bethel, and the high place which Jeroboam the son of Nebat, who made Israel sin, had made, both that altar and the high place he broke down; and he burned the high place and crushed it to powder, and burned the wooden image.*

i. This was more than a pronouncement of judgment against the altar; it also announced that the judgment would come through a ruler of Judah (**the house of David**). This was a special rebuke and source of concern to Jeroboam, who was always aware of the threat from his neighbor to the south (as in 1 Kings 12:27).

ii. *We* know that this didn't happen for some 350 years, but Jeroboam didn't know that in advance. He went to his grave worried about the fulfillment of this prophecy, which was a sort of immediate judgment on Jeroboam.

2. (3-5) Signs to confirm the prophet's words.

And he gave a sign the same day, saying, "This *is* the sign which the LORD has spoken: Surely the altar shall split apart, and the ashes on it shall be poured out." So it came to pass when King Jeroboam heard the saying of the man of God, who cried out against the altar in Bethel, that he stretched out his hand from the altar, saying, "Arrest him!" Then his hand, which he stretched out toward him, withered, so that he could not pull it back to himself. The altar also was split apart, and the ashes poured out from the altar, according to the sign which the man of God had given by the word of the LORD.

a. **He gave a sign the same day**: The prophecy of the man of God would not be fulfilled for hundreds of years, so an immediate sign was given to confirm the word to the present-day hearers.

b. **Surely the altar shall split apart, and the ashes on it shall be poured out**: This would be a convincing sign, and a direct rebuke to the idolatrous worship at that altar.

c. **Arrest him**: Jeroboam's reaction was immediate – he sought to silence the messenger rather than respond to the message. The prophecy from the man of God was like most every message of coming judgment – an implicit invitation to repentance. Jeroboam obviously did not accept this invitation.

i. "If Jeroboam would not have Jehovah's *priests*, God sends His *prophet* into his land." (Knapp)

d. **His hand, which he stretched out toward him, withered, so that he could not pull it back to himself**: God confirmed His word of judgment in two ways. First, He judged the disobedient king at the precise point of his most glaring sin (the outstretched hand against the man of God). Second, He fulfilled the immediate word against the altar (**the altar also was split apart**).

i. "This God did, partly, to chastise Jeroboam for offering violence to the Lord's prophet; partly, to secure the prophet against further violence; and partly, that in this example God might show how highly he resents the injuries done to his ministers in and for the faithful discharge of their office." (Poole)

3. (6) Jeroboam's plea.

Then the king answered and said to the man of God, "Please entreat the favor of the LORD your God, and pray for me, that my hand may be restored

to me." So the man of God entreated the LORD, and the king's hand was restored to him, and became as before.

a. **Please entreat the favor of the LORD your God, and pray for me, that my hand may be restored**: Under the evident judgment of God, Jeroboam had no use for golden calves or their altars. He knew that his only hope was in the LORD and in His representative.

i. As the subsequent chapters will show, Jeroboam didn't really repent here; or if he did, it was only for a moment. Wanting to receive something from God is not the same as repentance.

b. **So the man of God entreated the LORD, and the king's hand was restored to him**: To his credit, the man of God showed great grace to Jeroboam. He quickly moved from being under arrest to being an intercessor for his persecutor. This was great mercy from the man of God, and especially from God, who answered his prayer.

i. God did this, "Partly, to assure him that the stroke was from God; partly, because he repented of that violence which he intended against the prophet, for which God inflicted it; and partly, that the goodness of God to him might have led him to repentance; or if he continued impenitent, leave him without all excuse" (Poole).

4. (7-10) The man of God declines Jeroboam's invitation.

Then the king said to the man of God, "Come home with me and refresh yourself, and I will give you a reward." But the man of God said to the king, "If you were to give me half your house, I would not go in with you; nor would I eat bread nor drink water in this place. For so it was commanded me by the word of the LORD, saying, 'You shall not eat bread, nor drink water, nor return by the same way you came.'" So he went another way and did not return by the way he came to Bethel.

a. **I will give you a reward**: Jeroboam quickly - and naturally, given the circumstances – embraced the man of God as a friend. He wanted to **refresh** and **reward** him, without any *repentance* from the sin the man of God had denounced.

b. **If you were to give me half your house, I would not go in with you; nor would I eat bread nor drink water in this place**: The man of God refused the invitation, based on a prior warning from God. To accept Jeroboam's invitation would demonstrate fellowship with his idolatry.

B. The man of God's disobedience and death.

1. (11-17) An old prophet in Bethel invites the man of God to dinner.

Now an old prophet dwelt in Bethel, and his sons came and told him all the works that the man of God had done that day in Bethel; they also told

their father the words which he had spoken to the king. And their father said to them, "Which way did he go?" For his sons had seen which way the man of God went who came from Judah. Then he said to his sons, "Saddle the donkey for me." So they saddled the donkey for him; and he rode on it, and went after the man of God, and found him sitting under an oak. Then he said to him, "*Are* you the man of God who came from Judah?" And he said, "I *am.*" Then he said to him, "Come home with me and eat bread." And he said, "I cannot return with you nor go in with you; neither can I eat bread nor drink water with you in this place. For I have been told by the word of the LORD, 'You shall not eat bread nor drink water there, nor return by going the way you came.'"

a. **Now an old prophet dwelt in Bethel**: It seems that this was a faithful prophet to the LORD. This demonstrates that not every godly person left Israel for Judah; some still remained behind.

i. "Probably once a prophet of the Lord, who had fallen from his steadfastness, and yet not so deeply as to lose the knowledge of the true God, and join with Jeroboam with his idolatries." (Clarke)

b. **Come home with me and eat bread**: This prophet from Bethel invited the unnamed man of God to his home, as Jeroboam had invited him. The man of God refused, under the same reason he refused Jeroboam – that God had specifically told him to return to Judah without accepting hospitality, and to return a different way (also in 1 Kings 13:10).

2. (18-19) The prophet from Bethel lies to the man of God from Judah.

He said to him, "I too *am* a prophet as you *are,* and an angel spoke to me by the word of the LORD, saying, 'Bring him back with you to your house, that he may eat bread and drink water.'" (He was lying to him.) So he went back with him, and ate bread in his house, and drank water.

a. **He was lying to him**: The prophet from Bethel gave a false word from God, trying to persuade the man of God from Judah to change his course from doing exactly what God told him.

i. "As he found the man of God sitting under an oak, probably *faint* with *fatigue* and *fasting,* for he had no refreshment, his *humanity* might have led him to practise this deception, in order to persuade him to take some refreshment." (Clarke)

ii. "But his sin was great; for he did not only tell a premeditated lie, but also made God a liar, and to contradict himself, and all this without any pretence of necessity, or benefit to himself." (Poole)

b. **An angel spoke to me**: Perhaps this was true, and perhaps it was a *deceiving* angel. Satan and his messengers can appear as angels of light (2 Corinthians 11:14-15).

c. **So he went back with him, and ate bread in his house, and drank water**: The man of God from Judah listened to the lie from the prophet of Bethel. He did this for several reasons:

- The prophet from Bethel was probably older (*an old prophet*, 1 Kings 13:11) and had the respect of the man of God.
- The prophet from Bethel identified with the man of God (**I too am a prophet as you are**).
- The prophet from Bethel claimed a spectacular experience (**an angel spoke to me**).
- The prophet from Bethel claimed to speak for the LORD (**by the word of the LORD**).
- The prophet from Bethel did not seem to be an idolater who should be shunned (**Bring him back with you to your house**).
- The prophet from Bethel offered no reward, other than simple food (**he may eat bread and drink water**).

   i. No matter how natural and seductive this enticement was, it was the duty of the man of God to resist it. He had a word from God to guide his actions, and should receive *no other word* accept through dramatic and direct confirmation by God's Spirit. His failure at this point ended his usefulness as a man of God.

   ii. "When we have received a direct command fresh from the lips of Christ, we must act on it, and not be turned aside by a different suggestion, made to us through the lips of professing Christians… Deal with God at first-hand." (Meyer)

   iii. "God never contradicts Himself in His dealings with His servants. Let us be true to His commands, refusing to be deflected from the path of obedience, even by an angel from heaven." (Morgan)

3. (20-22) The prophet from Bethel prophesies the doom of the man of God.

Now it happened, as they sat at the table, that the word of the LORD came to the prophet who had brought him back; and he cried out to the man of God who came from Judah, saying, "Thus says the LORD: 'Because you have disobeyed the word of the LORD, and have not kept the commandment which the LORD your God commanded you, but you came back, ate bread, and drank water in the place of which *the Lord* said to you, "Eat no bread and drink no water," your corpse shall not come to the tomb of your fathers.'"

a. **The word of the LORD came to the prophet who had brought him back**: This prophet from Bethel spoke a *lie* in the name of the LORD in 1 Kings 13:18. Now he received a *true* prophecy while the man of God from Judah ate at his table.

b. **Because you have disobeyed the word of the LORD**: God promised great judgment against the man of God from Judah for his disobedience. This was a hard test, but he failed it. He should have **kept the commandment which the LORD your God commanded**, no matter how subtle and innocent the temptation was to disobey.

c. **Your corpse shall not come to the tomb of your fathers**: God judged the man of God from Judah far more strictly than He judged Jeroboam or the prophet from Bethel. It would seem that they were guilty of worse sins (leading national idolatry and a deliberate lying prophecy), yet the man of God received worse judgment.

i. "For a body to lie unburied was a curse, hence the emphasis on detail of the place of burial. It was a disgrace to be buried away from the family among strangers." (Wiseman)

ii. This is an example of an important principle of the way God works. We think that strict judgment should begin among the most ungodly, but often God begins strict judgment among His own people (1 Peter 4:17). Usually this is because God knows that the world will not be reached when His people live in compromise and disobedience.

iii. "By permitting himself to be seduced by the old prophet, when he should have acted only on the expressly declared counsel of God, he committed *the sin unto death* [1 John 5:16-17]; that is, such a sin as God will punish with the death of the body, while he extends mercy to his soul." (Clarke)

4. (23-25a) The word of the prophet from Bethel is fulfilled.

So it was, after he had eaten bread and after he had drunk, that he saddled the donkey for him, the prophet whom he had brought back. When he was gone, a lion met him on the road and killed him. And his corpse was thrown on the road, and the donkey stood by it. The lion also stood by the corpse. And there, men passed by and saw the corpse thrown on the road, and the lion standing by the corpse.

a. **A lion met him on the road and killed him**: The word – the *second* word – of the prophet from Bethel was fulfilled. He didn't say that the man of God would perish by a lion, but that he would not be buried in the tomb of his fathers.

i. "Lions were attested in Palestine until at least the thirteenth century A.D." (Wiseman)

b. **And there, men passed by and saw the corpse thrown on the road, and the lion standing by the corpse**: This demonstrates that this was no mere accident, but something unique from God. The lion did not attack the donkey (**the donkey stood by it**), nor did he attack the **men** who **passed by**. This lion was on a special mission of judgment from God, and seems to be more obedient than the man of God from Judah was.

5. (25b-32) The man of God is given a decent burial and the prophet from Bethel testifies to his prophecy.

Then they went and told *it* in the city where the old prophet dwelt. Now when the prophet who had brought him back from the way heard *it*, he said, "It *is* the man of God who was disobedient to the word of the LORD. Therefore the LORD has delivered him to the lion, which has torn him and killed him, according to the word of the LORD which He spoke to him." And he spoke to his sons, saying, "Saddle the donkey for me." So they saddled *it*. Then he went and found his corpse thrown on the road, and the donkey and the lion standing by the corpse. The lion had not eaten the corpse nor torn the donkey. And the prophet took up the corpse of the man of God, laid it on the donkey, and brought it back. So the old prophet came to the city to mourn, and to bury him. Then he laid the corpse in his own tomb; and they mourned over him, *saying,* "Alas, my brother!" So it was, after he had buried him, that he spoke to his sons, saying, "When I am dead, then bury me in the tomb where the man of God *is* buried; lay my bones beside his bones. For the saying which he cried out by the word of the LORD against the altar in Bethel, and against all the shrines on the high places which *are* in the cities of Samaria, will surely come to pass."

a. **So the old prophet came to the city to mourn, and to bury him**: The old prophet from Bethel was sympathetic to the man of God from Judah, even in his disobedience and resulting judgment. The prophet from Bethel was not a particularly righteous man or good prophet, having used a lying prophecy to lead the man of God into sin and judgment. He recognized the common weakness of this fellow servant of God.

i. How strange it was for the old prophet to look upon the carcass of the dead prophet, and to realize: "My sin was worse than his." The ways of God's judgment are sometimes past finding out, and only understandable from eternity.

b. **He laid the corpse in his own tomb**: Not in the tomb of the man of God from Judah's fathers, in fulfillment of the previous prophecy.

c. **When I am dead, then bury me in the tomb where the man of God is buried; lay my bones beside his bones**: Though he lied to him, led him into sin, and prophesied judgment against him, the prophet from Bethel still respected the man of God from Judah. Perhaps he understood that the word he spoke against Jeroboam required a courage he did not have; therefore he confirmed the word of the man of God against Jeroboam and the altar at Bethel.

6. (33-34) No repentance from Jeroboam.

After this event Jeroboam did not turn from his evil way, but again he made priests from every class of people for the high places; whoever wished, he consecrated him, and he became *one* of the priests of the high places. And this thing was the sin of the house of Jeroboam, so as to exterminate and destroy *it* from the face of the earth.

a. **After this event Jeroboam did not turn from his evil way**: He should have turned, but he did not. God's dealing with the man of God from Judah was warning enough to Jeroboam, but it was a warning he ignored.

   i. "All these wonderful accidents, as God's hammers, did but beat upon cold iron." (Trapp)

b. **He became one of the priests of the high places**: In ancient Israel, God commanded a strict separation between the office of king and priest. Jeroboam blurred this separation and **this thing was the sin of the house of Jeroboam**.

   i. Jeroboam had great opportunity, especially in light of the promise of God through Ahijah recorded in 1 Kings 11:38: *Then it shall be, if you heed all that I command you, walk in My ways, and do what is right in My sight, to keep My statutes and My commandments, as My servant David did, then I will be with you and build for you an enduring house, as I built for David, and will give Israel to you.* Jeroboam did not obey God and honor His commandments, and he never fulfilled his potential or promise.

   ii. The same principle works in servants of God today. We are not called because of obedience, or used out of merit; but our disobedience hinders our potential for full use. Paul put it this way in 2 Timothy 2:21: *Therefore if anyone cleanses himself from the latter* [works of dishonor]*, he will be a vessel for honor, sanctified and useful for the Master, prepared for every good work.* God uses vessels of honor, separation, usefulness, and preparation to their fullest potential.

   iii. In his failure, Jeroboam became the prototype of the disobedient kings of Israel. The phrase *He did evil in the sight of the LORD, and walked in the way of Jeroboam, and in his sin by which he had made Israel sin* was used of many subsequent kings of Israel. These include:

   • Baasha (1 Kings 15:33-34).
   • Omri (1 Kings 16:25-26).
   • Ahaziah (1 Kings 22:51-52).
   • Jehoram (2 Kings 3:1-3).
   • Jehu (2 Kings 10:29-31).
   • Jehoahaz (2 Kings 13:1-2).
   • Jehoash (2 Kings 13:10-11).
   • Jeroboam II (2 Kings 14:23-24).

- Zechariah (2 Kings 15:8-9).
- Menahim (2 Kings 15:17-18).
- Pekahiah (2 Kings 15:23-24).
- Pekah (2 Kings 15:27-28).

iv. One curious exception was Ahab, who was noted as *worse* than Jeroboam (1 Kings 16:30-31).

v. Jeroboam had great opportunity, but instead became a great curse to every generation of the northern kingdom after that. Even at the end of the Kingdom of Israel, Jeroboam's sin was remembered: *For He tore Israel from the house of David, and they made Jeroboam the son of Nebat king. Then Jeroboam drove Israel from following the LORD, and made them commit a great sin. For the children of Israel walked in all the sins of Jeroboam which he did; they did not depart from them, until the LORD removed Israel out of His sight, as He had said by all His servants the prophets. So Israel was carried away from their own land to Assyria, as it is to this day* (2 Kings 17:21-23).

vi. All in all, Jeroboam is an example of sinful failure.

- He failed despite great blessing and favor from God.
- He failed for the sake of mere political advantage.
- He failed and led an entire nation into idolatry.
- He failed despite specific warnings to repent.
- He failed despite specific judgment and deliverance from that judgment.
- He failed despite a clear message and example of integrity.

1 Kings 14 - The End of Jeroboam and Rehoboam

A. The end of Jeroboam, King of Israel.

1. (1-3) Jeroboam sends his wife on a mission.

At that time Abijah the son of Jeroboam became sick. And Jeroboam said to his wife, "Please arise, and disguise yourself, that they may not recognize you as the wife of Jeroboam, and go to Shiloh. Indeed, Ahijah the prophet *is* there, who told me that *I would be* king over this people. Also take with you ten loaves, *some* cakes, and a jar of honey, and go to him; he will tell you what will become of the child."

a. **At that time Abijah the son of Jeroboam became sick**: Jeroboam was a king, but even kings have trouble common to men. His sick son troubled him and prompted him to seek the help of a prophet.

i. "Prophets were commonly consulted on health matters (2 Kings 1:2; 4:22, 40; 5:3)." (Wiseman)

b. **Disguise yourself, that they may not recognize you as the wife of Jeroboam**: This was a familiar pattern for Jeroboam. In his time of need, he turned to the true God and men of God. He knew that idols could not help him in any true crisis. Yet he also knew that he had rejected God and His prophets, and so he told his wife to wear a **disguise**.

i. "How foolish! Jeroboam thought that the old prophet could penetrate the vail that hid the future, but not the disguise in which his wife wished to conceal herself." (Meyer)

c. **He will tell you what will become of the child**: Jeroboam did not tell his wife to pray for their son, or to ask the prophet to pray. He wanted to use Ahijah the prophet as a fortuneteller instead of seeking him as a man of God.

i. "It would have been more pious if he had begged the prophet's prayers, and cast away his idols from him; then the child might have been restored to him, as his hand was. But most people would rather be told their fortune than their faults or their duty." (Matthew Henry)

2. (4-6) Jeroboam's wife meets with Ahijah the prophet.

And Jeroboam's wife did so; she arose and went to Shiloh, and came to the house of Ahijah. But Ahijah could not see, for his eyes were glazed by reason of his age. Now the LORD had said to Ahijah, "Here is the wife of Jeroboam, coming to ask you something about her son, for he *is* sick. Thus and thus you shall say to her; for it will be, when she comes in, that she will pretend *to be* another *woman*." And so it was, when Ahijah heard the sound of her footsteps as she came through the door, he said, "Come in, wife of Jeroboam. Why do you pretend *to be* another *person?* For I *have been* sent to you *with* bad *news*.

a. **Ahijah could not see**: As it turned out, there was no reason for the wife of Jeroboam to wear a disguise. Old age made Ahijah unable to see.

b. **The LORD had said to Ahijah, "Here is the wife of Jeroboam, coming to ask you something about her son"**: The woman's disguise and Ahijah's blindness didn't matter, because God told Ahijah the truth of the matter.

c. **I have been sent to you with bad news**: From this, the wife of Jeroboam learned two things. First, that the news was bad. Second, that though she thought she was sent to Ahijah by her husband, in truth Ahijah was sent by God with a message to her and Jeroboam.

3. (7-11) Ahijah declares God's judgment on the house of Jeroboam.

Go, tell Jeroboam, 'Thus says the LORD God of Israel: "Because I exalted you from among the people, and made you ruler over My people Israel, and tore the kingdom away from the house of David, and gave it to you; and *yet* you have not been as My servant David, who kept My commandments and who followed Me with all his heart, to do only *what was* right in My eyes; but you have done more evil than all who were before you, for you have gone and made for yourself other gods and molded images to provoke Me to anger, and have cast Me behind your back—therefore behold! I will bring disaster on the house of Jeroboam, and will cut off from Jeroboam every male in Israel, bond and free; I will take away the remnant of the house of Jeroboam, as one takes away refuse until it is all gone. The dogs shall eat whoever belongs to Jeroboam and dies in the city, and the birds of the air shall eat whoever dies in the field; for the LORD has spoken!"'

a. **You have done more evil than all who were before you**: Saul was a bad man and a bad king. Solomon was a good king but a bad man. Though both men were bad, Jeroboam was far worse. He became the measuring line for the bad kings of Israel to come.

i. God compared Jeroboam unfavorably to David with the words, **as my servant David** "who though he fell into some sins, yet, first, he constantly persevered in the true worship of God, from which thou are revolted;

secondly, he heartily repented of and turned from all his sins, whereas thou are obstinate and incorrigible" (Poole).

b. **And have cast Me behind your back**: This was a powerful description of intense contempt towards God, as in Ezekiel 23:35 - *Because you have forgotten Me and cast Me behind your back, therefore you shall bear the penalty of your lewdness and your harlotry.*

> i. "The last reason implies a neglect, a scorning of God. It is the same figure of speech used to describe God's forgiveness of our sins. He puts them behind His back, or in other words, He forgets them. That is good news when it describes God's treatment of our sins [Isaiah 38:17], but it is tragically bad news when it describes a person's treatment of God." (Dilday)

c. **I will bring disaster on the house of Jeroboam, and will cut off from Jeroboam every male**: Jeroboam *could have* had a lasting dynasty, but he wasted the promise of God with his unbelief, idolatry, and outright rejection of God.

> i. **Every male**: "Means literally 'he who urinates against the wall'" (Patterson and Austel).

4. (12-16) The immediate judgment and the distant judgment.

"Arise therefore, go to your own house. When your feet enter the city, the child shall die. And all Israel shall mourn for him and bury him, for he is the only one of Jeroboam who shall come to the grave, because in him there is found something good toward the LORD God of Israel in the house of Jeroboam. Moreover the LORD will raise up for Himself a king over Israel who shall cut off the house of Jeroboam; this is the day. What? Even now! For the LORD will strike Israel, as a reed is shaken in the water. He will uproot Israel from this good land which He gave to their fathers, and will scatter them beyond the River, because they have made their wooden images, provoking the LORD to anger. And He will give Israel up because of the sins of Jeroboam, who sinned and who made Israel sin."

a. **When your feet enter the city, the child shall die**: Jeroboam sent his wife to discover the fate of his son. The bad news was that the child would die. Yet his death would be a demonstration of mercy, because at least he would be buried in honor and properly mourned. Such great judgment was coming upon the house of Jeroboam that all would see that by comparison, this son was *blessed* in his death.

b. **He will uproot Israel from this good land which He gave to their fathers, and will scatter them beyond the River**: This would finally be fulfilled some 300 years later. God knew that the root of Jeroboam's apostasy would eventually result in the bitter fruit of national exile.

5. (17-18) The immediate judgment is fulfilled.

Then Jeroboam's wife arose and departed, and came to Tirzah. When she came to the threshold of the house, the child died. And they buried him; and all Israel mourned for him, according to the word of the LORD which He spoke through His servant Ahijah the prophet.

a. **According to the word of the LORD which He spoke through His servant Ahijah the prophet**: The prophecy about Israel's national exile would not be fulfilled for centuries. Yet it was demonstrated as true because the immediate prophecy of the death of Jeroboam's son was exactly fulfilled.

6. (19-20) The death of Jeroboam and the summary of his reign.

Now the rest of the acts of Jeroboam, how he made war and how he reigned, indeed they *are* written in the book of the chronicles of the kings of Israel. The period that Jeroboam reigned *was* twenty-two years. So he rested with his fathers. Then Nadab his son reigned in his place.

a. **He rested with his fathers**: 2 Chronicles 13:20 tells us that *the LORD struck him, and he died.* "He died not the common death of all men, but by some remarkable stroke: beside the loss of five hundred thousand of his men in one battle with Abijah king of Judah (2 Chronicles 13:17)" (Trapp).

B. The end of Rehoboam, king of Judah.

1. (21-24) Judah's sin provokes God to jealousy.

And Rehoboam the son of Solomon reigned in Judah. Rehoboam *was* forty-one years old when he became king. He reigned seventeen years in Jerusalem, the city which the LORD had chosen out of all the tribes of Israel, to put His name there. His mother's name *was* Naamah, an Ammonitess. Now Judah did evil in the sight of the LORD, and they provoked Him to jealousy with their sins which they committed, more than all that their fathers had done. For they also built for themselves high places, *sacred* pillars, and wooden images on every high hill and under every green tree. And there were also perverted persons in the land. They did according to all the abominations of the nations which the LORD had cast out before the children of Israel.

a. **Judah did evil in the sight of the LORD, and they provoked Him to jealousy with their sins**: These sins **provoked** the LORD to jealousy because they were essentially sins of idolatry. Israel turned their back on the God who loved and redeemed them, and like an unfaithful spouse, they pursued spiritual adultery with idols.

b. **There were also perverted persons in the land**: This specifically describes prostitutes associated with the worship of idols. It is possible that the term **perverted persons** refers to both men and women cultic prostitutes. However, the term was used in Deuteronomy 23:17-18 in distinction to feminine cultic prostitutes.

c. **They did according to all the abominations of the nations which the LORD had cast out before the children of Israel**: Considering the depth of depravity among the Canaanite nations, this is a strong statement.

2. (25-26) God chastises Rehoboam through Egypt.

It happened in the fifth year of King Rehoboam *that* Shishak king of Egypt came up against Jerusalem. And he took away the treasures of the house of the LORD and the treasures of the king's house; he took away everything. He also took away all the gold shields which Solomon had made.

a. **In the fifth year of King Rehoboam**: This was not so far from the time of David and Solomon, years of strength and security in Israel. No foreign enemy ever did as much against God's people during the time of David and Solomon as happened during this occasion during the reign of Rehoboam.

b. **Shishak king of Egypt came up against Jerusalem**: Both 2 Chronicles and archeology confirm this account. The record in 2 Chronicles 12 gives many details that the writer of 1 Kings summarized. From 2 Chronicles 12 we learn:

• Exactly why this attack succeeded: *When Rehoboam had established the kingdom and had strengthened himself, that he forsook the law of the LORD, and all Israel along with him* (2 Chronicles 12:2).
• That Shishak brought an allied army of nations against Judah (2 Chronicles 12:3).
• That Shishak *took the fortified cities of Judah* on his way to Jerusalem (2 Chronicles 12: 4).
• That as the enemy army approached Jerusalem, the Prophet Shemaiah led the leaders of Judah in genuine repentance (2 Chronicles 12:6).
• In response to their repentance, God allowed Jerusalem to remain - but as servants of Shishak, king of Egypt (2 Chronicles 12:7-8).

   i. "Sheshonq I (Shishak) had founded the Egyptian (Libyan) Dynasty XXII (945-924 B.C.) and his raid into Palestine in this year (925 B.C.) is well attested on the Amon temple reliefs at Thebes (Karnak). From the one hundred and fifty place-names recorded there, his aim seems to have been to reassert Egyptian control over the main trade routes throughout Palestine and the Negeb." (Wiseman)

c. **He took away the treasures of the house of the LORD and the treasures of the king's house**: Solomon left great wealth to his son Rehoboam, both in the temple and in the palace. After only five years, that wealth was largely gone.

d. **He also took away all the gold shields which Solomon had made**: 1 Kings 10:16-17 mentions these 500 shields, 200 large and 300 small. These shields made beautiful displays in the House of the Forest of Lebanon, but they were of no use in battle. Gold was too heavy and too soft to be used as a metal for effective shields. This was an example of the emphasis of *image* over *substance* that began in the days of Solomon and worsened in the days of Rehoboam.

> i. "Rehoboam made in their stead shields of bronze, and with these pathetically tried to keep up former appearances. It is like souls, who, when despoiled of their freshness and power by the enemy, laboriously endeavor to keep up an outward appearance of spiritual prosperity; or, like a fallen church, shorn of its strength, and robbed of its purity, seeking to hide its helplessness, and cover its nakedness, with the tinsel of ritualism, spurious revivalism, union, and anything that promises to give them some appearance." (Knapp)

> ii. According to Dilday, each large shield was worth about $120,000. The smaller shields were worth $30,000. $33 million was invested in gold ceremonial shields – and now in the hands of the Egyptians.

3. (27-28) The decline of the Kingdom of Judah under Rehoboam.

Then King Rehoboam made bronze shields in their place, and committed *them* to the hands of the captains of the guard, who guarded the doorway of the king's house. And whenever the king entered the house of the LORD, the guards carried them, then brought them back into the guardroom.

> a. **King Rehoboam made bronze shields in their place**: The replacement of gold with bronze is a perfect picture of the decline under the days of Rehoboam. The dynasty of David went from gold to bronze in five years.

> > i. "They wished to emphasize how far Rehoboam fell in a mere few years. He had inherited an empire; five years later, master of a small state, he could protect his capital itself only by denuding his palace of its treasures. Solomon's court had despised silver; his son's court had to be content with bronze!" (Payne)

> b. **And committed them to the hands of the captains of the guard**: In the days of Solomon, the gold shields hung on display in the House of the Forest of Lebanon (1 Kings 10:16-17). Under Rehoboam, the replacement bronze shields were kept in a protected guardroom until they were specifically needed for state occasions.

4. (29-31) Rehoboam's death and the summary of his reign.

Now the rest of the acts of Rehoboam, and all that he did, *are* they not written in the book of the chronicles of the kings of Judah? And there was war between Rehoboam and Jeroboam all *their* days. So Rehoboam rested with his fathers, and was buried with his fathers in the City of David. His mother's name *was* Naamah, an Ammonitess. Then Abijam his son reigned in his place.

a. **Now the rest of the acts of Rehoboam**: 2 Chronicles summarized Rehoboam like this: *And he did evil, because he did not prepare his heart to seek the LORD.* (2 Chronicles 12:14) This speaks to the lack of his personal relationship with the LORD.

> i. "He was born of a heathen mother, and begotten of an apostate father. From such an impure fountain could sweet water possibly spring?" (Clarke)

> ii. "The account ends with the note that Rehoboam's mother was Naamah, an Ammonitess. Is this not the writer's way of reminding us that it was Solomon's marriage to foreign wives that started the precipitous decline in the first place?" (Dilday)

b. **There was war between Rehoboam and Jeroboam all their days**: These two were very different. Rehoboam governed as a tyrant, started bad and humbled himself to God towards the end of his life (2 Chronicles 12:6-7). Jeroboam governed as a populist, started with great promise but ended terribly.

1 Kings 15 - The Reigns of Abijam, Asa, Nadab and Baasha

A. Two kings of Judah.

1. (1-8) The reign of King Abijam (known as Abijah in 2 Chronicles 13).

In the eighteenth year of King Jeroboam the son of Nebat, Abijam became king over Judah. He reigned three years in Jerusalem. His mother's name *was* Maachah the granddaughter of Abishalom. And he walked in all the sins of his father, which he had done before him; his heart was not loyal to the LORD his God, as was the heart of his father David. Nevertheless for David's sake the LORD his God gave him a lamp in Jerusalem, by setting up his son after him and by establishing Jerusalem; because David did *what was* right in the eyes of the LORD, and had not turned aside from anything that He commanded him all the days of his life, except in the matter of Uriah the Hittite. And there was war between Rehoboam and Jeroboam all the days of his life. Now the rest of the acts of Abijam, and all that he did, *are* they not written in the book of the chronicles of the kings of Judah? And there was war between Abijam and Jeroboam. So Abijam rested with his fathers, and they buried him in the City of David. Then Asa his son reigned in his place.

a. **Abijam became king over Judah**: This son of Rehoboam only **reigned three years**, showing that God did not bless his reign.

i. From comparing this account with 2 Chronicles 13 we learn that Abijam knew something of the LORD and knew how to preach – but he did not uproot the idolatry and sexual immorality that was introduced by Rehoboam. The successor of Abijam (Asa) removed the centers of the sexually-charged idolatry that was so common in this land (1 Kings 15:12-13).

b. **His heart was not loyal to the LORD his God, as was the heart of his father David**: This was the real problem with Abijam's reign – his lack of a real personal relationship with God. David sinned during his reign, but his heart stayed **loyal to the LORD his God**.

> i. 2 Chronicles 13 fills in more interesting details about the reign of Abijam (called Abijah in 2 Chronicles). It tells us how there was war between Jeroboam of Israel and Abijam of Judah, and how Abijam challenged Jeroboam on the basis of righteousness and faithfulness to God. Jeroboam responded with a surprise attack, and victory seemed certain for Israel over Judah – but Abjiam cried out to the LORD, and God won a victory for Judah that day. 2 Chronicles 13:18 says of that war, *Thus the children of Israel were subdued at that time; and the children of Judah prevailed, because they relied on the LORD God of their fathers.*

> ii. "For David's sake and in response to his faith, he was allowed a spectacular victory over the encircling Israelites whom he had challenged, for being even more apostate than he… This is an instance of God blessing the unworthy for the sake of the worthy." (Wiseman)

> iii. Yet Chronicles also tells us his standing at the end of his brief reign: *But Abijah grew mighty, married fourteen wives, and begot twenty-two sons and sixteen daughters* (2 Chronicles 13:21). In the midst of his victory and good leadership for Judah, he never had the relationship with the LORD he should have had.

c. **For David's sake the LORD his God gave him a lamp in Jerusalem**: God preserved the dynasty of David in Jerusalem for the sake of David, not because of the character or quality of his descendants.

> i. "Chronicles spells his name Abijah, which means 'Yahweh is my father.' Kings spells the name Abijam, which means 'my father is Yam.' Yam was a Canaanite sea-god. Could it be that he started out as Abijah, a follower of Yahweh, and ended up as Abijam, a follower of a false god?" (Dilday)

2. (9-11) Summary of the reign of King Asa of Judah.

In the twentieth year of Jeroboam king of Israel, Asa became king over Judah. And he reigned forty-one years in Jerusalem. His grandmother's name *was* Maachah the granddaughter of Abishalom. Asa did *what was* right in the eyes of the LORD, as *did* his father David.

a. **Asa became king over Judah**: This great-grandson of Solomon took the throne of Judah at the end of Jeroboam's reign in Israel, after his father's brief reign.

b. **Asa did what was right in the eyes of the LORD, as did his father David**: The kings of Judah were usually measured against David, the founder of their dynasty. In contrast to his father Abijah (1 Kings 15:3), Asa followed in the same heart as David.

i. The phrase **his father David** shows us that in Hebrew literature the word **father** can be used of an ancestor in general, instead of strictly referring to one's father. David was actually the great-great-grandfather of Asa.

3. (12-15) The reforms of King Asa of Judah.

And he banished the perverted persons from the land, and removed all the idols that his fathers had made. Also he removed Maachah his grandmother from *being* queen mother, because she had made an obscene image of Asherah. And Asa cut down her obscene image and burned *it* by the Brook Kidron. But the high places were not removed. Nevertheless Asa's heart was loyal to the LORD all his days. He also brought into the house of the LORD the things which his father had dedicated, and the things which he himself had dedicated: silver and gold and utensils.

a. **He banished the perverted persons from the land**: These state-sanctioned homosexual idol-temple prostitutes were introduced into Judah during the reign of Rehoboam (1 Kings 14:24). Asa's father Abijam didn't remove these perversions and idols, but King Asa did.

b. **Also he removed Maachah his grandmother from being queen mother, because she had made an obscene image of Asherah**: This demonstrates the thoroughness of Asa's reforms. He was able to act righteously even when his family was wrong, in particular his own grandmother. "It is in a man's own family circle that his faithfulness is put fairly to the test" (Knapp).

i. "Maacah was apparently the daughter of Uriel of Gibeah (2 Chronicles 13:2) and Tamar (2 Samuel 14:27), hence the granddaughter of Absalom, David's rebellious son." (Patterson and Austel)

ii. **By the Brook Kidron**: "The *Kidron Valley* east of Jerusalem was then the city's main rubbish dump" (Wiseman).

iii. **An obscene image**: "This image is described as 'obscene' in our English translation, but the Hebrew word is closer in meaning to 'frightening,' 'horrible,' or 'abominable.' Some commentators believe it was some sort of phallic symbol consistent with the fertility cult of Asherah" (Dilday).

iv. "From the whole, it is pretty evident that the image was a mere *Priapus*, or something of the same nature, and that Maachah had an assembly in the grove where the image was set up, and doubtless worshipped it with the most impure rites. What the Roman *Priapus* was I need not tell the learned reader; and as to the unlearned, it would not profit him to know." (Clarke)

c. **But the high places were not removed**: 2 Chronicles 14:3 says that Asa did remove the high places, but it mentions these high places in connection with *altars of the foreign gods*. Therefore, Asa removed the high places that were dedicated to idols, but not the ones that were dedicated to the LORD.

d. **Nevertheless Asa's heart was loyal to the LORD all his days**: Asa's loyal heart was shown in his reforms against idolatry and state-sanctioned perversion, and in his restoration of certain **silver and gold utensils** to the temple.

4. (16-24) Asa buys the favor of Ben-Hadad, King of Syria.

Now there was war between Asa and Baasha king of Israel all their days. And Baasha king of Israel came up against Judah, and built Ramah, that he might let none go out or come in to Asa king of Judah. Then Asa took all the silver and gold *that was* left in the treasuries of the house of the LORD and the treasuries of the king's house, and delivered them into the hand of his servants. And King Asa sent them to Ben-Hadad the son of Tabrimmon, the son of Hezion, king of Syria, who dwelt in Damascus, saying, "*Let there be* a treaty between you and me, as there was between my father and your father. See, I have sent you a present of silver and gold. Come and break your treaty with Baasha king of Israel, so that he will withdraw from me." So Ben-Hadad heeded King Asa, and sent the captains of his armies against the cities of Israel. He attacked Ijon, Dan, Abel Beth Maachah, and all Chinneroth, with all the land of Naphtali. Now it happened, when Baasha heard *it*, that he stopped building Ramah, and remained in Tirzah. Then King Asa made a proclamation throughout all Judah; none *was* exempted. And they took away the stones and timber of Ramah, which Baasha had used for building; and with them King Asa built Geba of Benjamin, and Mizpah. The rest of all the acts of Asa, all his might, all that he did, and the cities which he built, *are* they not written in the book of the chronicles of the kings of Judah? But in the time of his old age he was diseased in his feet. So Asa rested with his fathers, and was buried with his fathers in the City of David his father. Then Jehoshaphat his son reigned in his place.

a. **Baasha king of Israel came up against Judah, and built Ramah, that he might let none go out or come in to Asa king of Judah**: This continues the struggle for dominance between the northern kingdom of Israel and the southern kingdom of Judah. Baasha gained the upper hand in the days of Asa because he effectively blocked a main route into Judah at the city of Ramah. He hoped this military and economic pressure on Judah would force Asa into significant concessions.

b. **Asa took all the silver and gold that was left in the treasuries of the house of the LORD and the treasuries of the king's house**: Asa used this treasure to buy the favor of Ben-Hadad of Syria, so that he would withdraw support from Israel. Apparently, Baasha of Israel could not stand against Judah by himself - he needed the backing of Syria.

i. 2 Chronicles 16:7-10 tells us that God was not pleased by this, and delivered this word by the prophet Hanani: *"Because you have relied on the king of Syria, and have not relied on the LORD your God, therefore the army of the king of Syria has escaped from your hand. Were the Ethiopians and the Lubim not a huge army with very many chariots and horsemen? Yet, because you relied on the Lord, He delivered them into your hand. For the eyes of the Lord run to and fro throughout the whole earth, to show Himself strong on behalf of those whose heart is loyal to Him. In this you have done foolishly; therefore from now on you shall have wars"* (2 Chronicles 16:7b-9).

ii. Sadly, Asa did not respond to this word properly. *Then Asa was angry with the seer, and put him in prison, for he was enraged at him because of this. And Asa oppressed some of the people at that time* (2 Chronicles 16:10). Asa shows us the tragedy of a man who rules well and seeks the Lord for many years, yet fails in a significant challenge of his faith and then refuses to hear God's correction.

iii. "Wherein he committed three great faults, amongst many others. First, He alienated things consecrated to God without necessity. Secondly, He did this out of carnal fear and distrust of that God whose power and goodness he had lately experienced. Thirdly, He did this for an ill intent, to hire him to the breach of his league and covenant with Baasha, and to take away part of that land which by right, and the special gift of God, belonged to the Israelites." (Poole)

c. **The rest of all the acts of Asa… are they not written in the book of the chronicles of the kings of Judah**: 2 Chronicles 14-16 provides many more details regarding the reign of Asa.

• He encouraged national piety: *He commanded Judah to seek the Lord God of their fathers, and to observe the law and the commandment.* (2 Chronicles 14:4).
• He built fortified cities and presided over a long period of peace (2 Chronicles 14:6).
• In response to Asa's prayer, God defeated a huge Ethiopian army that came against Judah (2 Chronicles 14:9-13).
• He had an encouraging word from the prophet Azariah that encouraged him to continue his reforms (2 Chronicles 15:1-9).
• Asa led a national re-commitment to the covenant (2 Chronicles 15:10-15).

d. **But in the time of his old age he was diseased in his feet**: 2 Chronicles gives us the more complete analysis: *his malady was severe; yet in his disease he did not seek the Lord, but the physicians.* (2 Chronicles 16:12). This happened after he refused to hear God's word of correction through Hanani the seer.

i. Some think that Asa's foot ailment was gout, "but gout was uncommon in Palestine and ancient Egypt and it is more likely, in view of Asa's age, the severity of the disease and death within two years, to have been a peripheral obstructive vascular disease with ensuing gangrene" (Wiseman).

ii. Morgan on Asa: "It is the record of a faulty life, but one in which the deepest thing, that of desire, was right; and so it is the record of a life, the influence of which was a blessing rather than a curse. It is a revealing story."

iii. All in all, Asa was a good man who did not finish well. The last years of his life were marked by unbelief, hardness against God, oppression against his people, and disease. Age and time do not necessarily make us better; they only do if we continue to follow God in faith.

iv. "Jeremiah 41:9 refers to a pit (or cistern) made by Asa 'for fear of Baasha king of Israel.' God would thus, in this incidental way, remind us by this late and last historical notice of King Asa what was the beginning of his decline – 'the fear of man, which bringeth a snare.'" (Knapp)

B. Two kings of Israel.

1. (25-32) The short reign of Nadab, king of Israel.

Now Nadab the son of Jeroboam became king over Israel in the second year of Asa king of Judah, and he reigned over Israel two years. And he did evil in the sight of the LORD, and walked in the way of his father, and in his sin by which he had made Israel sin. Then Baasha the son of Ahijah, of the house of Issachar, conspired against him. And Baasha killed him at Gibbethon, which *belonged* to the Philistines, while Nadab and all Israel laid siege to Gibbethon. Baasha killed him in the third year of Asa king of Judah, and reigned in his place. And it was so, when he became king, *that* he killed all the house of Jeroboam. He did not leave to Jeroboam anyone that breathed, until he had destroyed him, according to the word of the LORD which He had spoken by His servant Ahijah the Shilonite, because of the sins of Jeroboam, which he had sinned and by which he had made Israel sin, because of his provocation with which he had provoked the LORD God of Israel to anger. Now the rest of the acts of Nadab, and all that he did, *are* they not written in the book of the chronicles of the kings of Israel? And there was war between Asa and Baasha king of Israel all their days.

a. **And he did evil in the sight of the LORD, and walked in the way of his father**: Nadab, this son of Jeroboam, did as his father did continuing in his idolatry and hardness towards God.

i. 2 Chronicles 11:14 specifically tells us that *both* Jeroboam and his sons were responsible for driving God's priests out of the land of Israel. In this, Nadab directly shared in the sins of his father Jeroboam.

ii. "Nadab's name means *willing*, and he appears to have been too willing to continue in, and perpetuate, the sin of his iniquitous father." (Knapp)

b. **Baasha killed him in the third year of Asa king of Judah, and reigned in his place. And it was so, when he became king, that he killed all the house**

of Jeroboam: This was the end of the dynasty of Jeroboam. Had Jeroboam remained obedient to the LORD, God promised him a lasting dynasty like the house of David (1 Kings 11:38). Because of Jeroboam's sin, though he enjoyed a long reign, his son only reigned two years before assassination of Nadab and the murder of all Jeroboam's descendants.

 i. "Thus God made use of one wicked man to destroy another." (Clarke)

 ii. "Nadab was king little more than one year, but since it covered parts of two years, Hebrew time measurement reckons his reign as two years." (Dilday)

c. **According to the word of the LORD which He had spoken by His servant Ahijah**: This word is recorded in 1 Kings 14:7-16.

 i. "So ended the first of the nine dynasties that for two hundred and fifty years ruled (or misruled) the kingdom of Israel." (Knapp)

2. (33-34) The reign of Baasha, king of Israel.

In the third year of Asa king of Judah, Baasha the son of Ahijah became king over all Israel in Tirzah, and *reigned* twenty-four years. He did evil in the sight of the LORD, and walked in the way of Jeroboam, and in his sin by which he had made Israel sin.

a. **Baasha the son of Ahijah became king over all Israel**: As expected with a man who came to the throne through assassination, Baasha was a wicked man and ushered in a dreadful period for Israel, both spiritually and politically.

b. **He did evil in the sight of the LORD, and walked in the way of Jeroboam**: The summary puts it simply. Though Baasha was not a genetic descendent of Jeroboam (having murdered his family), he was certainly a *spiritual* descendent of Jeroboam.

1 Kings 16 - Five Successive Kings of Israel

A. Two short dynasties over Israel: Baasha and Zimri.

1. (1-4) Baasha's rebuke and prophecy of judgment.

Then the word of the LORD came to Jehu the son of Hanani, against Baasha, saying: "Inasmuch as I lifted you out of the dust and made you ruler over My people Israel, and you have walked in the way of Jeroboam, and have made My people Israel sin, to provoke Me to anger with their sins, surely I will take away the posterity of Baasha and the posterity of his house, and I will make your house like the house of Jeroboam the son of Nebat. The dogs shall eat whoever belongs to Baasha and dies in the city, and the birds of the air shall eat whoever dies in the fields."

a. **I lifted you out of the dust and made you ruler over My people Israel**: 1 Kings 15:27 tells us that Baasha was head of a conspiracy to kill Nadab, the son of Jeroboam. It tells us nothing of God's hand with Baasha, but here we learn that behind-the-scenes God moved even *through* the conspiracy of Baasha against Nadab.

   i. "Baasha was of plebian stock, yet his name, *he who lays waste*, tells only too accurately what kind of a ruler he proved himself to be." (Knapp)

b. **You have walked in the way of Jeroboam... I will make your house like the house of Jeroboam**: Because Baasha was a wicked king after the pattern of Jeroboam, he would face the same judgment as Jeroboam and his house. This had special relevance to Baasha, because he was the instrument of judgment God used to bring justice to the house of Jeroboam.

   i. "God, who looks upon the heart, sees him but as an assassin for the accomplishment of his ambitious designs, slaying king Nadab and the entire house of Jeroboam." (Knapp)

c. **You have walked in the way of Jeroboam... I will make your house like the house of Jeroboam**: Baasha was not a blood descendant of Jeroboam, but he was a spiritual descendent of this great idolater of the northern kingdom.

Because he walked in the way of Jeroboam, the house of Baasha would face the same judgment as the house of Jeroboam.

d. **The dogs shall eat whoever belongs to Baasha and dies in the city**: This same judgment was promised and fulfilled against the house of Jeroboam (1 Kings 14:11). It was considered a special disgrace to have your dead corpse desecrated and kept from proper burial.

2. (5-7) The death of Baasha.

Now the rest of the acts of Baasha, what he did, and his might, *are* they not written in the book of the chronicles of the kings of Israel? So Baasha rested with his fathers and was buried in Tirzah. Then Elah his son reigned in his place. And also the word of the LORD came by the prophet Jehu the son of Hanani against Baasha and his house, because of all the evil that he did in the sight of the LORD in provoking Him to anger with the work of his hands, in being like the house of Jeroboam, and because he killed them.

a. **The word of the LORD came by the prophet Jehu**: Apparently, Jehu had a long career as a prophet. 2 Chronicles 19:2 mentions another word of Jehu, the son of Hanani. Some 50 years after this word to Baasha, he spoke to Jehoshaphat the King of Judah.

> i. Jehu the Prophet also wrote specific books of history regarding kings of Israel (2 Chronicles 20:34). His father Hanani is also mentioned in 2 Chronicles 16:7-10, where it describes how he suffered imprisonment because he was a faithful prophet in speaking to King Asa.

b. **Because of all the evil that he did in the sight of the LORD in provoking Him to anger**: The Bible tells us that by nature, God *is merciful and gracious, slow to anger, and abounding in mercy* (Psalm 103:8). Because He is *slow to anger*, it took a lot of wickedness on the part of Baasha to succeed in **provoking Him to anger**.

c. **In being like the house of Jeroboam, and because He killed them**: In 1 Kings 16:2 God said that He lifted Baasha out of the dust and set him as ruler over Israel. In doing this, God used Baasha to bring judgment upon the house of Jeroboam; yet God did not *cause* Baasha to do this, so He rightly judged Baasha, even though God used the wickedness of Baasha in bringing judgment upon Jeroboam.

> i. God did not need to coerce a reluctant Baasha to conspire against and assassinate Nadab the son of Jeroboam. That wicked desire was already in the heart of Baasha. In using Baasha to bring judgment on the house of Jeroboam, God only needed to let Baasha do *what he wanted to do*. Therefore, it was proper of God to judge Baasha for something that ultimately furthered God's eternal plan.

ii. "God is ever represented in Scripture as *doing* those things which, in the course of his providence, he *permits* to be done." (Clarke)

3. (8-14) The two-year reign of Elah.

In the twenty-sixth year of Asa king of Judah, Elah the son of Baasha became king over Israel, *and reigned* two years in Tirzah. Now his servant Zimri, commander of half *his* chariots, conspired against him as he was in Tirzah drinking himself drunk in the house of Arza, steward of *his* house in Tirzah. And Zimri went in and struck him and killed him in the twenty-seventh year of Asa king of Judah, and reigned in his place. Then it came to pass, when he began to reign, as soon as he was seated on his throne, *that* he killed all the household of Baasha; he did not leave him one male, neither of his relatives nor of his friends. Thus Zimri destroyed all the household of Baasha, according to the word of the LORD, which He spoke against Baasha by Jehu the prophet, for all the sins of Baasha and the sins of Elah his son, by which they had sinned and by which they had made Israel sin, in provoking the LORD God of Israel to anger with their idols. Now the rest of the acts of Elah, and all that he did, *are* they not written in the book of the chronicles of the kings of Israel?

a. **Elah the son of Baasha became king over Israel, and reigned two years in Tirzah**: The hope of every king is to pass the throne on to his son and to further a lasting dynasty. Because Baasha was a wicked king, God did not bless his dynasty and his son only **reigned two years**.

b. **And Zimri went in and struck him and killed him in the twenty-seventh year of Asa king of Judah, and reigned in his place**: Even as Baasha gained the throne through assassination, so the son of Baasha was assassinated by Zimri, an officer in the army of Israel.

c. **Then it came to pass, when he began to reign, as soon as he was seated on his throne, that he killed all the household of Baasha**: This was common practice in the ancient world, and was exactly what Baasha did to the house of Jeroboam (1 Kings 15:29). David's treatment of the house of Saul was a glorious exception to this common practice.

i. This massacre was an exact fulfillment of the word of the LORD through the prophet Jehu, the son of Hanani (1 Kings 16:2-4).

ii. "In less than fifty years the first two dynastys of Israel's kings had come to an end and every member of their families been exterminated. God meant to make their doom an example to those who should thereafter live ungodly." (Knapp)

4. (15-20) The seven-day reign of Zimri.

In the twenty-seventh year of Asa king of Judah, Zimri had reigned in Tirzah seven days. And the people *were* encamped against Gibbethon,

which *belonged* to the Philistines. Now the people *who were* encamped heard it said, "Zimri has conspired and also has killed the king." So all Israel made Omri, the commander of the army, king over Israel that day in the camp. Then Omri and all Israel with him went up from Gibbethon, and they besieged Tirzah. And it happened, when Zimri saw that the city was taken, that he went into the citadel of the king's house and burned the king's house down upon himself with fire, and died, because of the sins which he had committed in doing evil in the sight of the LORD, in walking in the way of Jeroboam, and in his sin which he had committed to make Israel sin. Now the rest of the acts of Zimri, and the treason he committed, *are* they not written in the book of the chronicles of the kings of Israel?

a. **Zimri had reigned in Tirzah seven days**: The man who assassinated Elah, the son of Baasha, did not enjoy a blessed reign. His end came soon.

b. **So all Israel made Omri, the commander of the army, king over Israel that day**: This shows that the democratic influence in Israel was greater than is often thought. The people – especially it would seem the army – simply did not want Zimri to reign as king over them. They therefore rejected his authority and appointed **Omri, the commander of the army, king over Israel**.

c. **When Zimri saw that the city was taken, that he went into the citadel of the king's house and burned the king's house down upon himself with fire, and died, because of the sins which he had committed**: Zimri is one of the few suicides in the Bible, along with Samson (Judges 9:54), Saul (1 Samuel 31:4) and Ahithophel (2 Samuel 17:23).

i. The Bible never approves of suicide. It is sin; the sin of self-murder. Yet we are wrong if we regard it as the unforgivable sin, and anyone who does commit suicide has given in to the lies and deceptions of Satan, whose purpose is to kill and destroy (John 10:10).

ii. "Suicide is always the ultimate action of cowardice. In the case of Saul, and in many similar cases, it is perfectly natural; but let it never be glorified as heroic. It is the last resort of the man who dare not stand up to life." (Morgan)

d. **In walking in the way of Jeroboam**: Zimri only reigned seven days, but in those days, he **walked in the way of Jeroboam**. God allowed many of the wicked kings of Israel to reign much longer than this, but He was under no obligation to do so. God is within His rights to bring judgment sooner rather than later.

i. "Let Zimri's end warn intentional regicides and traitors." (Knapp)

B. The fourth dynasty of the northern kingdom of Israel: The House of Omri.

1. (21-28) The 12-year reign of Omri, King of Israel.

Then the people of Israel were divided into two parts: half of the people followed Tibni the son of Ginath, to make him king, and half followed Omri. But the people who followed Omri prevailed over the people who followed Tibni the son of Ginath. So Tibni died and Omri reigned. In the thirty-first year of Asa king of Judah, Omri became king over Israel, *and reigned* twelve years. Six years he reigned in Tirzah. And he bought the hill of Samaria from Shemer for two talents of silver; then he built on the hill, and called the name of the city which he built, Samaria, after the name of Shemer, owner of the hill. Omri did evil in the eyes of the LORD, and did worse than all who *were* before him. For he walked in all the ways of Jeroboam the son of Nebat, and in his sin by which he had made Israel sin, provoking the LORD God of Israel to anger with their idols. Now the rest of the acts of Omri which he did, and the might that he showed, *are* they not written in the book of the chronicles of the kings of Israel? So Omri rested with his fathers and was buried in Samaria. Then Ahab his son reigned in his place.

a. **The people of Israel were divided into two parts… So Tibni died and Omri reigned**: Omri defeated the forces loyal to Tibni, **so Tibni died**, presumably killed by Omri after the defeat of his forces.

i. "*The people of Israel* fell into a civil war; yet neither this nor any other of God's dreadful judgments could win them to repentance; which is an evidence of their prodigious impiety and incorrigibleness, and how ripe they were for ruin." (Poole)

ii. "The division of the kingdom between Tibni and Omri began in the *twenty-seventh* year of Asa; this division lasted *five years*, during which Omri, had but a *share* of the kingdom. Tibni dying, Omri came into the possession of the *whole* kingdom, which he held *seven years*; this was in the *thirty-first* year of Asa." (Clarke)

b. **He built on the hill, and called the name of the city which he built, Samaria**: This became the capital city of the Northern Kingdom of Israel. Omri built a capital that was politically neutral (being a new city with no previous tribal associations) and in a strong defensive position (on top of a hill).

i. "Excavations at Samaria… show that Omri was the first builder on the one-hundred-metre-high hill. This site was a good choice, for it was to withstand several sieges." (Wiseman)

c. **He walked in all the ways of Jeroboam the son of Nebat**: This makes Omri the sixth king of Israel since the division of the once-unified kingdom. Jeroboam was the first king, and each of the five kings after him followed in the evil **ways of Jeroboam**.

i. "He seems to have formulated laws [see Micah 6:16], making Jeroboam's calf-worship, or other forms of idolatry, obligatory throughout his realm, which remained in force till the end of the kingdom, more than two hundred years later." (Knapp)

ii. In the records of secular history, Omri is one of the more *successful* and famous kings of ancient Israel. "Omri's fame as a monarch, while downplayed by the author of Kings, was widely recognized in other places. The Moabite stone, discovered in 1868, refers to him as the conqueror of Moab. Assyrian inscriptions make mention of him as a great warrior. For years the Assyrians referred to Israel as 'the house of Omri'" (Dilday).

iii. "His name means *heaping*; and by his iniquity he helped to heap up wrath against his dynasty, executed finally, thirty-six years later, on his great-grandson Joram, to the total extinction of the guilty house." (Knapp)

2. (29-34) Ahab begins his 22-year reign.

In the thirty-eighth year of Asa king of Judah, Ahab the son of Omri became king over Israel; and Ahab the son of Omri reigned over Israel in Samaria twenty-two years. Now Ahab the son of Omri did evil in the sight of the LORD, more than all who *were* before him. And it came to pass, as though it had been a trivial thing for him to walk in the sins of Jeroboam the son of Nebat, that he took as wife Jezebel the daughter of Ethbaal, king of the Sidonians; and he went and served Baal and worshiped him. Then he set up an altar for Baal in the temple of Baal, which he had built in Samaria. And Ahab made a wooden image. Ahab did more to provoke the LORD God of Israel to anger than all the kings of Israel who were before him. In his days Hiel of Bethel built Jericho. He laid its foundation with Abiram his firstborn, and with his youngest *son* Segub he set up its gates, according to the word of the LORD, which He had spoken through Joshua the son of Nun.

a. **In the thirty-eighth year of Asa king of Judah**: Asa reigned for 41 years in total (1 Kings 15:10). During his 41 years, there were seven different kings of Israel.

b. **Ahab the son of Omri did evil in the sight of the LORD, more than all who were before him**: Each of the previous kings of Israel walked in the wicked pattern of Jeroboam. Ahab distinguished himself in being *worse* than Jeroboam.

i. His father Omri was a political and economic success for Israel but a spiritual failure. Ahab picked up where his father left off. "Reinforcing the father-son relationship is the name *Ahab*, which can be translated 'brother of the father' or 'resembling the father'" (Dilday). It can be said of some sons, "He has his father's eyes." It could be said of Ahab, "He has his father's lies."

ii. Jeroboam intended to serve the LORD through idolatrous images (such as the golden calf) and in disobedient ways (altars and high places other than Jerusalem). Ahab introduced the worship of completely new, pagan gods. In his disobedience Jeroboam said, "I will worship the LORD, but do it my way." Ahab said, "I want to forget about the LORD completely and worship Baal."

iii. In his later years, Solomon tragically worshipped pagan gods. Yet Omri and Ahab were far worse in that they *commanded* the worship of idols. "He made *statutes* in favour of idolatry, and obliged the people by law to commit it. See Micah 6:16, where this seems to be intended: *For the statutes of Omri are kept, and all the works of the house of Ahab*" (Clarke).

c. **He took as wife Jezebel the daughter of Ethbaal, king of the Sidonians; and he went and served Baal and worshiped him**: Even as the foreign wives of Solomon led to his spiritual downfall, so Ahab's foreign wife **Jezebel** led him and the nation into deep idolatry.

i. Ethbaal means, *With Baal.* "Jezebel's name may come from a cultic cry used in the worship of Baal meaning 'Where is Baal?' Translated into Hebrew the name was also a verbal pun that the Israelites must have relished. *Zebel* in Hebrew means dung!" (Dilday).

ii. Jezebel was "A woman infamous for her idolatry, and cruelty, and sorcery, and filthiness" (Poole).

iii. Meyer on the bad reign of Ahab: "This came to pass, not so much because his character was more depraved: but because he was a weak man, the tool of a crafty, unscrupulous, and cruel woman: and some of the worst crimes that have ever been committed have been wrought by weak men, at the instigation of worse – but stronger – spirits than themselves."

iv. "So well known was the hostility of Jezebel to all good, that his marrying her was esteemed the highest pitch of vice, and an act the most provoking to God, and destructive to the prosperity of the kingdom." (Clarke)

v. "Had a secular historian been recording these events, the marriage of Ahab and Jezebel would likely have been applauded as a prudent political move. Both Phoenicia and Israel were being threatened by Syria, and the marriage gave Ahab a powerful military ally at a crucial time." (Dilday)

vi. It seemed like the marriage partnership between Tyre and Israel was ideal for Israel. Tyre was at the height of its glory. "Her colonies dotted the shores of the Mediterranean as far as Spain; her ships whitened every sea with their sails, and ventured to the coasts of our own Cornwall for tin;

her daughter, Carthage, nursed the lion-cup Hannibal, and was strong enough to make Rome tremble" (Meyer).

d. **In his days Hiel of Bethel built Jericho**: It seems that Ahab wanted to challenge the prophecy of Joshua after the destruction of the city. *Then Joshua charged them at that time, saying, "Cursed be the man before the LORD who rises up and builds this city Jericho; he shall lay its foundation with his firstborn, and with his youngest he shall set up its gates"* (Joshua 6:26). If Ahab did think that he could rebuild Jericho without being affected by this curse, he was wrong: **He laid its foundation with Abiram his firstborn, and with his youngest son Segub he set up its gates, according to the word of the LORD, which He had spoken through Joshua the son of Nun**.

i. We don't know how the sons of Hiel died; they may have died as a curse or Hiel may have sacrificed them. "Archaeological excavations have uncovered evidence of a practice in ancient biblical times called 'foundation sacrifices' in which children were buried, maybe alive, in the foundations of buildings" (Dilday).

ii. This was a merciful warning to Ahab that he ignored. God told him, "You cannot go against my word without paying the price. Hiel of Bethel, the man you directed to rebuild Jericho, has found this to be true. Take this warning seriously." Yet Ahab did not take this warning seriously.

1 Kings 17 - The Early Ministry of Elijah

A. Elijah prays for drought and experiences God's provision.

1. (1) Elijah tells of the LORD's judgment.

And Elijah the Tishbite, of the inhabitants of Gilead, said to Ahab, "*As* the LORD God of Israel lives, before whom I stand, there shall not be dew nor rain these years, except at my word."

    a. **Elijah the Tishbite**: At this crucial time in the history of Judah and Israel, the Prophet **Elijah** suddenly appeared. He became the dominant spiritual force in Israel during the dark days of Ahab's apostasy.

        i. The name **Elijah** means, *Yahweh is my God*. In the days when Ahab's government officially supported the worship of Baal and other gods, even the *name* of this prophet told the truth.

        ii. It was a crucial time in the history of Israel. It looked as if the worship of the true God might be completely eliminated in the northern kingdom. "The land swarmed with the priests of Baal and of the groves - proud of Court favour; glorying in their sudden rise to power; insolent, greedy, licentious, and debased. The fires of persecution were lit, and began to burn with fury" (Meyer).

        iii. "The whole land seemed apostate. Of all the thousands of Israel, only seven thousand remained who had not bowed the knee or kissed the hand to Baal. But they were paralysed with fear; and kept so still, that their very existence was unknown by Elijah in the hour of his great loneliness." (Meyer)

    b. **There shall not be dew nor rain these years, except at my word**: This was a dramatic demonstration against the pagan god Baal, who was thought to be the sky god, the god of the weather. Elijah showed that through his prayers to the God of Israel, Yahweh was mightier than Baal.

i. "The old religion against the new; the child of nature against the effeminate child of the courts; camel's hair against soft clothing; moral strength against moral weakness." (Meyer)

ii. Elijah was not merely the *prophet* of this drought – in the sense of prayer – he was *the cause* of the drought. He prayed and it happened. James 5:17-18 makes this clear: *Elijah was a man with a nature like ours, and he prayed earnestly that it would not rain; and it did not rain on the land for three years and six months. And he prayed again, and the heaven gave rain, and the earth produced its fruit.*

c. **As the LORD God of Israel lives, before whom I stand**: This statement of Elijah shows the source of his strength. It is specifically said *Elijah was a man with a nature like ours* (James 5:17). Yet he showed a strength greater than most of us in our life with God. We must pay attention to these indications to the source of Elijah's strength.

i. **As the LORD God of Israel lives**: Everyone else felt that the LORD was dead, but for Elijah the LORD lived. He was the supreme reality of Elijah's life.

ii. **Before whom I stand**: He stood in the presence of Ahab, but he was conscious of the presence of someone greater than any earthly king. Gabriel himself could not choose a higher title (Luke 1:19).

2. (2-5) Elijah escapes to Cherith.

Then the word of the LORD came to him, saying, "Get away from here and turn eastward, and hide by the Brook Cherith, which flows into the Jordan. And it will be *that* you shall drink from the brook, and I have commanded the ravens to feed you there." So he went and did according to the word of the LORD, for he went and stayed by the Brook Cherith, which flows into the Jordan.

a. **Get away from here and turn eastward, and hide by the Brook Cherith**: The drought announced by Elijah in the previous verse was a great threat to the northern kingdom of Israel and the reign of Ahab. Therefore, his life was in danger, and God sent him to **the Brook Cherith** for his own safety.

i. God led Elijah one step at a time. He did not tell him to go to Cherith until he first delivered the message to Ahab. He did not tell him to go to Zarephath until the brook dried up at Cherith. God led Elijah by faith, one step at a time, and Elijah followed in faith.

ii. **Hide by the Brook Cherith**: Through this, God taught Elijah the value of the *hidden* life. He had just become famous as an adversary of Ahab, so mighty that his prayers could stop the rain. At the moment of his new-found fame, God wanted Elijah to **hide** and be alone with God. "We must not be surprised, then, if sometimes our Father says: 'There, child, thou hast had enough of this hurry, and publicity, and excitement; get thee hence, and hide thyself by the brook - hide thyself in the Cherith of the sick chamber; or in the Cherith of disappointed hopes; or in the Cherith of bereavement; or in some solitude from which the crowds have ebbed away'" (Meyer).

iii. "Elijah could not be alone, so long as he had God and himself to converse with. A good man is never less alone, than when alone." (Trapp)

b. **And it will be that you shall drink from the brook, and I have commanded the ravens to feed you there**: The escape to the Brook Cherith was for more than protection. It was also to train Elijah in dependence upon the LORD. In a season of drought, he had to trust that God could keep this brook flowing. He also had to accept food from **the ravens**, which were unclean animals.

i. The name **Cherith** comes from the ancient Hebrew root meaning, *to cut away, to cut up or off.* This shows that God had some cutting to do in the life of Elijah during this period.

ii. **I have commanded the ravens to feed you there**: There is an emphasis on the word **there**. God promised that the ravens would feed Elijah as he stayed at Cherith. Of course, theoretically the ravens could feed him anywhere - but God commanded that it be at Cherith. Elijah perhaps wanted to be somewhere else, or be preaching, or doing anything else. Yet God wanted him **there** and would provide for him **there**.

3. (6) Elijah's provision.

The ravens brought him bread and meat in the morning, and bread and meat in the evening; and he drank from the brook.

a. **The ravens brought him bread and meat**: Every bit of food that came to Elijah came from the beak of an unclean animal. Elijah had to put away his traditional ideas of clean and unclean or he would die of starvation. Through this, God taught Elijah to emphasize the spirit of the law before the letter of the law.

i. Charles Spurgeon drew two points of application from this event, likening the food the ravens brought to spiritual food. First, he recognized that God may bring a good word to us through an unclean vessel, spiritually unclean, like a raven. Second, that one can bring spiritual food to others and still be unclean spiritually themselves. "But see, too, how possible it is for us to carry bread and meat to God's servants, and do, some good things for his church, and yet be ravens still!" (Spurgeon).

b. **Bread and meat in the morning, and bread and meat in the evening**: As faithfully has He provided manna for Israel in the wilderness, God provided for Elijah's needs. He came to trust more than ever in the miraculous provision of God.

i. "A little boy, having read this incident with his widowed mother one wintry night, as they sat in a fireless room, beside a bare table, asked her if he might set the door open for God's ravens to come in; he was so sure that they must be on their way. The burgomaster of that German town, passing by, was attracted by the sight of the open door, and entered, inquiring the cause. When he learnt the reason, he said, 'I will be God's raven'; and relieved their need then and afterwards." (Meyer)

4. (7) Elijah and the dry brook.

And it happened after a while that the brook dried up, because there had been no rain in the land.

a. **After a while that the brook dried up**: Elijah saw the flow of the brook slow down until it **dried up**. His source of water was gone.

i. "Ah, it is hard to sit beside a drying brook - much harder than to face the prophets of Baal on Carmel." (Meyer) Meyer also mentioned different kinds of drying brooks we might experience:

• The drying brook of popularity, ebbing away as from John the Baptist.
• The drying brook of health, sinking under a creeping paralysis, or a slow consumption.
• The drying brook of money, slowly dwindling before the demands of sickness, bad debts, or other people's extravagance.
• The drying brook of friendship, which for long has been diminishing, and threatens soon to cease.

ii. "Why does God let them dry? He wants to teach us not to trust in His gifts but in Himself. He wants to drain us of self, as He drained the apostles by ten days of waiting before Pentecost. He wants to loosen our roots ere He removes us to some other sphere of service and education. He wants to put in stronger contrast the river of throne-water that never dries." (Meyer)

b. **Because there had been no rain in the land**: This was the drought Elijah prayed for. He did not pray for rain to come again, even for his own survival. He kept the purpose of God first, even when it adversely affected him.

B. God provides for Elijah through a widow.

1. (8-9) God calls Elijah to go to Zarephath.

Then the word of the LORD came to him, saying, "Arise, go to Zarephath, which *belongs* to Sidon, and dwell there. See, I have commanded a widow there to provide for you."

a. **Arise, go to Zarephath**: God led Elijah from the dry brook to a *Gentile* city. This was an unusual and challenging move for Elijah to make.

i. God kept transplanting Elijah: From home to Jezreel to Cherith to Zarephath. This transplanting made him stronger and stronger.

ii. We should also remember that this was the general region that the wicked queen Jezebel was from. "Elijah was visiting enemy territory and showing the power of God in an area where Baal was worshipped, though ineffective through drought" (Wiseman).

b. **See, I have commanded a widow there to provide for you**: Widows were notorious for their poverty in the ancient world. God told Elijah to go to a Gentile widow and receive provision; it probably seemed to make more sense to wait beside a dry brook.

i. When He was rejected by His own people, Jesus used this example of Elijah's coming to the widow of Zarephath as an illustration of God's right to choose a people to Himself: *Then He said, "Assuredly, I say to you, no prophet is accepted in his own country. But I tell you truly, many widows were in Israel in the days of Elijah, when the heaven was shut up three years and six months, and there was a great famine throughout all the land; but to none of them was Elijah sent except to Zarephath, in the region of Sidon, to a woman who was a widow"* (Luke 4:24-26).

2. (10-11) Elijah addresses a widow.

So he arose and went to Zarephath. And when he came to the gate of the city, indeed a widow *was* there gathering sticks. And he called to her and said, "Please bring me a little water in a cup, that I may drink." And as she was going to get *it*, he called to her and said, "Please bring me a morsel of bread in your hand."

a. **Indeed a widow was there gathering sticks**: This showed that she was a poor woman, gathering meager scraps for firewood. Elijah perhaps thought that God would lead him to an unusual *rich* widow, but God led him to a poor Gentile widow.

i. "You learn this from the fact that she had not even firewood. Now, there was no reason why she should not have had that even in time of famine of bread, for there was no famine of wood, unless she had been extremely poor." (Spurgeon)

ii. God told Elijah (1 Kings 17:9) that He *commanded* a widow to feed the prophet. Yet this woman seemed unaware of the command. This shows how God's unseen hand often works. "She does not appear to have been at all aware that she was to feed a prophet. She went out that morning to gather sticks, not to meet a guest. She was thinking about feeding her son and herself upon the last cake; certainly she had no idea of sustaining a man of God out of that all but empty barrel of meal. Yet the Lord, who never lieth, spoke a solemn truth when he said, 'I have commanded a widow woman there.' He had so operated upon her mind that he had prepared her to obey the command when it did come by the lip of his servant the prophet" (Spurgeon).

b. **Please bring me a little water in a cup… Please bring me a morsel of bread in your hand**: Elijah boldly put this request in faith. Common sense and circumstances told him that the widow would not give so generously to a Jewish stranger, but faith made him ask.

i. "This was certainly putting the widow's faith to an extraordinary trial: to take and give to a stranger, of whom she knew nothing, the small pittance requisite to keep her child from perishing, was too much to be expected." (Clarke)

ii. God indeed chose this woman, but He chose her for more than a miracle. He chose her for *service*. "The choice of this woman, while it brought such blessedness to her, involved service. She was not elected merely to be saved in the famine, but to feed the prophet. She must be a woman of faith; she must make the little cake first, and afterwards she shall have the multiplication of the meal and of the oil. So the grace of God does not choose men to sleep and wake up in heaven, nor choose them to live in sin and find themselves absolved at the last; nor choose them to be idle and go about their own worldly business, and yet to win a reward at the last for which they never toiled. Ah, no! The sovereign electing grace of God chooses us to repentance, to faith, and afterwards to holiness of living, to Christian service, to zeal, to devotion" (Spurgeon).

3. (12) The response of the widow of Zarephath.

So she said, "As the LORD your God lives, I do not have bread, only a handful of flour in a bin, and a little oil in a jar; and see, I *am* gathering a couple of sticks that I may go in and prepare it for myself and my son, that we may eat it, and die."

a. **As the LORD your God lives**: This polite address showed that she respected God, yet recognized that the God of Israel was *Elijah's* God and not her own.

b. **I do not have bread**: Elijah quickly found out that she was not only poor, but *desperately* poor. Elijah found her right before she was going to prepare her last morsel of food for herself and her son, and then resign themselves to death.

4. (13-14) Elijah's words to her.

And Elijah said to her, "Do not fear; go *and* do as you have said, but make me a small cake from it first, and bring *it* to me; and afterward make *some* for yourself and your son. For thus says the LORD God of Israel: 'The bin of flour shall not be used up, nor shall the jar of oil run dry, until the day the LORD sends rain on the earth.'"

a. **Do not fear**: This was God's first word to the widow through Elijah. Her present crisis rightly made her afraid, and God wanted her to put away fear and replace it with trust in Him.

b. **Go and do as you have said, but make me a small cake from it first**: This was an audaciously bold request from the prophet. He asked this destitute widow to **first** give *him* something from her last bit of food. This seemed like the worst kind of predatory fund-raising.

c. **The bin of flour shall not be used up, nor shall the jar of oil run dry, until the day the LORD sends rain on the earth**: This shows why Elijah could make such an audacious request. It was because God told him that He would provide a never-ending supply of food for the widow, her son, and Elijah himself. He asked the widow to put her trust in this great promise of God.

5. (15-16) The widow's obedience and God's great blessing.

So she went away and did according to the word of Elijah; and she and he and her household ate for *many* days. The bin of flour was not used up, nor did the jar of oil run dry, according to the word of the LORD which He spoke by Elijah.

a. **So she went away and did according to the word of Elijah**: The widow actually did it – she willingly gave at great risk, based on her trust in the promise of God.

b. **She and he and her household ate for many days**: God fulfilled the promise to the widow, her son, and Elijah. God used her as a channel of supply and her needs were met as a result.

i. "Why did not God give her a granary full of meal at once, and a vat full of oil instantly? I will tell you. It was not merely because of God's intent to try her, but there was wisdom here. Suppose he had given her a granary full of meal, how much of it would have been left by the next day? I question whether any would have remained, for in days of famine men are sharp of scent, and it would soon have been noised about the city, 'The old widow woman who lives in such-and-such a street, has a great store of food.' Why, they would have caused a riot, and robbed the house, and perhaps, have killed the woman and her son. She would have been despoiled of her treasure, and in four and twenty hours the barrel of meal would have been as empty as it was at first, and the cruse of oil would have been spilled upon the ground." (Spurgeon)

C. Elijah raises the widow's son.

1. (17-18) The widow's grief at the death of her son.

Now it happened after these things *that* the son of the woman who owned the house became sick. And his sickness was so serious that there was no

breath left in him. So she said to Elijah, "What have I to do with you, O man of God? Have you come to me to bring my sin to remembrance, and to kill my son?"

a. **After these things that the son of the woman who owned the house became sick**: We can imagine the happy days of provision in the household of the widow. Their needs were supplied by a continuing miracle of God. Yet those happy days were eventually covered by a dark shadow – the sickness and death of the widow's son.

i. The death of the son was a double blow to the widow. Not only did she suffer as any mother who loses a child, but she also suffered as one who lost her only hope for the future. The expectation was that her son would grow and provide for her in her old age. Now that expectation was shattered.

b. **Have you come to me to bring my sin to remembrance, and to kill my son**: At the death of her son, the widow indirectly blamed Elijah. She more directly blamed herself and her unnamed **sin**. Whatever her sin was, the guilty memory of it was always close to her.

2. (19-20) Elijah's prayer.

And he said to her, "Give me your son." So he took him out of her arms and carried him to the upper room where he was staying, and laid him on his own bed. Then he cried out to the LORD and said, "O LORD my God, have You also brought tragedy on the widow with whom I lodge, by killing her son?"

a. **He took him out of her arms**: This vivid detail shows that the widow clutched the dead child tightly in her arms.

b. **The upper room where he was staying**: The term **upper room** "Refers to a temporary shelter or room on the roof, accessible from outside the house. Such structures are common in the Near East. This arrangement would allow the widow not only her needed privacy but would safeguard her reputation" (Patterson and Austel).

c. **Then he cried out to the LORD**: Elijah prayed with great heart and intimacy with God. He brought this seemingly unexplainable and irredeemable tragedy to God in prayer. Since he knew God led him to this widow, Elijah laid this **tragedy** on God and asked Him to remedy it.

3. (21-24) The son is raised from the dead.

And he stretched himself out on the child three times, and cried out to the LORD and said, "O LORD my God, I pray, let this child's soul come back to him." Then the LORD heard the voice of Elijah; and the soul of the child came back to him, and he revived. And Elijah took the child and brought him down from the upper room into the house, and gave him to his mother. And Elijah said, "See, your son lives!" Then the woman said to Elijah, "Now by this I know that you *are* a man of God, *and* that the word of the LORD in your mouth *is* the truth."

a. **He stretched himself out on the child three times, and cried out to the LORD**: This was an unusual prayer technique, but Elijah had no precedent for this. It was not because of his prayer technique, but because of his faith that God answered this prayer.

i. There is an almost irresistible desire to embellish on these wonderful accounts of the power of God. Patterson and Austel speak of one such attempt: "Syriac translation, followed by Jerome, that the lad was the prophet Jonah is totally unsatisfactory and historically impossible (cf. 2 Kings 14:25)."

b. **O LORD my God, I pray, let this child's soul come back to him**: "A prayer full of powerful arguments. Thou art *the Lord*, that canst revive the child; and *my God*, and therefore wilt not, do not, deny me. She is *a widow*; add not affliction to the afflicted; deprive her not of the great support and staff of her age. She hath given me kind entertainment; let her not fare the worse for her kindness to a prophet, whereby wicked men will take occasion to reproach both her and religion" (Poole).

c. **Then the LORD heard the voice of Elijah**: The son was raised and God provided for the widow on every level, not only with the miraculous supply of food, but also with the resuscitation of her son.

i. "This first example in the Bible of revival from death cannot be explained away as contactual magic nor as the prophet's life-force transmitted by the mouth-to-mouth method of resuscitation." (Wiseman)

1 Kings 18 - Elijah's Victory at Carmel

A. Elijah meets Ahab.

1. (1-2) The end of the drought.

And it came to pass *after* many days that the word of the LORD came to Elijah, in the third year, saying, "Go, present yourself to Ahab, and I will send rain on the earth." So Elijah went to present himself to Ahab; and *there was* a severe famine in Samaria.

> a. **In the third year**: This remarkable drought lasted three-and-one-half years by the fervent prayer of Elijah.

> b. **Go, present yourself to Ahab**: Earlier, God told Elijah to *hide* himself. Now it was time to *present* himself. There is a time to hide and be alone with God, and there is also a time to present yourself to the world. Some wish to always remain hidden when they should step up and **present** themselves.

>> i. Elijah simply obeyed God's command. Though it happened through the prayers of Elijah, his prayers were sensitive to the leading of God. The drought did not begin or end as a result of Elijah's will, but at God's will.

2. (3-14) Elijah meets Obadiah.

And Ahab had called Obadiah, who *was* in charge of *his* house. (Now Obadiah feared the LORD greatly. For so it was, while Jezebel massacred the prophets of the LORD, that Obadiah had taken one hundred prophets and hidden them, fifty to a cave, and had fed them with bread and water.) And Ahab had said to Obadiah, "Go into the land to all the springs of water and to all the brooks; perhaps we may find grass to keep the horses and mules alive, so that we will not have to kill any livestock. So they divided the land between them to explore it; Ahab went one way by himself, and Obadiah went another way by himself. Now as Obadiah was on his way, suddenly Elijah met him; and he recognized him, and fell on his face, and said, "*Is* that you, my lord Elijah?" And he answered him, "*It is* I. Go, tell your master, 'Elijah *is here*.'" So he said, "How have I sinned, that you

are delivering your servant into the hand of Ahab, to kill me? *As* the LORD your God lives, there is no nation or kingdom where my master has not sent someone to hunt for you; and when they said, *'He is* not *here,'* he took an oath from the kingdom or nation that they could not find you. And now you say, 'Go, tell your master, "Elijah *is here"'*! And it shall come to pass, *as soon as* I am gone from you, that the Spirit of the LORD will carry you to a place I do not know; so when I go and tell Ahab, and he cannot find you, he will kill me. But I your servant have feared the LORD from my youth. Was it not reported to my lord what I did when Jezebel killed the prophets of the LORD, how I hid one hundred men of the Lord's prophets, fifty to a cave, and fed them with bread and water? And now you say, 'Go, tell your master, "Elijah *is here.*"' He will kill me!"

a. **While Jezebel massacred the prophets of the LORD, that Obadiah had taken one hundred prophets and hidden them, fifty to a cave, and had fed them with bread and water**: This man Obadiah was a brave man who stood for God and His prophets in a difficult time.

i. This may be the same Obadiah whose prophecy against Edom is recorded among the Minor Prophets. It is a little difficult to be certain, because there were 13 Obadiahs in the Old Testament. The Hebrew name **Obadiah** means "Worshipper of Yahweh" or "Servant of Yahweh."

• An Obadiah was sent out by King Jehoshaphat of Judah to teach the law in the cities of Judah (2 Chronicles 17:7).
• An Obadiah was one of the overseers who helped repair the temple in the days of Josiah, King of Judah (2 Chronicles 34:12).
• An Obadiah was a priest in the days of Nehemiah (Nehemiah 10:5).

ii. **One hundred prophets**: "*Prophets*: this name is not only given to such as are endowed with an extraordinary spirit of prophecy, but to such ministers as devoted themselves to the service of God in preaching, praying, praising God, and the like" (Poole).

iii. "Account for it how you may, it is a singular circumstance that in the center of rebellion against God there was one whose devotion to God was intense and distinguished. As it is horrible to find a Judas among the apostles, so it is grand to discover an Obadiah among Ahab's courtiers. What grace must have been at work to maintain such a fire in the midst of the sea, such godliness in the midst of the vilest iniquity!" (Spurgeon)

iv. "That Obadiah would have little difficulty in finding caves for the sons of the prophets can be seen in that over two thousand caves have been counted in the Mount Carmel area." (Patterson and Austel)

b. **Now as Obadiah was on his way, suddenly Elijah met him**: The drought was so severe that King Ahab himself and his trusted servant Obadiah were out searching for pastureland. God arranged this unexpected meeting between Obadiah and the prophet Elijah.

> i. "We might have supposed that he would set himself to alleviate the miseries of his people; and, above all, that he would have turned back to God: but no - his one thought was about the horses and mules of his stud; his only care was to save some of them alive... What selfishness is here! Mules and asses before his people! Seeking for grass, instead of seeking for God!" (Meyer)

c. **How have I sinned, that you are delivering your servant into the hand of Ahab, to kill me**: Obadiah knew that King Ahab conducted an exhaustive search for Elijah to punish him for the drought that his prayers imposed on Israel. Obadiah feared that if he announced that he met Elijah, and the prophet disappeared again, Ahab would punish Obadiah for letting Elijah get away.

3. (15-16) Elijah assures Obadiah that he will meet with Ahab.

Then Elijah said, "As the LORD of hosts lives, before whom I stand, I will surely present myself to him today." So Obadiah went to meet Ahab, and told him; and Ahab went to meet Elijah.

a. **I will surely present myself to him today**: Kindly and wisely, Elijah responded to Obadiah's legitimate fears. He would not make Obadiah a martyr on Elijah's behalf.

4. (17-19) Elijah and Ahab trade accusations.

Then it happened, when Ahab saw Elijah, that Ahab said to him, *"Is that* you, O troubler of Israel?" And he answered, "I have not troubled Israel, but you and your father's house *have,* in that you have forsaken the commandments of the LORD and have followed the Baals. Now therefore, send *and* gather all Israel to me on Mount Carmel, the four hundred and fifty prophets of Baal, and the four hundred prophets of Asherah, who eat at Jezebel's table."

a. **Is that you, O troubler of Israel?** Ahab was easily the worst, most ungodly king that Israel ever had. Yet he did not hesitate to blame the godly prophet Elijah for the problems of Israel. If Ahab would at least stop the active persecution of the people of God, God would relent in the drought. But the wicked king of Israel found it easier to blame the godly prophet.

> i. According to his theology, it made sense for Ahab to blame Elijah. Ahab believed in Baal, so much so that his government promoted and supported Baal worship and persecuted the worshippers of Yahweh. Ahab believed that Elijah had angered the sky-god Baal and therefore Baal withheld rain. Ahab probably thought that Baal would hold back the rain until Elijah was caught and executed.

ii. Instead, Ahab should have turned to the Word of God. Deuteronomy 28:23-24 promised that drought would come to a disobedient Israel.

b. **Now therefore, send and gather all Israel to me on Mount Carmel**: Elijah challenged King Ahab to gather the idol prophets of Baal and Asherah for this meeting at Mount Carmel.

i. "*Gather to me all Israel*, by their deputies, or heads, or representatives, that they may be witnesses of all our transactions." (Poole)

ii. 1 Kings 18:36 makes it clear that Elijah did all this at the command of God. This wasn't his clever idea or strategy. This was a God-inspired plan that Elijah obeyed.

iii. It was important to confront and eliminate these prophets of Baal *before* God sent rain to the land of Israel. It was crucial that everyone understand that the rain came from Yahweh, not from Baal.

c. **Who eat at Jezebel's table**: This refers to the fact that these prophets of Baal and Asherah were sponsored and supported by the government of Israel, having a special patron in the wicked Queen Jezebel.

i. "Jezebel was not content with a private chapel, nor with her husband's readiness to pay lip-service to Baal; she meant to dethrone the God of Israel, and make her Baal the chief deity and her faith in the official state religion." (Payne)

B. Elijah's victory on Mount Carmel.

1. (20-21) Elijah challenges Israel to make a decision.

So Ahab sent for all the children of Israel, and gathered the prophets together on Mount Carmel. And Elijah came to all the people, and said, "How long will you falter between two opinions? If the LORD *is* God, follow Him; but if Baal, follow him." But the people answered him not a word.

a. **Ahab sent for all the children of Israel**: It is hard to know why Ahab did this, carrying out the instructions of Elijah. Perhaps he hoped that the people would be so angry with Elijah for the last three years of drought that this crowd would turn against the prophet.

b. **And gathered the prophets together on Mount Carmel**: These prophets of Baal *hated* Elijah. They loved the favor of King Ahab and Queen Jezebel, and they enthusiastically promoted the persecution of any true follower of Yahweh. But over the last three years, they had been severely humbled by Elijah and the drought sustained by his prayers. All their cries to the weather-god Baal were ineffective for three years. They *hated* this prophet of God who humiliated them and their sham priesthood so thoroughly.

i. "See, with what malignant glances his every movement is watched by the priests. No tiger ever watched its victim more fiercely! If they may have their way, he will never touch yonder plain again." (Meyer)

ii. "That lone man, of heroic soul, stemmed the fearful torrent of idolatry, and like a rock in mid-current, firmly stood his ground. He, alone and single-handed, was more than a match for all the priests of the palace and the groves, even as one lion scatters a flock of sheep." (Spurgeon)

c. **How long will you falter between two opinions? If the LORD is God, follow Him; but if Baal, follow him**: This was a logical and useful question. In general, the people of Israel were in a spiritually lukewarm condition. They wanted to give some devotion to *both* Yahweh and Baal, but the God of Israel was not interested in such divided devotion.

i. Spiritually speaking, Israel was like an unfaithful partner in a marriage who doesn't want to give up their marriage partner, but also does not want to give up their illicit lover. The marriage partner has a legitimate claim to the *exclusive* devotion of their spouse.

ii. **How long will you falter**: The ancient Hebrew word translated **falter** means "to limp, halt, hop, dance, or leap" (Dilday). It is the same word used in 1 Kings 18:26 where the prophets of Baal leaped about the altar. It may be that Elijah meant, "How long will you dance between two opinions?"

iii. Adam Clarke had a slightly different understanding: "Literally, 'How long hop ye about upon two boughs?' This is a metaphor taken from birds hopping about from bough to bough, not knowing on which to settle."

iv. The appeal of Elijah made it clear that there was a *difference* between the service of Baal and the service of Yahweh. Perhaps in the minds of many, there was not a great difference - the only important thing was to have *some kind* of religion, and to be sincere about that, following your heart to whatever god your heart might lead you to. Yet Elijah knew that it could never be this way. You either served Baal *or* you served Yahweh; there was a difference.

v. Elijah's appeal also called his hearers to account for the period of time in which they had not made a decision between Yahweh and Baal. "**How long**," he asked them. "How many more sermons do you want? How many more Sundays must roll away wasted? How many warnings, how many sicknesses, how many toilings of the bell to warn you that you must die? How many graves must be dug for your family before you will be impressed? How many plagues and pestilences must ravage this city before you will turn to God in truth? How long halt ye between two opinions?" (Spurgeon).

d. **But the people answered him not a word**: There was no objection and no repentance. They lacked the courage to either defend their position or to change it. They were willing to live unexamined lives of low conviction.

i. Elijah could so accurately see their hearts because he could see their *actions*. Spurgeon explained Elijah's idea: "I know you are not decided in opinion, because you are *not decided in practice*. If God be God, *follow him*; if Baal, *follow* him. You are not decided in practice."

2. (22-24) Elijah proposes a test between God and Baal.

Then Elijah said to the people, "I alone am left a prophet of the LORD; but Baal's prophets *are* four hundred and fifty men. Therefore let them give us two bulls; and let them choose one bull for themselves, cut it in pieces, and lay *it* on the wood, but put no fire *under it;* and I will prepare the other bull, and lay *it* on the wood, but put no fire *under it*. Then you call on the name of your gods, and I will call on the name of the LORD; and the God who answers by fire, He is God." So all the people answered and said, "It is well spoken."

a. **I alone am left a prophet of the LORD**: This was not true and Elijah had reason to know that it was not true. In the recent past, Obadiah told him that he sheltered 100 prophets of God against the persecution of Jezebel and Ahab.

b. **Let them give us two bulls; and let them choose one bull for themselves**: In this proposed test, Elijah was careful to give the prophets of Baal every potential advantage. They picked the two bulls, and picked which one they would sacrifice and which one Elijah would sacrifice.

c. **And the God who answers by fire, He is God**: The fire would not come from either Elijah or the prophets of Baal. It had to be supernatural in origin, and supplied by either Baal or Yahweh.

i. Again, Elijah gave plenty of advantage to the prophets of Baal. It was thought that Baal was the sky-god, lord of the weather and the sender of lightning (thought to be fire from the sky). If Baal were real, he certainly could send fire from heaven.

ii. To put God and himself on the line before the gathered nation of Israel took a lot of faith. Elijah learned this faith over the many months of daily dependence on God, both at the Brook Cherith and at the widow's house at Zarapeth.

iii. Of course, Elijah had plenty of reasons for confidence in the LORD God. First, he was following express instructions from the LORD (1 Kings 18:36). Second, he knew from the history of Israel that God could and would send fire from heaven upon a sacrifice (Judges 6:20-21 and 2 Chronicles 7:1-7).

3. (25-27) The prophets of Baal pray for fire from their god.

Now Elijah said to the prophets of Baal, "Choose one bull for yourselves and prepare *it* first, for you *are* many; and call on the name of your god, but put no fire *under it*." So they took the bull which was given them, and they prepared *it*, and called on the name of Baal from morning even till noon, saying, "O Baal, hear us!" But *there was* no voice; no one answered. Then they leaped about the altar which they had made. And so it was, at noon, that Elijah mocked them and said, "Cry aloud, for he *is* a god; either he is meditating, or he is busy, or he is on a journey, *or* perhaps he is sleeping and must be awakened."

> a. **Called on the name of Baal from morning even till noon, saying, "O Baal, hear us"**: The prophets of Baal had a devoted prayer life. Here, they prayed long and with great passion. Yet because they did not pray to the *real* God, their prayer meant nothing. **There was no voice; no one answered.**

> b. **They leaped about the altar which they had made**: The prophets of Baal had an energetic prayer life. Their worship was filled with enthusiasm and activity. Yet because it was not directed to the *real* God, their prayer meant nothing.

> c. **Elijah mocked them**: Elijah could not resist the opportunity to mock the prophets of Baal for their evidently foolish faith.

>> i. "Elijah's irony bordered on sarcasm" (Patterson and Austel). The words **meditating** and **busy** can be translated "to be engaged in business" and may be a euphemism for bodily elimination.

>> ii. "Rabbi S. Jarchi gives this the most degrading meaning; I will give it in Latin, because it is too coarse to be put in English; *Fortassis ad locum secretum abiit, ut ventrem ibi exoneret*; 'Perhaps he has gone to the ----------
---.' This certainly reduces Baal to the lowest degree of contempt, and with it the ridicule and sarcasm are complete." (Clarke)

4. (28-29) The prophets of Baal work harder at their prayer.

So they cried aloud, and cut themselves, as was their custom, with knives and lances, until the blood gushed out on them. And when midday was past, they prophesied until the *time* of the offering of the *evening* sacrifice. But *there was* no voice; no one answered, no one paid attention.

> a. **They cried aloud, and cut themselves, as was their custom, with knives and lances, until the blood gushed out on them**: The prophets of Baal were utterly *sincere* and completely *devoted* to their religion. They were so committed that they expressed it in their own blood. They had zeal, but without knowledge - therefore their zeal profited them *nothing*.

i. "The practice of self-inflicted wounds to arouse a deity's pity or response is attested in Ugarit when men 'bathed in their own blood like an ecstatic prophet.'" (Wiseman)

ii. "This was done according to the *rites* of that barbarous religion; of the blood of the bullock would not move him they thought their *own blood* might; and with it they smeared themselves and their sacrifice." (Clarke)

b. **But there was no voice; no one answered, no one paid attention**: This is the sad result of worshipping an imaginary god or the god of our own making. We may dedicate great sincerity, sacrifice, and devotion to such gods, but it means nothing. There is no one there to answer.

5. (30-35) Elijah prepares his altar.

Then Elijah said to all the people, "Come near to me." So all the people came near to him. And he repaired the altar of the LORD *that was* broken down. And Elijah took twelve stones, according to the number of the tribes of the sons of Jacob, to whom the word of the LORD had come, saying, "Israel shall be your name." Then with the stones he built an altar in the name of the LORD; and he made a trench around the altar large enough to hold two seahs of seed. And he put the wood in order, cut the bull in pieces, and laid *it* on the wood, and said, "Fill four waterpots with water, and pour *it* on the burnt sacrifice and on the wood." Then he said, "Do *it* a second time," and they did *it* a second time; and he said, "Do *it* a third time," and they did *it* a third time. So the water ran all around the altar; and he also filled the trench with water.

a. **Come near to me**: When it was Elijah's turn to sacrifice, he first wanted to get the *attention* of the people. This was for their benefit, not his own or really primarily for the benefit of God. They needed to pay attention so they would see that the LORD was a true God, in contrast to the silent Baal.

b. **He repaired the altar of the LORD that was broken down**: Elijah was very aware that he repaired something that once stood strong. There was once an altar of the LORD at Carmel and in Israel in general. Elijah looked to *revive* something that *once was*.

c. **Fill four waterpots with water, and pour it on the burnt sacrifice and on the wood**: In wanting to make a deep impression upon the people, Elijah required more of Yahweh than he did of Baal. Elijah did not even suggest to the prophets of Baal that they wet down their sacrifice once or twice, much less three times. Yet Elijah did this, confident that it was no harder for God to ignite a wet sacrifice than it was for Him to set a dry one ablaze.

i. "There can be no question of trickery, such as the use of naptha [a flammable liquid often used as a solvent] instead of water, or mirrors for ignition as suggested by some scholars. The opposition was observant and close." (Wiseman)

6. (36-37) Elijah's prayer.

And it came to pass, at *the time of* the offering of the *evening* sacrifice, that Elijah the prophet came near and said, "Lord God of Abraham, Isaac, and Israel, let it be known this day that You *are* God in Israel and I *am* Your servant, and *that* I have done all these things at Your word. Hear me, O Lord, hear me, that this people may know that You *are* the Lord God, and *that* You have turned their hearts back *to You* again."

a. **At the time of the offering of the evening sacrifice**: Some 50 years before this, Jeroboam the King of Israel officially disassociated the citizens of the northern kingdom from the worship of the God of Israel at the temple in Jerusalem. Nevertheless, Elijah still remembered the **evening sacrifice** that was offered according to God's commandment every day at the temple in Jerusalem.

b. **Let it be known this day that You are God in Israel and I am Your servant**: Both were important. It was important for the people of Israel to know who their God was, and who *God's servant* was.

c. **And that I have done all these things at Your word**: This also was essential, and helps us to understand the whole event. Elijah did this according to the word of God. It wasn't prompted because of his own cleverness, because of presumption or because of vainglory. *God* led Elijah to this showdown with the prophets of Baal.

i. "It was no whim of his to chastise the nation with a drought. It was no scheme of his, concocted in his own brain, that he should put the Godhead of Jehovah or of Baal to the test by a sacrifice to be consumed by miraculous fire." (Spurgeon)

ii. Spurgeon recommended that believers use the same principle in prayer, especially those who preach the Word of God: "Go you to the mercy-seat with this as one of your arguments, 'Lord, I have done according to thy word. Now let it be seen that it is even so. I have preached thy word, and thou hast said, "It shall not return unto me void." I have prayed for these people, and thou hast said, "The effectual fervent prayer of a righteous man availeth much"; let it be seen that this is according to thy word.'"

7. (38-40) The result: Yahweh answers by fire.

Then the fire of the Lord fell and consumed the burnt sacrifice, and the wood and the stones and the dust, and it licked up the water that *was* in the trench. Now when all the people saw *it,* they fell on their faces; and they said, "The Lord, He *is* God! The Lord, He *is* God!" And Elijah said to them, "Seize the prophets of Baal! Do not let one of them escape!" So

they seized them; and Elijah brought them down to the Brook Kishon and executed them there.

a. **Then the fire of the LORD fell**: The prophets of Baal had passion, commitment, sincerity, devotion, and great energy. What they did *not* have was a God in heaven who answered by **fire**.

i. "The action of this fire was in every case *downward*, contrary to the nature of all earthly and material fire." (Clarke)

ii. "Elijah's petition had lasted less than a minute but produced spectacular results. The difference lay in the One addressed." (Patterson and Austel)

b. **The fire of the LORD fell and consumed the burnt sacrifice, and the wood and the stones and the dust, and it licked up the water that was in the trench**: When the fire of God fell, its work was *beyond expectation*. It would have been enough if merely the cut-up pieces of bull on the altar were ignited, but God wanted more than simple vindication – He wanted to *glorify* Himself among the people.

c. **Now when all the people saw it, they fell on their faces; and they said, "The LORD, He is God! The LORD, He is God!"** At this moment, the people were completely persuaded. Asked to choose between Baal and Yahweh, there was no choice to make, obviously, the LORD was God.

i. Tragically, this was only a momentary persuasion. This was no lasting revival in Israel. The people were decidedly persuaded, but not lastingly changed.

d. **Elijah said to them, "Seize the prophets of Baal! Do not let one of them escape"**: Since this was a contest between Yahweh and Baal, the prophets of each deity had to be responsible for their respective results. The great sin of King Ahab was his official sponsorship of the prophets of Baal, and now that the fraud of Baal was exposed, his prophets had to answer for it and were dealt with according to the Law of Moses (Deuteronomy 13:5, 13:13-18, 17:2-5, and 18:9-22).

i. Elijah simply demanded that the prophets of Baal receive the treatment they promoted for the prophets of Yahweh.

C. Elijah goes to Jezreel.

1. (41-44) Elijah prays for rain.

Then Elijah said to Ahab, "Go up, eat and drink; for *there is* the sound of abundance of rain." So Ahab went up to eat and drink. And Elijah went up to the top of Carmel; then he bowed down on the ground, and put his face between his knees, and said to his servant, "Go up now, look toward the sea." So he went up and looked, and said, *"There is* nothing." And seven times he said, "Go again." Then it came to pass the seventh *time,* that he

said, "There is a cloud, as small as a man's hand, rising out of the sea!" So he said, "Go up, say to Ahab, 'Prepare *your chariot,* and go down before the rain stops you.'"

a. **Go up, eat and drink; for there is the sound of abundance of rain**: Elijah knew that once the *official* worship of Baal had been defeated, the purpose for the drought was fulfilled. Rain was on the way. Elijah and Ahab would now each do what they wanted to do - Elijah would pray and Ahab would eat.

b. **He bowed down on the ground, and put his face between his knees**: This was an unusual posture of prayer for Elijah. He wasn't kneeling, he wasn't sitting, he wasn't standing, and he didn't lay prostrate before the LORD. This shows that the power in prayer resides in faith in the living God.

> i. "We scarcely recognize him, he seems so to have lost his identity. A few hours before, he stood erect as an oak of Bashan; now, he is bowed as a bulrush. Then as God's ambassador he pleaded with man; now as man's intercessor he pleads with God. Is it not always so - that the men who stand straightest in the presence of sin bow lowest in the presence of God." (Meyer)

c. **It came to pass the seventh time**: This was stubbornly *persistent* prayer. It was as if Elijah would not take "no" for an answer, because he had confidence that God's will was to send rain. He stubbornly furthered the will of God by his persistent prayer.

> i. "*Go again seven times*; let us not be dejected for some disappointments, but continue to wait upon God, who will answer me, and that speedily." (Poole)

> ii. "God's promises are given, not to restrain, but to incite to prayer. They show the direction in which we may ask, and the extent to which we may expect an answer They are the mould into which we may pour our fervid spirits without fear." (Meyer)

d. **There is a cloud, as small as a man's hand, rising out of the sea**: Elijah prayed, asking in faith for God to send the rain. Elijah obviously *sensed* this was the will of God, yet it was his fervent prayer that brought the rain. The evidence of the rain came slowly and in a small way, but out of this small evidence God brought a mighty work.

> i. In the November 9, 1904, edition of *The Life of Faith*, a London newspaper dedicated to the deeper life movement, a writer named Jessie Penn-Lewis reported on a remarkable work just beginning in Wales under the ministry of men like Evan Roberts and Seth Joshua. She reported that a *cloud no bigger than a man's hand* had arisen in Wales. It was a fitting description of the clear but small beginning of what became a mighty work.

ii. Charles Spurgeon used this text as an illustration of the small signs that precede a mighty work of God. He spoke of four "certain signs and tokens for good which prayerful faith clearly perceives when an awakening, a genuine revival is about to come." Christians should regard the following things as clouds, **as small as a man's hand, rising out of the sea**:

> • A growing dissatisfaction with the present state of things, and an increasing anxiety among the members of the church for the salvation of souls.
> • When this anxiety leads believers to be exceedingly earnest and importunate in prayer.
> • When ministers begin to take counsel one with another, and to say, "What must we do?"
> • When we shall see the doctrine of the individual responsibility of each Christian fully felt and carried out into individual action.

e. **Prepare your chariot, and go down before the rain stops you**: This was a word of faith from Elijah to Ahab. Based only on the sighting of a **cloud** that was **as small as a man's hand**, he knew a torrent was on the way.

2. (45-46) Elijah's amazing 14-mile cross-country run.

Now it happened in the meantime that the sky became black with clouds and wind, and there was a heavy rain. So Ahab rode away and went to Jezreel. Then the hand of the LORD came upon Elijah; and he girded up his loins and ran ahead of Ahab to the entrance of Jezreel.

a. **There was a heavy rain**: God's word through Elijah was proved true. The long drought was over, and it was demonstrated that the prayers of Elijah both *withheld* the rain and then subsequently *brought* the rain.

b. **Then the hand of the LORD came upon Elijah; and he girded up his loins and ran ahead of Ahab**: This was an obviously supernaturally empowered 14-mile cross-country run. We don't know exactly why it was important to God for Elijah to reach Jezreel first; perhaps it was so that he would be the first to tell Queen Jezebel.

i. "To demonstrate that he was neither ashamed of, nor afraid for, what he had done, though he knew how Jezebel would resent it, but durst venture himself in the midst of his enemies, as being confident of the Divine power and protection." (Poole)

ii. "That Elijah could have made such a run is assured in the Arab runners could easily cover one hundred miles in two days." (Patterson and Austel)

1 Kings 19 - God Encourages Discouraged Elijah

A. Elijah flees to the wilderness.

1. (1-3) Jezebel's threat.

And Ahab told Jezebel all that Elijah had done, also how he had executed all the prophets with the sword. Then Jezebel sent a messenger to Elijah, saying, "So let the gods do *to me*, and more also, if I do not make your life as the life of one of them by tomorrow about this time." And when he saw *that*, he arose and ran for his life, and went to Beersheba, which *belongs* to Judah, and left his servant there.

a. **Ahab told Jezebel all that Elijah had done**: The report came as a great shock to this champion of Baal and Astarte worship in Israel. She thought so much of these priests that she supported them from the royal treasury, and now they were dead at the hand of Elijah.

b. **So let the gods do to me, and more also, if I do not make your life as the life of one of them by tomorrow about this time**: Jezebel heard about **all that Elijah had done**, encompassing the great confrontation at Mount Carmel. Yet her response was *not* to say, "The silence of Baal and the fire from Yahweh proves that I am wrong and Yahweh is God." Instead, she responded with a vow to kill within 24 hours the man who *exposed* the lie of Baal worship and *displayed* the glory of Yahweh.

   i. "He probably thought that the miracle at Carmel would have been the means of effecting the conversion of the whole court and of the country, but, finding himself mistaken, he is greatly discouraged." (Clarke)

c. **When he saw that, he arose and ran for his life, and went to Beersheba**: We cannot say for certain if this was led of God or not. It is clear that God wanted to protect Elijah, but we cannot say if God wanted to protect him at Jezreel or protect him by getting him out of Jezreel. Nevertheless, Elijah went about 80 miles south to Beersheba.

i. "Probably Elijah had played into Jezebel's hand. Had she really wanted Elijah dead, she surely would have seized him without warning and slain him. What she desired was that Elijah and his God be discredited before the new converts what had aided Elijah by executing the prophets of Baal." (Patterson and Austel)

ii. "Elijah failed in the very point at which he was strongest, and that is where most men fail. In Scripture, it is the wisest man who proves himself to be the greatest fool; just as the meekest man, Moses, spoke hasty and bitter words. Abraham failed in his faith, and Job in his patience; so, he who was the most courageous of all men, fled from an angry woman." (Spurgeon)

2. (4) Elijah's depression.

But he himself went a day's journey into the wilderness, and came and sat down under a broom tree. And he prayed that he might die, and said, "It is enough! Now, Lᴏʀᴅ, take my life, for I *am* no better than my fathers!"

a. **He himself went a day's journey into the wilderness**: *Beyond* the distant city of Beersheba, Elijah secluded himself even more.

b. **And he prayed that he might die**: This mighty man of prayer - mighty enough to make the rain and the dew stop for three and a half years, and then mighty enough to make it start again at his prayer - now **he prayed that he might die**.

i. Thankfully, this was a prayer *not answered* for Elijah. In fact, *Elijah was one of the few men in the Bible to never die!* We can imagine that as he was caught up into heaven, he smiled and thought of this prayer - and the blessed *no* that answered his prayer. To receive a *no* answer from God can be better than receiving a *yes* answer.

c. **It is enough**: We sense that Elijah meant, "I can't do this anymore, Lᴏʀᴅ." The work was stressful, exhausting, and seemed to accomplish nothing. The great work on Mount Carmel did not result in a lasting national revival or return to the Lᴏʀᴅ.

i. Perhaps Elijah had especially hoped that the events on Mount Carmel would turn around Ahab and Jezebel and the leadership of Israel in general. If so, Elijah forgot that people reject God *despite* the evidence, not *because* of the evidence.

ii. "Elijah said, 'It is enough,' yet it was not enough even for his own enjoyment, for the Lord had more blessings in store for him... It was so with Elijah, for he was to have that wonderful revelation of God on Mount Horeb. He had more to enjoy, and the later life of Elijah appears to have been one of calm communion with his God; he seems never to have had another fainting fit, but to the end his sun shone brightly without a cloud. So it was not enough; how could he know that it was? It is God alone who knows when we have done enough, and enjoyed enough; but we do not know." (Spurgeon)

d. **Now, LORD, take my life, for I am no better than my fathers**: When Elijah examined the apparent failure of his work, he instinctively set the blame on his own unworthiness. It was because he was a sinner as the rest of his ancestors that the work seemed to fail.

B. God's ministry to the despairing Elijah.

1. (5-8) God ministers to the physical needs of Elijah.

Then as he lay and slept under a broom tree, suddenly an angel touched him, and said to him, "Arise *and* eat." Then he looked, and there by his head *was* a cake baked on coals, and a jar of water. So he ate and drank, and lay down again. And the angel of the LORD came back the second time, and touched him, and said, "Arise *and* eat, because the journey *is* too great for you." So he arose, and ate and drank; and he went in the strength of that food forty days and forty nights as far as Horeb, the mountain of God.

a. **As he lay and slept under a broom tree**: This was the mercy of God extended to Elijah. Physically speaking, he needed rest and replenishment. God gave him rest **under a broom tree**, and provided miraculous food for the replenishment.

i. God first ministered to Elijah's physical needs. This is not always His order, but physical needs are important. Sometimes the most *spiritual* thing a person can do is get enough rest and replenishment.

ii. "And how many are there at this day that sit under Elias's juniper, willing and wishing to lay down that heavy burden imposed upon them by the Almighty!" (Trapp)

b. **So he ate and drank, and lay down again**: Elijah received this rest and replenishment repeatedly from the LORD. One quick nap and one quick meal wasn't enough.

i. "Before entering into that communion with him which was for the correction of his false attitude of fear, He commanded him to eat, thus ministering to his physical weakness." (Morgan)

ii. "The spirit needs to be fed, and the body needs feeding also. Do not forget these matters; it may seem to some people that I ought not to mention such small things as food and rest, but these may be the very first elements in really helping a poor depressed servant of God." (Spurgeon)

iii. "It was very gracious for God to deal this with his servant. We might have expected rebuke or remonstrance, chiding or chastisement; but we would hardly have expected such loving, gentle treatment as this." (Meyer)

c. **Arise and eat, because the journey is too great for you**: God set Elijah on a 200-mile, 40-day trip to Mount **Horeb**, also known as Mount Sinai. This shows that God did not demand an *immediate* recovery from Elijah. He allowed the prophet time to recover from his spiritual depression.

> i. "Elijah's forty-day journey is not without significance. Indeed, a straight trip from Beersheba would require little more than a quarter of that time. Therefore the period is designedly symbolic. As the children of Israel had a notable spiritual failure and so were to wander forty years in the wilderness, so a defeated Elijah was to spend forty days in the desert." (Patterson and Austel)

2. (9-10) God allows Elijah to vent his frustrations.

And there he went into a cave, and spent the night in that place; and behold, the word of the LORD *came* to him, and He said to him, "What are you doing here, Elijah?" So he said, "I have been very zealous for the LORD God of hosts; for the children of Israel have forsaken Your covenant, torn down Your altars, and killed Your prophets with the sword. I alone am left; and they seek to take my life."

a. **He went into a cave**: Literally, the Hebrew is definite describing *the cave*. "*The cave* may well have been the specific 'cleft of the rock' where God appeared to Moses (AV, Exodus 33:22) rather than the 'cave-region' generally." (Wiseman)

> i. "Perhaps no spot on earth is more associated with the manifested presence of God than that sacred mount." (Meyer)

b. **What are you doing here, Elijah**: God knew the answer to this question, but it was good for Elijah to speak to the LORD freely and to unburden his heart.

> i. "God has ways of teaching all of us in our bones and in our flesh, but he specially knows how to do this with those upon whom he puts any honor in his service. You must not marvel, if God should be pleased to bless you to the conversion of souls, that he should also make you sometimes smart." (Spurgeon)

c. **I have been very zealous for the LORD God of hosts**: Elijah protested to God, "I have faithfully served You and now look at the danger I am in." To Elijah - and many servants of God since - it seemed unfair that a faithful servant of God should be made to suffer.

d. **I alone am left**: This was not *accurate*, but it reflected how Elijah felt. Even back at the confrontation at Mount Carmel, Elijah said *I alone am left a prophet of the LORD* (1 Kings 18:22). Discouraging times make God's servants feel more isolated and alone than they are.

e. **I alone am left; and they seek to take my life**: Strangely, the reasons Elijah provided were actually important reasons for him to remain alive. If he really was the last prophet or believer alive, should not he seek to live as long as possible? If the enemies of God like Jezebel wanted him dead, should he not seek to defeat her wicked will? Elijah, here, powerfully showed the *unreasonable nature* of unbelief and fear.

3. (11-12) God reveals Himself to Elijah.

Then He said, "Go out, and stand on the mountain before the LORD." And behold, the LORD passed by, and a great and strong wind tore into the mountains and broke the rocks in pieces before the LORD, *but* the LORD *was* not in the wind; and after the wind an earthquake, *but* the LORD *was* not in the earthquake; and after the earthquake a fire, *but* the LORD *was* not in the fire; and after the fire a still small voice.

a. **Go out, and stand on the mountain before the LORD**: God knew what the depressed and discouraged Elijah needed. He needed a *personal encounter with God*. There was nothing fundamentally wrong with Elijah's *theology*, but at the time there was something lacking in his experience.

b. **Behold, the LORD passed by**: God brought His presence before Elijah, but first, to show *where He was not*. The LORD was **not in the wind**; He was **not in the earthquake**; He was **not in the fire**. Like many others, Elijah probably only looked for God in dramatic manifestations. Certainly, God sometimes appears in such ways, but He often appears in less dramatic surroundings.

i. "This same lesson has to be learned over and over by us all: let us repeat it, 'Not by might, nor by power, but by my Spirit, saith the Lord.' It is to be lamented that the most of professors obstinately cling to the fatal error of looking for displays of power of one kind or another. I hear that a certain church is seeking for a very clever man: she thinks that God is in the wind… That still small voice will be hushed and silent, while the boastings of your wisdom resound like a howling wind or a thunder unaccompanied by rain." (Spurgeon)

c. **After the fire a still small voice**: This final phenomenon was a marked contrast to the previous manifestations. God actually met Elijah in the quiet whisper of a voice, instead of the earth-shaking phenomenon that had gone before.

i. Wiseman called the **still small voice** a *gentle whisper*.

ii. "And now the thunder ceased, and the lightning was gone, and the earth was still, and the wind was hushed, and there was a dead calm, and out of the midst of the still air there came what the Hebrew calls 'a voice of gentle silence,' as if silence had become audible. There is nothing more terrible than an awful stillness after a dread uproar." (Spurgeon)

iii. Elijah perhaps thought that the dramatic display of power at Mount Carmel would turn the nation around. Or perhaps he thought that the radical display of God's judgment against the priests of Baal following the vindication at Mount Carmel would change the hearts of the nation. Neither of these worked. This example is important for Christian ministers today, especially preachers. It shows that *displays of power* and *preaching God's anger* don't necessarily change hearts. Instead, the **still small voice** of God speaking to the human heart is actually more powerful than outward displays of power or displays of God's judgment.

iv. "Because the success of Carmel melted like the morning mist, he thought that his career had been a failure all along, and that he had brought no one to reverence Jehovah; but he was reading with the eyes of unbelief, and his imagination was leading him rather than the facts of the case. Here are seven thousand people scattered up and down the country to whom God has blessed Elijah's testimony. If he had not blessed his big things as he had desired, yet his little things had prospered greatly. It was Elijah's daily conduct rather than his miracles which had impressed these seven thousand and led them to hold fast their integrity." (Spurgeon)

4. (13-15) After this ministry, God gives Elijah work to do.

So it was, when Elijah heard *it*, that he wrapped his face in his mantle and went out and stood in the entrance of the cave. Suddenly a voice *came* to him, and said, "What are you doing here, Elijah?" And he said, "I have been very zealous for the LORD God of hosts; because the children of Israel have forsaken Your covenant, torn down Your altars, and killed Your prophets with the sword. I alone am left; and they seek to take my life." Then the LORD said to him: "Go, return on your way to the Wilderness of Damascus; and when you arrive, anoint Hazael *as* king over Syria.

a. **He wrapped his face in his mantle and went out and stood in the entrance of the cave**: Immediately, Elijah sensed that God was present in the *still small voice* in a way that He was not in the previous, more dramatic phenomena. Because he sensed the special presence of God, Elijah immediately humbled himself when he **wrapped his face in his mantle**.

i. "Through horror and dread of God's presence, being sensible that he was neither worthy nor able to endure the sight of God with open face." (Poole)

ii. "He first wrapped his mantle about his face – he became subdued and awe-stricken – full of reverence. Oh! it is a great thing when a sinner is willing to wrap his face when he is confounded, and say, 'I cannot defend my course; I am guilty.' We know that if at our judgment-seat a man pleads guilty, he is punished; but at the judgment-seat of the gospel whoever pleads guilty is forgiven. Wrap your face." (Spurgeon)

b. **What are you doing here, Elijah**: God asked Elijah the same question – and received the same response – as in 1 Kings 19:9-10. There was something helpful for Elijah in this question-and-answer process.

c. **Go, return on your way... anoint Hazael as king over Syria**: God gave Elijah *something to do*. He needed a task to focus on so he could avoid excessive introspection. He needed to stop looking at himself and his own (admittedly difficult) circumstances. He needed to get on with what God wanted him to do.

> i. "Then the Lord did what perhaps was best of all for Elijah, *he gave him some more work to d*o. He sent him off about his Master's business again; and I warrant you that, when Elijah went back over that road, it was with a very different step from that which brought him down to Beersheba. He had come along terrified and distressed; but now he goes back with the majesty that belongs to the Tishbite, he is afraid of no Jezebel now." (Spurgeon)

5. (16-18) Further assurance to Elijah.

"Also you shall anoint Jehu the son of Nimshi *as* king over Israel. And Elisha the son of Shaphat of Abel Meholah you shall anoint *as* prophet in your place. It shall be *that* whoever escapes the sword of Hazael, Jehu will kill; and whoever escapes the sword of Jehu, Elisha will kill. Yet I have reserved seven thousand in Israel, all whose knees have not bowed to Baal, and every mouth that has not kissed him."

a. **You shall anoint Jehu the son of Nimshi as king over Israel**: God had more work for Elijah to do. He would also demonstrate God's choice of **Jehu** to be the king to succeed the corrupt Ahab and his wife Jezebel.

b. **Elisha the son of Shaphat of Abel Meholah you shall anoint as prophet in your place**: God gave something else to the discouraged and depressed prophet, beyond work to do. He also gave him *a friend* and a *successor*.

> i. Elijah needed a *friend*; the core of his complaint before God was that he was alone. God let him know that there was a man ready to learn from the great prophet and be his disciple and companion.

> ii. Elijah also needed *hope*, and since Elisha would be raised up as a successor to Elijah's prophetic office, Elijah then knew that his work would continue even after his death.

c. **It shall be that whoever escapes the sword of Hazael, Jehu will kill; and whoever escapes the sword of Jehu, Elisha will kill**: This was another source of encouragement to Elijah. With this promise he knew that ultimately justice would be done, and God would not allow the institutionalized persecution and promotion of idolatry to go unpunished.

d. Yet I have reserved seven thousand in Israel, all whose knees have not bowed to Baal: This was a final encouragement to Elijah. He repeatedly bemoaned that he was alone among the true followers of God (1 Kings 18:22, 19:10, and 19:14). This both assured Elijah that he was not alone and that his work as a prophet had indeed been fruitful.

> i. This showed Elijah that his *quiet ministry* over the years actually bore more fruit than the *spectacular ministry* at Mount Carmel. "Yet, all the while that vile idolatry was spreading in Israel, the worship of the true God was being retained by seven thousand faithful souls, though Elijah did not know that there was even one beside himself. How were they won to Jehovah? Certainly not by Elijah's impressive demonstration on the top of Carmel, for they were loyal to the Lord before that... The still small voice had been doing for Israel what Elijah could not do" (Spurgeon).

6. (19-21) The call of Elisha.

So he departed from there, and found Elisha the son of Shaphat, who *was* plowing *with* twelve yoke *of oxen* before him, and he was with the twelfth. Then Elijah passed by him and threw his mantle on him. And he left the oxen and ran after Elijah, and said, "Please let me kiss my father and my mother, and *then* I will follow you." And he said to him, "Go back again, for what have I done to you?" So *Elisha* turned back from him, and took a yoke of oxen and slaughtered them and boiled their flesh, using the oxen's equipment, and gave it to the people, and they ate. Then he arose and followed Elijah, and became his servant.

a. He departed from there, and found Elisha the son of Shaphat: Elijah did what the *still small voice* of God told him to do. He happened to do it in reverse order than God described to him in the previous passage. Perhaps Elijah believed that he *first* needed a friend and apprentice.

b. Who was plowing with twelve yoke of oxen before him: Elijah found Elisha and commissioned him to ministry when Elisha was at work.

c. Elijah passed by him and threw his mantle on him: The mantle was the symbol of Elijah's prophetic authority. This was a dramatic symbol that said, "I call upon you to join in my work as a prophet."

> i. "The *mantle*, or *pallium*, was the peculiar garb of the prophet, as we may learn from Zechariah 13:4; and this was probably made of *skin dressed with the hair on*. See also 2 Kings 1:8." (Clarke)

d. What have I done to you: This question "Could mean, 'Go back, but remember what I have done to you.' It might be a rebuke at any delay in following." (Wiseman)

i. "Elijah's reply indicates that he himself had not called Elisha; it was God's call. Whether Elisha would follow that call was his own decision." (Patterson and Austel)

e. **Took a yoke of oxen and slaughtered them and boiled their flesh, using the oxen's equipment, and gave it to the people, and they ate**: This demonstrated Elisha's complete commitment to following Elijah. He destroyed the tools of his trade in a going-away party for his family and friends.

i. "Elisha must have had a considerable estate, when he kept *twelve* yoke of oxen to till the ground. If, therefore, he obeyed the prophetic call, he did it to considerable secular loss." (Clarke)

ii. "Hereby he showed how willingly and joyfully he forsook all his friends, that he might serve God in that high and honourable employment." (Poole)

1 Kings 20 - God Leads Israel to Two Victories Over Syria

A. Ben-Hadad comes against Samaria.

1. (1-6) The demands of Ben-Hadad, king of Syria.

Now Ben-Hadad the king of Syria gathered all his forces together; thirty-two kings *were* with him, with horses and chariots. And he went up and besieged Samaria, and made war against it. Then he sent messengers into the city to Ahab king of Israel, and said to him, "Thus says Ben-Hadad: 'Your silver and your gold *are* mine; your loveliest wives and children are mine.'" And the king of Israel answered and said, "My lord, O king, just as you say, I and all that I have *are* yours." Then the messengers came back and said, "Thus speaks Ben-Hadad, saying, 'Indeed I have sent to you, saying, "You shall deliver to me your silver and your gold, your wives and your children"; but I will send my servants to you tomorrow about this time, and they shall search your house and the houses of your servants. And it shall be, *that* whatever is pleasant in your eyes, they will put *it* in their hands and take *it*.'"

> a. **Ben-Hadad the King of Syria gathered all his forces together; thirty-two kings were with him**: This was a formidable military attack against Israel. Though they were outwardly strong politically and militarily during the reign of Ahab, they were not strong enough to discourage such an attack.
>
> > i. "Ben-Hadad may be the same king Asa enlisted against Baasha in 15:18; or he may be that king's son or grandson by the same name." (Dilday)
> >
> > ii. "The *thirty-two* kings would include minor tribal chiefs." (Wiseman)
>
> b. **My lord, O king, just as you say, I and all that I have are yours**: Ahab's response to Ben-Hadad fit his general personality. He was a man concerned with the luxuries and comforts of living, and so he did not have the character to stand in the face of such a threat. Ahab surrendered unconditionally to Ben-Hadad.

i. Ahab believed he was in no position to resist Ben-Hadad. No doubt, the national and military might of Israel was greatly weakened by the three-and-a-half-year drought and famine that had just ended.

c. **They shall search your house and the houses of your servants**: This was a greater demand than what Ben-Hadad made at first. "When Ahab agreed to his terms readily, Ben-Hadad demanded the additional right to unlimited search of the palace and the houses of Ahab's officials so as to carry away anything of value." (Patterson and Austel)

2. (7-9) Ahab is counseled by his elders to resist.

So the king of Israel called all the elders of the land, and said, "Notice, please, and see how this *man* seeks trouble, for he sent to me for my wives, my children, my silver, and my gold; and I did not deny him." And all the elders and all the people said to him, "Do not listen or consent." Therefore he said to the messengers of Ben-Hadad, "Tell my lord the king, 'All that you sent for to your servant the first time I will do, but this thing I cannot do.'" And the messengers departed and brought back word to him.

a. **The king of Israel called all the elders of the land**: It was wiser for Ahab to seek the counsel of the **elders of the land** *before* he surrendered to the Syrians. Now, in the brief time between the message of surrender and the actual abduction of his women and the plundering of his goods he sought counsel.

b. **Do not listen or consent**: The elders of Israel rightly saw that such surrender to Ben-Hadad and the Syrians was the first step to a total loss of sovereignty for Israel. If they wanted to remain a kingdom at all, they had to resist this threat.

c. **But this thing I cannot do**: Ahab told Ben-Hadad that he would do *most* of what he requested, but not *all*. But to deny a tyrant on one point is to deny him on every point. Ahab could expect a harsh reaction.

3. (10-12) Ben-Hadad threatens and readies his army.

Then Ben-Hadad sent to him and said, "The gods do so to me, and more also, if enough dust is left of Samaria for a handful for each of the people who follow me." So the king of Israel answered and said, "Tell *him*, 'Let not the one who puts on *his armor* boast like the one who takes *it off.*'" And it happened when *Ben*-Hadad heard this message, as he and the kings *were* drinking at the command post, that he said to his servants, "Get ready." And they got ready to attack the city.

a. **The gods do so to me, and more also**: Jezebel swore a similar oath of vengeance against Elijah (1 Kings 19:2).

b. **Let not the one who puts on his armor boast like the one who takes it off**: Though it was uncharacteristically bold speech from Ahab, it was also a wonderful piece of wisdom. The idea is that you should do your boasting *after* the battle, not before.

c. **They got ready to attack the city**: Syria and its allies readied, and the city of Samaria braced for a furious attack.

B. Victory for Israel.

1. (13-15) The prophet promises victory.

Suddenly a prophet approached Ahab king of Israel, saying, "Thus says the LORD: 'Have you seen all this great multitude? Behold, I will deliver it into your hand today, and you shall know that I *am* the LORD.'" So Ahab said, "By whom?" And he said, "Thus says the LORD: 'By the young leaders of the provinces.'" Then he said, "Who will set the battle in order?" And he answered, "You." Then he mustered the young leaders of the provinces, and there were two hundred and thirty-two; and after them he mustered all the people, all the children of Israel—seven thousand.

a. **A prophet approached Ahab king of Israel**: This nameless prophet does not seem to be either Elijah or Elisha. He was one of the 7,000 in Israel that were quietly faithful to Yahweh.

i. Adam Clarke had an interesting (though unlikely) idea: "It is strange that on such an occasion we hear nothing of Elijah or Elisha. Is it not possible that this was one of them disguised?"

b. **Behold, I will deliver it into your hand today, and you shall know that I am the LORD**: This was a generous promise of God towards Ahab and Israel. Their hardened idolatry and rejection of God *deserved* divine abandonment. God had every right to just leave them alone and let them perish without His help. Yet God is rich in mercy, and He showed that mercy to Ahab and Israel.

i. There is a small irony in the statement, "**and you shall know that I am the LORD**." Ahab saw the victory of Yahweh over the pagan god Baal on Mount Carmel – yet he was not completely convinced. Graciously, God would give him even *more* evidence.

c. **So Ahab said, "By whom"**: Ahab looked around at his army and military leaders and naturally wondered how God could bring a victory against a mighty enemy with them. Ahab wondered who would lead the battle and God told him, "**You**." God wanted to win this victory by working through the unlikely people Ahab already had.

i. Whenever a work for God is to be done, we often ask Ahab's question: "**By whom?**" When many Christian leaders ask God that question, they expect God will answer by bringing someone new to them, a leader or champion that can do the work or at least help with it. However, God's normal way of working is to use the people already with the Christian leader, even if they seem to be a very unlikely army.

ii. God would do this work against Syria and Ben-Hadad with an army of only **seven thousand**. Undoubtedly, these were not the same **seven thousand** that stayed faithful to God in Israel, but there was a correspondence between their numbers to show that God could and would work through each group.

2. (16-21) Victory for Israel.

So they went out at noon. Meanwhile Ben-Hadad and the thirty-two kings helping him were getting drunk at the command post. The young leaders of the provinces went out first. And Ben-Hadad sent out *a patrol,* and they told him, saying, "Men are coming out of Samaria!" So he said, "If they have come out for peace, take them alive; and if they have come out for war, take them alive." Then these young leaders of the provinces went out of the city with the army which followed them. And each one killed his man; so the Syrians fled, and Israel pursued them; and Ben-Hadad the king of Syria escaped on a horse with the cavalry. Then the king of Israel went out and attacked the horses and chariots, and killed the Syrians with a great slaughter.

a. **Ben-Hadad and the thirty-two kings helping him were getting drunk at the command post**: The same sinful heart that made Ben-Hadad attack Israel also made him a drunk. In part, his own weak character defeated him.

b. **If they have come out for peace, take them alive; and if they have come out for war, take them alive**: It may be that Ben-Hadad *intended* to say that if the men from Israel had come for war, they should be attacked and killed. Perhaps he spoke in a drunken confusion, giving foolish orders to his soldiers.

c. **The Syrians fled, and Israel pursued them**: God blessed the army of Israel and the leaders that Ahab had, even blessing Ahab's own leadership of the army. Despite great odds, they won the battle.

i. "The battle strategy appears to have been to send out the small but well trained advance party who could perhaps draw near to the Syrians without arousing too much alarm and then, at a given signal, initiate a charge that, joined by Ahab's main striking force, would both catch the drunken Arameans off guard and throw them into confusion. The plan was more successful than Ahab dared to imagine." (Patterson and Austel)

3. (22) The prophet advises preparation.

And the prophet came to the king of Israel and said to him, "Go, strengthen yourself; take note, and see what you should do, for in the spring of the year the king of Syria will come up against you."

a. **The prophet came to the king of Israel**: This nameless prophet again advised Ahab. The victory over Ben-Hadad did not end the conflict between Israel and Syria.

b. **Go, strengthen yourself; take note, and see what you should do**: The prophet directed Ahab to prepare for a Syrian attack in the coming spring. The prophet knew that God works through the careful preparation of His people.

C. A second victory over Syria.

1. (23-25) The Syrians try again.

Then the servants of the king of Syria said to him, "Their gods *are* gods of the hills. Therefore they were stronger than we; but if we fight against them in the plain, surely we will be stronger than they. So do this thing: Dismiss the kings, each from his position, and put captains in their places; and you shall muster an army like the army that you have lost, horse for horse and chariot for chariot. Then we will fight against them in the plain; surely we will be stronger than they." And he listened to their voice and did so.

a. **Their gods are gods of the hills**: The idea of the *localized deity* was prominent in the ancient world. They felt that particular gods had authority over particular areas. Because the recent victory was won on hilly terrain, the **servants of the king of Syria** believed that the God of Israel was a localized deity with power over the hills, not the plains.

i. Here they imagined that God could be molded into an image that they wanted or could relate to. "The art of god-making is very common among men. Instead of going to revelation to see what God is, and humbly believing in him as he reveals himself, men sit down and consider what sort of God he ought to be, and in so doing they are no wiser than the man who makes a god of mud or wood or stone" (Spurgeon).

ii. Many today think that God is a God of hills but not of the plains. They think God is a God of the past but not of the present. They think God is a God of a few special favorites but not of all His people. They think that God is God of one kind of trial, but not of another kind. "Depend upon it, since Satan could not kill the church by roaring at her like a lion, he is now trying to crush her by hugging her like a bear. There is truth in this, but it is not all the truth. Do you really think, my brethren, that God cannot preserve his Church in the particular trial through which she is now passing? Is he the God of the hills of persecution, but not the God of the valleys of prosperity?" (Spurgeon).

iii. "Will God aid a Whitfield and not help a poor local preacher holding forth upon the green? Will he assist the earnest minister who addresses thousands, and desert the simple girl who teaches a dozen little children the old, old story of the cross? Is this after the fashion of God, to patronise the eminent and neglect the lowly? Does Jesus despise the day of small things?" (Spurgeon)

b. **Then we will fight against them in the plain; surely we will be stronger than they**: The action they recommended was logical, given their theology. Their theological belief directed their advice and action.

2. (26-28) The armies muster and God promises victory.

So it was, in the spring of the year, that Ben-Hadad mustered the Syrians and went up to Aphek to fight against Israel. And the children of Israel were mustered and given provisions, and they went against them. Now the children of Israel encamped before them like two little flocks of goats, while the Syrians filled the countryside. Then a man of God came and spoke to the king of Israel, and said, "Thus says the LORD: 'Because the Syrians have said, "The LORD *is* God of the hills, but He *is* not God of the valleys," therefore I will deliver all this great multitude into your hand, and you shall know that I *am* the LORD.'"

a. **Now the children of Israel encamped before them like two little flocks of goats, while the Syrians filled the countryside**: When Ben-Hadad came to avenge their previous loss, he came with overwhelming force. Ben-Hadad didn't want to risk another humiliation.

b. **Because the Syrians have said, "The LORD is God of the hills, but He is not God of the valleys," therefore I will deliver all this great multitude into your hand**: God took the flawed theology of the Syrians as a personal insult. Our flawed and wrong ideas about God always take away from His glory and majesty, never adding to them.

i. "God resents their blasphemy, and is determined to punish it. They shall now be discomfited in such a way as to show that God's power is every where, and that the multitude of a host is nothing against him." (Clarke)

3. (29-30) A second victory for Israel against Syria.

And they encamped opposite each other for seven days. So it was that on the seventh day the battle was joined; and the children of Israel killed one hundred thousand foot soldiers *of* the Syrians in one day. But the rest fled to Aphek, into the city; then a wall fell on twenty-seven thousand of the men *who were* left. And Ben-Hadad fled and went into the city, into an inner chamber.

a. **The children of Israel killed one hundred thousand foot soldiers of the Syrians in one day**: This was clearly a miracle, yet it was a miracle working *through* the existing Israeli army, not by another outside agency. God wanted to show that as unlikely as it seemed, He *could* work through this outwardly weak and ineffective instrument.

b. **Then a wall fell on twenty-seven thousand of the men who were left**: After the great victory on the battlefield, God moved in other extraordinary ways to defeat the Syrians, who had defamed His character through their flawed understanding of Him.

> i. "The 27,000 killed in Aphek would include everyone in the city when the walls fell." (Wiseman)

4. (31-34) Ahab's willingness to make peace with an enemy of God.

Then his servants said to him, "Look now, we have heard that the kings of the house of Israel *are* merciful kings. Please, let us put sackcloth around our waists and ropes around our heads, and go out to the king of Israel; perhaps he will spare your life." So they wore sackcloth around their waists and *put* ropes around their heads, and came to the king of Israel and said, "Your servant Ben-Hadad says, 'Please let me live.'" And he said, "*Is* he still alive? He *is* my brother." Now the men were watching closely to see whether *any sign of mercy would come* from him; and they quickly grasped *at this word* and said, "Your brother Ben-Hadad." So he said, "Go, bring him." Then Ben-Hadad came out to him; and he had him come up into the chariot. So *Ben*-Hadad said to him, "The cities which my father took from your father I will restore; and you may set up marketplaces for yourself in Damascus, as my father did in Samaria." Then *Ahab said,* "I will send you away with this treaty." So he made a treaty with him and sent him away.

a. **Please, let us put sackcloth around our waists and ropes around our heads, and go out to the king of Israel**: Not long before this, Ben-Hadad spoke severe threats against Ahab and the Kingdom of Israel (1 Kings 20:1-6). Now, he humbled himself as much as he could to win mercy and favor from the unexpectedly triumphant King of Israel.

> i. "The rope around the head was a sign of supplication, the figure being that of the porter at the wheel of the victor's chariot." (Patterson and Austel)

> ii. Sinners should come to God the King with the same manner as Ben-Hadad. They should come with *sincerity*, with *humility*, with *surrender*, with *earnestness*, and with close watching to **see whether any sign of mercy would come** to them.

b. **Is he still alive? He is my brother**: Ahab felt a kinship towards this pagan king with exceedingly pagan ideas of God. Perhaps Ahab wanted Ben-Hadad and Syria's friendship as protection against the powerful and threatening Assyrian Empire. If so, he looked for friends in the wrong places.

> i. "This was not courtesy, but foolery. Brother Ben-Hadad will ere long fight against Ahab with that life which he had given him (chapter 22:31)." (Trapp)

c. **I will send you away with this treaty**: Ahab had no business making this treaty. The victory was the Lord's and did not belong to Ahab; he had no right to negotiate away the victory.

5. (35-38) A prophet prepares to confront the king.

Now a certain man of the sons of the prophets said to his neighbor by the word of the Lord, "Strike me, please." And the man refused to strike him. Then he said to him, "Because you have not obeyed the voice of the Lord, surely, as soon as you depart from me, a lion shall kill you." And as soon as he left him, a lion found him and killed him. And he found another man, and said, "Strike me, please." So the man struck him, inflicting a wound. Then the prophet departed and waited for the king by the road, and disguised himself with a bandage over his eyes.

a. **A certain man of the sons of the prophets**: This seems to be a different prophet from the man mentioned earlier in the chapter. This is another reminder that the 7,000 faithful followers of Yahweh were active in Israel.

i. "Although he is not named, Josephus believed the anonymous 'man of God' introduced in verse 35 was Micaiah who figures so prominently in the next story. He suggested it was in retaliation for Micaiah's prophetic condemnation that the king put him in prison." (Dilday)

ii. "This is the first reference to these special bands of prophets (2 Kings 2:3-7, 2:15; 4:1, 4:38; 5:22; 6:1; 9:1) who appear during the critical period of the Omride dynasty but are otherwise not well attested." (Wiseman)

b. **Strike me, please**: Directed by God, the prophet needed an injury to display to King Ahab. When his neighbor refused, the prophet announced coming judgment on the neighbor, through the unusual method of a lion attack (**a lion found him and killed him**).

i. The **neighbor** was not just another man in the kingdom of Israel. The implication was that he was a fellow member of the **sons of the prophets**. He himself was a man given to following God and sensitive to God's work in the prophets. He should have known better. Though this is not as clear in the New King James translation, it is clearer in other translations: *his companion* (NIV), *a certain member of a company of prophets said to another* (NRSV) *another* (NASB) *to another man* (NLB).

ii. "This seems a hard measure, but there was ample reason for it. This person was also one of the sons of the prophets, and he knew that God frequently delivered his counsels in this way, and should have immediately obeyed; for the smiting could have had no evil in it when God commanded it, and it could be no outrage or injury to his fellow when he himself required him to do it." (Clarke)

c. **Disguised himself with a bandage over his eyes**: Ready with his injury, the prophet waited for the arrival of King Ahab so he could deliver his message from God to the king.

6. (39-40) The prophet gives an object lesson.

Now as the king passed by, he cried out to the king and said, "Your servant went out into the midst of the battle; and there, a man came over and brought a man to me, and said, 'Guard this man; if by any means he is missing, your life shall be for his life, or else you shall pay a talent of silver.' While your servant was busy here and there, he was gone." Then the king of Israel said to him, "So *shall* your judgment *be;* you yourself have decided it."

a. **Your servant went out into the midst of the battle**: After the pattern of other prophets, this anonymous prophet brought a message to King Ahab through a made-up story.

b. **While your servant was busy here and there, he was gone**: The prophet's story told of a man who was responsible to guard the life of another, and proved himself unfaithful. In the story, the guilty man's excuse was that he was **busy here and there**, which was no excuse at all. He should have paid attention to the job he had to do.

i. "This was likely enough to happen on a battlefield. It would not be possible to hold your prisoner, and to busy yourself about other things at the same time." (Meyer)

ii. The prophet's made-up story with the fictional excuse becomes *real* in the life of many, especially many ministers of the Gospel. "If a man is called to preach the Word, and becomes busy over a hundred things other than that of his central work, and so loses the opportunity to preach, his failure is complete. That which is our God-appointed work, we must do. If we fail in that, the fact that we have been 'busy here and there,' doing all sorts of other things, is of no avail" (Morgan).

iii. **He was gone**: Even as the fictional prisoner escaped, so many opportunities escape us in the Christian life. "I want you all to remember this morning that if any portion of life has not been spent in God's service *it is gone*. Time past is gone. You can never have it back again, not even the last moment which just now glided by" (Spurgeon).

c. **So shall your judgment be; you yourself have decided it**: In the prophet's story, he was unfaithful in guarding something that was entrusted to him. Ahab rightly judged that he should be held responsible for his failure to guard what was entrusted to him.

7. (41-43) The rebuke from God.

And he hastened to take the bandage away from his eyes; and the king of Israel recognized him as one of the prophets. Then he said to him, "Thus says the LORD: 'Because you have let slip out of *your* hand a man whom I appointed to utter destruction, therefore your life shall go for his life, and your people for his people.'" So the king of Israel went to his house sullen and displeased, and came to Samaria.

a. **The king of Israel recognized him as one of the prophets**: This showed why the prophet found it wise to disguise himself as a soldier recently returned from battle, and why the wound was necessary. Ahab consciously shielded himself from the prophets.

b. **Because you have let slip out of your hand a man whom I appointed to utter destruction, therefore your life shall go for his life, and your people for his people**: God intended that Ben-Hadad should be utterly destroyed, but He *also intended* that this happen by the hand of the army of Israel. God was interested in more than the mere death of Ben-Hadad, but also in the way that death came about.

c. **So the king of Israel went to his house sullen and displeased**: Ahab was **sullen and displeased**, but he was not *repentant*. He had the sorrow of being a sinner and knowing the consequences of sin, without having the sorrow for the sin itself.

1 Kings 21 - The Murder of Naboth

A. Naboth is murdered for his vineyard.

1. (1-3) Naboth refuses to give up his land.

And it came to pass after these things *that* Naboth the Jezreelite had a vineyard which *was* in Jezreel, next to the palace of Ahab king of Samaria. So Ahab spoke to Naboth, saying, "Give me your vineyard, that I may have it for a vegetable garden, because it *is* near, next to my house; and for it I will give you a vineyard better than it. *Or,* if it seems good to you, I will give you its worth in money." But Naboth said to Ahab, "The Lord forbid that I should give the inheritance of my fathers to you!"

a. **Give me your vineyard**: This account begins as a simple attempted real estate transaction. Ahab wanted the vineyard near his royal house in Jezreel so that he might have it as a **vegetable garden**. He was willing to trade for the land or to pay for it.

b. **The Lord forbid that I should give the inheritance of my fathers to you**: Naboth's response was an emphatic "No." His rejection of the otherwise reasonable offer was rooted in the ancient Israelite idea of the land. They believed that the land was an inheritance from God, parceled out to individual tribes and families according to His will. Therefore, land was never really sold, only leased - and that only under the most dire circumstances. Real Estate offices in ancient Israel didn't do very good business.

i. "For God hath expressly, and for divers weighty reasons, forbidden the alienation of lands from the tribes and families to which they were allotted, Leviticus 25:15, 25:23, 25:25; Numbers 36:7; Ezekiel 46:18." (Poole)

2. (4-7) Ahab pouts before Jezebel.

So Ahab went into his house sullen and displeased because of the word which Naboth the Jezreelite had spoken to him; for he had said, "I will not give you the inheritance of my fathers." And he lay down on his bed, and turned away his face, and would eat no food. But Jezebel his wife

came to him, and said to him, "Why is your spirit so sullen that you eat no food?" He said to her, "Because I spoke to Naboth the Jezreelite, and said to him, 'Give me your vineyard for money; or else, if it pleases you, I will give you *another* vineyard for it.' And he answered, 'I will not give you my vineyard.'" Then Jezebel his wife said to him, "You now exercise authority over Israel! Arise, eat food, and let your heart be cheerful; I will give you the vineyard of Naboth the Jezreelite."

a. **Ahab went into his house sullen and displeased**: This seemed entirely characteristic of Ahab. He seemed to be a spineless, pouting man who reacted this way when he met any kind of adversity.

i. "So the scene is a vivid picture of peevish Ahab turning his face to the wall and refusing to eat. He was like a sulking child who could not get his own way." (Dilday)

ii. "Poor soul! He was lord over ten-twelfths of the land, and became miserable because he could not get a poor man's vineyard added to all that he possessed!" (Clarke)

b. **You now exercise authority over Israel… I will give you the vineyard of Naboth**: Jezebel's manner of speech revealed who really exercised **authority** in the palace of Israel.

i. "Alas, was it not *she* that governed it really, with more daring ungodliness than Ahab, her puppet husband?" (Knapp)

3. (8-14) Jezebel plots and orders the murder of Naboth.

And she wrote letters in Ahab's name, sealed *them* with his seal, and sent the letters to the elders and the nobles who *were* dwelling in the city with Naboth. She wrote in the letters, saying, Proclaim a fast, and seat Naboth with high honor among the people; and seat two men, scoundrels, before him to bear witness against him, saying, "You have blasphemed God and the king." *Then* take him out, and stone him, that he may die. So the men of his city, the elders and nobles who were inhabitants of his city, did as Jezebel had sent to them, as it *was* written in the letters which she had sent to them. They proclaimed a fast, and seated Naboth with high honor among the people. And two men, scoundrels, came in and sat before him; and the scoundrels witnessed against him, against Naboth, in the presence of the people, saying, "Naboth has blasphemed God and the king!" Then they took him outside the city and stoned him with stones, so that he died. Then they sent to Jezebel, saying, "Naboth has been stoned and is dead."

a. **She wrote letters in Ahab's name, sealed them with his seal, and sent the letters to the elders and the nobles**: This shows that Ahab was in agreement with what Jezebel did and had to know *something* of her plot.

i. "She involved Ahab by the use of his seal on the directives to the local magistrates. The use of the king's royal, dynastic, administrative or even personal seal to gain his authority would require Ahab's collusion." (Wiseman)

ii. Alexander Maclaren noted three types of dangerous characters in this chapter: (1) Ahab, who was wicked and weak. (2) Jezebel, who was wicked and strong. (3) The Elders of Jezreel, who were wicked and subservient.

b. **Proclaim a fast**: The idea was that some evil or calamity came upon Israel, and a scapegoat had to be found for the evil. Jezebel intended that Naboth be revealed as the scapegoat.

c. **Seat Naboth with high honor among the people**: This was a treacherous plan; first, to set Naboth in a high place of **honor**, and then to destroy him with lies from the mouths of **scoundrels**.

d. **Naboth has blasphemed God and the king**: Jesus was charged with similar crimes, accused of offending both God and Caesar. Naboth, just like Jesus, was completely innocent of such accusations and was murdered without cause. The stoning of Naboth over a piece of land for a vegetable garden shows the brutal and amoral character of Jezebel and Ahab.

i. 2 Kings 9:26 indicates that the crime was even worse than this, connecting the murder of Naboth with the *blood of his sons*. It is likely that the entire family of Naboth was murdered, so no heirs were left to claim his property.

4. (15-16) Ahab takes possession of Naboth's land.

And it came to pass, when Jezebel heard that Naboth had been stoned and was dead, that Jezebel said to Ahab, "Arise, take possession of the vineyard of Naboth the Jezreelite, which he refused to give you for money; for Naboth is not alive, but dead." So it was, when Ahab heard that Naboth was dead, that Ahab got up and went down to take possession of the vineyard of Naboth the Jezreelite.

a. **Ahab got up and went down to take possession of the vineyard of Naboth**: This added evil to evil. Even with Naboth dead, the land did not belong to Ahab or the royal house of Israel. It belonged to the heirs or family of Naboth. Ahab probably claimed the land as a royal right because the crown seized the land of any executed criminal.

i. Although, "Some say that Ahab was his next kinsman, his sons being dead; which they judge more likely, because his land was next to the king's" (Poole). "Hence some make Naboth to have been Ahab's uncle; but that is uncertain" (Trapp).

B. Elijah confronts Ahab.

1. (17-24) God pronounces judgment upon Ahab.

Then the word of the LORD came to Elijah the Tishbite, saying, "Arise, go down to meet Ahab king of Israel, who *lives* in Samaria. There *he is,* in the vineyard of Naboth, where he has gone down to take possession of it. You shall speak to him, saying, 'Thus says the LORD: "Have you murdered and also taken possession?"' And you shall speak to him, saying, 'Thus says the LORD: "In the place where dogs licked the blood of Naboth, dogs shall lick your blood, even yours."'" So Ahab said to Elijah, "Have you found me, O my enemy?" And he answered, "I have found *you,* because you have sold yourself to do evil in the sight of the LORD: 'Behold, I will bring calamity on you. I will take away your posterity, and will cut off from Ahab every male in Israel, both bond and free. I will make your house like the house of Jeroboam the son of Nebat, and like the house of Baasha the son of Ahijah, because of the provocation with which you have provoked *Me* to anger, and made Israel sin.' And concerning Jezebel the LORD also spoke, saying, 'The dogs shall eat Jezebel by the wall of Jezreel.' The dogs shall eat whoever belongs to Ahab and dies in the city, and the birds of the air shall eat whoever dies in the field."

a. **Arise, go down to meet Ahab**: Ahab ran out to get his new toy (the land gained by betrayal, lies, and murder), and instead he ran into the prophet of God.

b. **Have you murdered and also taken possession**: Elijah did what few other men had the courage to do – confront this wicked, brutal, and amoral king and queen of Israel. He pointedly charged them with the two crimes of both murder and theft of Naboth's land.

i. We notice that Elijah confronted Ahab (**you murdered**) over the sin of Jezebel and her wicked associates. God clearly held Ahab responsible for this sin as *husband*, as *king*, and as *beneficiary* of this crime.

ii. "This is added to show that temptations to sin are no excuse to the sinner." (Poole)

c. **In the place where dogs licked the blood of Naboth, dogs shall lick your blood, even yours**: This was a strong and startling prophecy. It was not fulfilled, because Ahab died in *Samaria* and the dogs licked his blood *there* (1 Kings 22:38), instead of in Jezreel where Naboth was murdered.

i. This unfulfilled prophecy has needlessly troubled some. Various explanations have been made, including the ideas that Elijah meant a general area and not a specific place, or that there were pools or streams that carried the blood from Ahab's chariot to the waters of Jezreel, or that this was fulfilled in the blood that ran in the veins of Ahab's son Joram

(2 Kings 9:25). A far better explanation is found in the fact that because of Ahab's sorrow and repentance at the end of the chapter, God relented from this judgment and instead brought it upon Ahab's son (in 2 Kings 9:24-26) as the LORD said He would in 1 Kings 21:29.

ii. "And see how literally the prediction concerning *his son* was fulfilled, see 2 Kings 9:25, where we find that the body of Jehoram his son, just then slain by an arrow that had passed through his heart, was thrown *into the portion of the field of Naboth the Jezreelite*; and there, doubtless, the dogs licked his blood, if they did not even devour his body." (Clarke)

d. **Have you found me, O my enemy**: "Though the king knew it not, Elijah was his best friend; Jezebel his direst foe." (Meyer)

i. "To the widow of Zarephath Elijah was an angel of light; whilst to Ahab he was an enemy... What you are, determines whether Elijah will be your friend or your enemy." (Meyer)

e. **You have sold yourself to do evil in the sight of the LORD**: "See a similar form of speech, Romans 7:14. Thou hast totally abandoned thyself to the service of sin. Satan is become thy *absolute master*, and thou his *undivided slave*." (Clarke)

f. **I will take away your posterity, and cut off from Ahab every male in Israel**: This was a severe judgment against anyone, in particular against a king. A king's legacy was in his **posterity** succeeding him on the throne, and here God announced an end to the dynasty of Omri (Ahab's father). His dynasty would come to a dead-end, just like the dynasties of **Jeroboam** and **Baasha**.

i. "Ahab never possessed the vineyard of Naboth. He held it, but that very fact became to him a torment. However fine the vintage, for him the grapes were acrid, poisonous... That which is gained by fraud is never possessed." (Morgan)

g. **The dogs shall eat Jezebel by the wall of Jezreel**: Though the prophecy of judgment was focused against Ahab, it did not forget Jezebel. Her end would be both horrible and disgraceful.

2. (25-26) Ahab's great wickedness.

But there was no one like Ahab who sold himself to do wickedness in the sight of the LORD, because Jezebel his wife stirred him up. And he behaved very abominably in following idols, according to all *that* the Amorites had done, whom the LORD had cast out before the children of Israel.

a. **There was no one like Ahab who sold himself to do wickedness in the sight of the LORD, because Jezebel his wife stirred him up**: Ahab's sin was multiplied not only because of the sin itself, but because by his permission, **his wife stirred him up** to do it.

i. This reminds us of what God said to Adam in pronouncing the curse after the sin in the Garden of Eden: *Because you have heeded the voice of your wife* (Genesis 3:17). Apparently, God holds husbands who follow their wives into sin to a special accountability.

b. **According to all that the Amorites had done, whom the LORD had cast out**: In likening the sin of Ahab to the sin of the **Amorites**, God prepared the ground for the future eviction of Israel from the Promised Land. As the **Amorites** were cast out of Canaan for their continued idolatry and rejection of God, so would the northern kingdom of Israel be cast out.

3. (27-29) Ahab humbles himself and God relents from judgment in his life.

So it was, when Ahab heard those words, that he tore his clothes and put sackcloth on his body, and fasted and lay in sackcloth, and went about mourning. And the word of the LORD came to Elijah the Tishbite, saying, "See how Ahab has humbled himself before Me? Because he has humbled himself before Me, I will not bring the calamity in his days. In the days of his son I will bring the calamity on his house."

a. **When Ahab heard those words, that he tore his clothes and put sackcloth on his body**: For all his wickedness, Ahab received this prophecy of judgment exactly as he should have. He understood that the prophecy of judgment was in fact an invitation to repent, humble one's self, and to seek God for mercy.

i. "But this humiliation or repentance of Ahab's was only external and superficial, arising from the terror of God's judgments; and not sincere and serious, proceeding from the love of God, or a true sense of his sin, or a solemn purpose of amendment of his life, as appears, because all the particulars of his repentance here, are external and ritual only; nor is there the least intimation of any one sign or fruit of his true repentance, as that he restored Naboth's land, or reproved his infamous wife; but in the very next chapter you find him returning to his former vomit." (Poole)

ii. Three years later, Ahab was dead under God's judgment. "I will recompense his temporary repentance with a temporary deliverance." (Trapp)

b. **Because he has humbled himself before Me, I will not bring the calamity in his days**: God honored Ahab's initiative. This shows the power of both prayer and humble repentance. If Ahab *did not* humble himself in this way, then the judgment would have come in his own day. This shows that God gave the prophecy of judgment as an invitation to repentance, and God opened the door of mercy when Ahab properly responded to that invitation.

i. There is no record of Jezebel's humility or repentance; therefore, we can expect that God's judgment will come upon her *exactly* as He first announced.

ii. "The *penitent* heart ever meets the *merciful* eye of God; repentance is highly esteemed by the Father of compassion, even where it is comparatively shallow and short-lived." (Clarke)

iii. This shows us the character of God's mercy: *it is given to the undeserving.* By nature, the innocent does not *need* mercy. Ahab was a great sinner, but he won great mercy (in this life) through humble repentance. The worst sinner should not disqualify himself from receiving God's mercy, if that sinner should only approach God in humble repentance.

1 Kings 22 - The Death of Ahab

A. God foretells Ahab's doom.

1. (1-4) Ahab sets his eyes upon Ramoth-Gilead.

Now three years passed without war between Syria and Israel. Then it came to pass, in the third year, that Jehoshaphat the king of Judah went down to *visit* the king of Israel. And the king of Israel said to his servants, "Do you know that Ramoth in Gilead *is* ours, but we hesitate to take it out of the hand of the king of Syria?" So he said to Jehoshaphat, "Will you go with me to fight at Ramoth Gilead?" Jehoshaphat said to the king of Israel, "I *am* as you *are,* my people as your people, my horses as your horses."

> a. **Do you know that Ramoth in Gilead is ours, but we hesitate to take it out of the hand of the king of Syria**: Previously, the King of Syria promised to return certain cities to Israel (1 Kings 20:34) in exchange for leniency after defeat in battle. Apparently, this was a city that Ben-Hadad never returned to Israel and it was in a strategically important location.

> b. **Will you go with me to fight at Ramoth Gilead**: King Ahab of Israel asked King Jehoshaphat of Judah to help him in this dispute against Syria. This made some sense, because Ramoth-Gilead was only 40 miles from Jerusalem.

2. (5-9) Jehoshaphat proposes that they seek God in the matter.

Also Jehoshaphat said to the king of Israel, "Please inquire for the word of the LORD today." Then the king of Israel gathered the prophets together, about four hundred men, and said to them, "Shall I go against Ramoth Gilead to fight, or shall I refrain?" So they said, "Go up, for the Lord will deliver *it* into the hand of the king." And Jehoshaphat said, "*Is there* not still a prophet of the LORD here, that we may inquire of Him?" So the king of Israel said to Jehoshaphat, "*There is* still one man, Micaiah the son of Imlah, by whom we may inquire of the LORD; but I hate him, because he does not prophesy good concerning me, but evil." And Jehoshaphat said, "Let not the king say such things!" Then the king of Israel called an officer and said, "Bring Micaiah the son of Imlah quickly!"

a. **Please inquire for the word of the LORD today**: Considering the generally adversarial relationship between Ahab and the prophets of Yahweh, this was a bold request for Jehoshaphat to ask of Ahab. It wasn't surprising that Ahab picked prophets who would tell them what they wanted to hear.

b. **Go up, for the Lord will deliver it into the hand of the king**: When Ahab gathered the prophets, they were not *faithful* prophets of the LORD. These were prophets happy to please their kings, and to tell them what they wanted to hear. Jehoshaphat still wanted to hear from a prophet of Yahweh, the LORD (**Is there not still a prophet of the LORD here, that we may inquire of Him?**).

c. **I hate him, because he does not prophesy good concerning me, but evil**: Ahab hated the messenger because of the message. His real conflict was with God, but he focused his hatred against the prophet Micaiah. Yet he was willing to listen to the King of Judah when he advised that Ahab *should* listen to the Prophet Micaiah.

3. (10-12) An object lesson from the unfaithful prophets.

The king of Israel and Jehoshaphat the king of Judah, having put on *their* robes, sat each on his throne, at a threshing floor at the entrance of the gate of Samaria; and all the prophets prophesied before them. Now Zedekiah the son of Chenaanah had made horns of iron for himself; and he said, "Thus says the LORD: 'With these you shall gore the Syrians until they are destroyed.'" And all the prophets prophesied so, saying, "Go up to Ramoth Gilead and prosper, for the LORD will deliver *it* into the king's hand."

a. **Sat each on his throne, at a threshing floor at the entrance of the gate of Samaria**: This illustrates the ancient custom of holding court and making decisions at the gates of the city. There were even thrones for high officials to sit on at the gates of the city of Samaria.

b. **Thus says the LORD**: These unfaithful prophets (such as **Zedekiah**) prophesied in the name of the LORD, but they did not prophesy truthfully. Many commentators believe these prophets were *pagan* prophets, perhaps representatives of Asherah or other pagan gods or goddesses. Yet they clearly prophesied in the name of **the LORD**. It is best to regard these *not as pagan prophets*, but unfaithful prophets to the true God.

   i. Perhaps these were true followers of Yahweh who were seduced by Ahab's sincere but shallow repentance three years before (1 Kings 21:27-29). After that, they began to align with Ahab uncritically. Three years later, they were willing to prophesy lies to Ahab if that was what he wanted to hear.

c. **With these you shall gore the Syrians until they are destroyed**: Zedekiah used a familiar tool of ancient prophets – the object lesson. He used **horns of iron** to illustrate the thrust of two powerful forces, armies that would defeat the Syrians. Zedekiah had the agreement of 400 other prophets (**all the prophets prophesied so**).

> i. This must have been a vivid and entertaining presentation. We can be certain that every eye was on Zedekiah when he used the **horns of iron** to powerfully illustrate the point. It was certainly persuasive to have 400 prophets speak in agreement on one issue. No matter how powerful and persuasive the presentation, *their message was unfaithful.*

4. (13-16) The prophecy of Micaiah, the faithful prophet.

Then the messenger who had gone to call Micaiah spoke to him, saying, "Now listen, the words of the prophets with one accord encourage the king. Please, let your word be like the word of one of them, and speak encouragement." And Micaiah said, "*As* the LORD lives, whatever the LORD says to me, that I will speak." Then he came to the king; and the king said to him, "Micaiah, shall we go to war against Ramoth Gilead, or shall we refrain?" And he answered him, "Go and prosper, for the LORD will deliver *it* into the hand of the king!" So the king said to him, "How many times shall I make you swear that you tell me nothing but the truth in the name of the LORD?"

a. **As the LORD lives, whatever the LORD says to me, that I will speak**: The assistants of King Ahab tried to persuade Micaiah to speak in agreement with the 400 other prophets. Micaiah assured him that he would simply repeat what God said to him.

> i. This was a dramatic scene. Micaiah was brought out from prison (1 Kings 22:26 indicates that he came from prison). We see a prophet in rags and chains stand before two kings, ready to speak on behalf of the LORD.
>
> ii. "This might have daunted the good prophet, but that he had lately seen the Lord sitting upon His throne with all the host of heaven standing by Him, and hence he so boldly looked in the face these two kings in their majesty; for he beheld them as so many mice." (Trapp)

b. **Go and prosper, for the LORD will deliver it into the hand of the king**: When Micaiah said this, his tone was probably mocking and sarcastic. He said similar *words* to the 400 unfaithful prophets, but delivered a completely different *message.*

c. **How many times shall I make you swear that you tell me nothing but the truth in the name of the LORD**: King Ahab recognized the mocking tone of Micaiah's prophecy and knew it contradicted the message of the 400 prophets. He demanded that Micaiah tell **nothing but the truth** – which Ahab believed and hoped was the message of the 400 other prophets.

5. (17-18) Micaiah speaks the true prophecy from the LORD.

Then he said, "I saw all Israel scattered on the mountains, as sheep that have no shepherd. And the LORD said, 'These have no master. Let each return to his house in peace.'" And the king of Israel said to Jehoshaphat, "Did I not tell you he would not prophesy good concerning me, but evil?"

a. **I saw all Israel scattered on the mountains, as sheep that have no shepherd**: Micaiah was challenged to tell the truth, and now he changed his tone from mocking to serious. He said that not only would Israel be defeated, but also that their leader (**shepherd**) would perish.

b. **Did I not tell you he would not prophesy good concerning me, but evil**: King Ahab said that he wanted the truth - but he couldn't handle the truth. What he didn't consider was that though Micaiah prophesied **evil** towards Ahab, he prophesied *truth*.

i. "Ahab knew in his heart that Micaiah would not fear or flatter him, but only declare the word of Jehovah. This he construed into personal hatred... Hatred of the messenger of God is clear evidence of willful wickedness." (Morgan)

6. (19-23) Micaiah reveals the inspiration behind the 400 prophets.

Then *Micaiah* said, "Therefore hear the word of the LORD: I saw the LORD sitting on His throne, and all the host of heaven standing by, on His right hand and on His left. And the LORD said, 'Who will persuade Ahab to go up, that he may fall at Ramoth Gilead?' So one spoke in this manner, and another spoke in that manner. Then a spirit came forward and stood before the LORD, and said, 'I will persuade him.' The LORD said to him, 'In what way?' So he said, 'I will go out and be a lying spirit in the mouth of all his prophets.' And the LORD said, 'You shall persuade *him,* and also prevail. Go out and do so.' Therefore look! The LORD has put a lying spirit in the mouth of all these prophets of yours, and the LORD has declared disaster against you."

a. **I saw the LORD sitting on His throne, and all the host of heaven standing by**: King Ahab and others at the court found it hard to explain how one prophet could be right and 400 prophets could be wrong. Here, Micaiah explained the message of the 400 prophets. It is possible that this was just a parable, but it is more likely that Micaiah had an accurate prophetic glimpse into the heavenly drama behind these events.

b. **On His right hand and on His left**: Since the **right hand** was the place of favor, this may indicate that God spoke to the *combined* **host of heaven**, both faithful and fallen angelic beings.

i. Some people forget that Satan and his fellow fallen angels have access to heaven (Job 1:6, Revelation 12:10). There is a well-intentioned but mistaken teaching that *God can allow no evil in His presence,* meaning that

Satan and other fallen angels could not be in His presence. These passages show that God *can* allow evil in His presence, though He can have no *fellowship* with evil and one day all evil will be removed from His presence (Revelation 20:14-15).

c. **Who will persuade Ahab to go up, that he may fall at Ramoth Gilead**: God wanted to bring judgment against Ahab, so He asked this group of **the host of heaven** for a volunteer to lead Ahab into battle.

d. **I will go out and be a lying spirit in the mouth of all his prophets**: Apparently, one of the *fallen* angels volunteered for this task. Since Ahab wanted to be deceived, God would give him what He wanted, using a willing fallen angel who worked through willing unfaithful prophets.

i. "It is rather a personified spirit of prophecy (Zechariah 13:2; 1 John 4:6), for even the false prophets may be governed by supernatural or spiritual forces rather than merely human reason. It represents the power of a lie in the mouth of someone opposed to the truth and speaking for his own ends." (Wiseman)

7. (24-28) The reaction of the false prophets and Ahab.

Now Zedekiah the son of Chenaanah went near and struck Micaiah on the cheek, and said, "Which way did the spirit from the LORD go from me to speak to you?" And Micaiah said, "Indeed, you shall see on that day when you go into an inner chamber to hide!" So the king of Israel said, "Take Micaiah, and return him to Amon the governor of the city and to Joash the king's son; and say, 'Thus says the king: "Put this *fellow* in prison, and feed him with bread of affliction and water of affliction, until I come in peace."'" But Micaiah said, "If you ever return in peace, the LORD has not spoken by me." And he said, "Take heed, all you people!"

a. **Now Zedekiah the son of Chenaanah went near and struck Micaiah**: Zedekiah responded the way many do when they are defeated in argument - he responded with violence.

b. **Put this fellow in prison**: King Ahab responded the way many tyrants do when they are confronted with the truth. Ahab wanted Micaiah imprisoned and deprived (**feed him with the bread of affliction and water of affliction**).

i. **Take Micaiah, and return him** tells us that they took Micaiah from the prison to speak to these kings.

ii. "The phrase '*bread of affliction and water of affliction*' may be translated 'bread and water of scant measure.'" (Dilday)

c. **If you ever return in peace, the LORD has not spoken by me**: The prophet Micaiah made one final and ultimate appeal. He was willing to be judged by whether his prophecy came to pass or not.

B. Ahab dies in battle.

1. (29-30) Jehoshaphat and Ahab go into battle.

So the king of Israel and Jehoshaphat the king of Judah went up to Ramoth Gilead. And the king of Israel said to Jehoshaphat, "I will disguise myself and go into battle; but you put on your robes." So the king of Israel disguised himself and went into battle.

> a. **So the king of Israel and Jehoshaphat the king of Judah went up to Ramoth Gilead**: It is easy to understand why King Ahab of Israel went to this battle; he didn't want to believe that Micaiah's prophecy was true and wanted to courageously oppose it. It is less easy to understand why King Jehoshaphat of Judah went to this battle with Ahab. He should have believed the prophecy of Micaiah and known that the battle would end in disaster and the death of at least Ahab.

> > i. It may be that Jehoshaphat had a *fatalistic* attitude towards the will of God, figuring that if it all was God's will, then there was nothing he or anyone else could do about it.

> b. **I will disguise myself and go into battle; but you put on your robes**: Going into the battle, Ahab did not want to be identified as a king and therefore be a special target. He thought this would help protect him against Micaiah's prophecy of doom. It is more difficult to explain why Jehoshaphat agreed to go into the battle as the only clearly identified king. Perhaps he was either not very smart or he had very great faith.

2. (31-36) Jehoshaphat is saved and Ahab dies in battle.

Now the king of Syria had commanded the thirty-two captains of his chariots, saying, "Fight with no one small or great, but only with the king of Israel." So it was, when the captains of the chariots saw Jehoshaphat, that they said, "Surely it *is* the king of Israel!" Therefore they turned aside to fight against him, and Jehoshaphat cried out. And it happened, when the captains of the chariots saw that it *was* not the king of Israel, that they turned back from pursuing him. Now a *certain* man drew a bow at random, and struck the king of Israel between the joints of his armor. So he said to the driver of his chariot, "Turn around and take me out of the battle, for I am wounded." The battle increased that day; and the king was propped up in his chariot, facing the Syrians, and died at evening. The blood ran out from the wound onto the floor of the chariot. Then, as the sun was going down, a shout went throughout the army, saying, "Every man to his city, and every man to his own country!"

> a. **Fight with no one small or great, but only with the king of Israel**: Ahab's previous mercy to Ben-Hadad did not win any lasting favor with the rulers

of Syria. This strategy of the Syrian army made Ahab's counter-strategy of disguising himself in battle seem very wise.

> i. "Thus doth the unthankful infidel repay the mercy of his late victory… but God had a holy hand in it." (Trapp)

b. **Jehoshaphat cried out**: Finding himself as the only identifiable king in the battle, Jehoshaphat found himself quickly in danger. He **cried out** unto the LORD and was rescued when **they turned back from pursuing him**.

> i. 2 Chronicles 18:31 makes it clear that the LORD heard Jehoshaphat's cry and rescued him.

> ii. After the close escape at Ramoth Gilead, Jehoshaphat rededicated himself to the spiritual reform of Judah: *he went out again among the people from Beersheba to the mountains of Ephraim, and brought them back to the LORD God of their fathers* (2 Chronicles 19:4).

c. **Now a certain man drew a bow at random, and struck the king of Israel**: This seemed to be pure chance. It was a **certain man**, and he pulled his **bow at random** - but it struck as if it were a sin-seeking missile. God orchestrated the unintended actions of man to result in an exercise of His judgment.

> i. "And now what joy could Ahab's black soul, ready to depart, have of his ivory house? Who had not rather be a Micaiah in the jail than Ahab in the chariot? Wicked men have the advantage of the way, godly men of the end." (Trapp)

d. **The king was propped up in his chariot, facing the Syrians, and died at evening**: Ahab faced the end of his life bravely, dying **propped up in his chariot** to inspire his troops. When his death became known, the battle was over.

> i. "It appears that the Israelites and Jews maintained the fight the whole of the day; but when at evening the king died, and this was known, there was a proclamation made, probably with the consent of both Syrians and Israelites, that the war was over." (Clarke)

3. (37-40) God's word to Ahab is fulfilled.

So the king died, and was brought to Samaria. And they buried the king in Samaria. Then *someone* washed the chariot at a pool in Samaria, and the dogs licked up his blood while the harlots bathed, according to the word of the LORD which He had spoken. Now the rest of the acts of Ahab, and all that he did, the ivory house which he built and all the cities that he built, *are* they not written in the book of the chronicles of the kings of Israel? So Ahab rested with his fathers. Then Ahaziah his son reigned in his place.

a. **So the king died**: The word through the prophet Micaiah proved true. King Ahab never returned to Samaria or Israel in peace.

b. **The dogs licked up his blood while the harlots bathed**: This was an *almost* fulfillment of God's word through Elijah in 1 Kings 21:19, where Elijah prophesied that dogs would lick the blood of Ahab. This proved true, but not in the *place* Elijah said it would happen. God relented from His original judgment against Ahab announced in 1 Kings 21, but because of Ahab's false repentance and continued sin, a very similar judgment came upon him.

c. **According to the word of the LORD which He had spoken**: There was another prophecy fulfilled in the death of Ahab. It was the word from the anonymous prophet of 1 Kings 20:42, that Ahab spared Ben-Hadad's life at the expense of his own.

d. **The ivory house which he built and all the cities that he built**: By material standards, the reign of Ahab was a success. He was generally militarily successful and enjoyed a generally prosperous economy. Yet spiritually his reign was a disaster, one of the worst ever for Israel.

C. The reigns of Jehoshaphat and Ahaziah.

1. (41-50) Summary of the reign of Jehoshaphat.

Jehoshaphat the son of Asa had become king over Judah in the fourth year of Ahab king of Israel. Jehoshaphat *was* thirty-five years old when he became king, and he reigned twenty-five years in Jerusalem. His mother's name *was* Azubah the daughter of Shilhi. And he walked in all the ways of his father Asa. He did not turn aside from them, doing *what was* right in the eyes of the LORD. Nevertheless the high places were not taken away, *for* the people offered sacrifices and burned incense on the high places. Also Jehoshaphat made peace with the king of Israel. Now the rest of the acts of Jehoshaphat, the might that he showed, and how he made war, *are* they not written in the book of the chronicles of the kings of Judah? And the rest of the perverted persons, who remained in the days of his father Asa, he banished from the land. *There was* then no king in Edom, only a deputy of the king. Jehoshaphat made merchant ships to go to Ophir for gold; but they never sailed, for the ships were wrecked at Ezion Geber. Then Ahaziah the son of Ahab said to Jehoshaphat, "Let my servants go with your servants in the ships." But Jehoshaphat would not. And Jehoshaphat rested with his fathers, and was buried with his fathers in the City of David his father. Then Jehoram his son reigned in his place.

a. **Jehoshaphat the son of Asa**: Asa was a good king and Jehoshaphat his son followed in his footsteps and did **what was right in the eyes of the LORD**.

i. The writer of 1 Kings actually summarized many of the remarkable accomplishments of Jehoshaphat, who was one of the better kings of Judah. From 2 Chronicles we learn many of Jehoshaphat's other accomplishments.

• He sent teachers of God's Word out to his entire kingdom (2 Chronicles 17:7-10). "By this little band of princes, Levites and priests, sixteen in all, Jehoshaphat did more toward impressing the surrounding nations with a sense of his power than the largest and best-equipped standing army could have secured to him" (Knapp).

• He established a permanent military garrison along the northern frontier (2 Chronicles 17:1-2, 12).

• He trained and equipped a sizeable army (2 Chronicles 17:14-19) that was able to quell a Transjordan invasion (2 Chronicles 20:1-30).

• He placed Edom under Judean control, controlling an important caravan route to the south (2 Kings 3:8-27; 2 Chronicles 20:36).

• God blessed his reign so much that the fear of the LORD came upon neighboring nations so that they did not make war against Jehoshaphat (2 Chronicles 17:10).

• Jehoshaphat was also an able administrator, implementing judicial reforms (2 Chronicles 19:5-11) and religious reforms (2 Chronicles 17:3-9).

• Jehoshaphat was also the king connected to the famous incident when the army of Judah saw a great victory won as the Levites led the battle with praise (2 Chronicles 20:15-23).

b. **Nevertheless the high places were not taken away**: Jehoshaphat did not do *everything* he should have as a king. Yet he reformed Israel even more deeply than Asa did (**the rest of the perverted persons, who remained in the days of his father Asa, he banished from the land**).

i. "In 2 Chronicles 17:6, it is expressly said, that he *did take way the high places*. Allowing that the text is right in 2 Chronicles the two places may be easily recognized. There were *two kinds* of *high places* in the land: 1. Those used for *idolatrous* purposes. 2. Those that were *consecrated to God*, and were used before the temple was built. The former he did take away, the latter he did not." (Clarke)

c. **There was then no king in Edom**: "This note is introduced by the writer to account for Jehoshaphat's building ships at *Ezion-geber*, which was in the *territory* of the *Edomites*, and which showed them to be at that time under the Jewish yoke." (Clarke)

d. **Let my servants go with your servants in the ships**: After a disastrous shipping venture, Jehoshaphat was tempted to make an alliance with Israel, but **Jehoshaphat would not**. This was to his credit. He learned the lesson of not entering a partnership with the ungodly.

i. 2 Chronicles 20:35-37 tells us more about this shipping venture with Israel. It tells us that Jehoshaphat *did* make an alliance with Ahaziah and it ended in disaster. The LORD told Jehoshaphat why: *Because you have allied yourself with Ahaziah, the* LORD *has destroyed your works* (2 Chronicles 20:37). It was *after* this word of the LORD that Jehoshaphat turned down the offer of a continued alliance with King Ahaziah of Israel.

e. **Then Jehoram his son reigned in his place**: Jehoshaphat gave his son Jehoram to Athaliah in marriage, the daughter of Ahab and Jezebel (2 Chronicles 18:1). This was a serious error because the reign of Ahaziah was a spiritual and national disaster for Judah because Jehoram *walked in the ways of the kings of Israel, just as the house of Ahab had done, for he had the daughter of Ahab as a wife* (2 Chronicles 21:6). The ill effects of this were felt even to the next generation, because Ahaziah the son of Jehoram was also a bad king for Judah (2 Chronicles 22:2-4).

2. (51-53) The evil reign of King Ahaziah of Israel, the son of Ahab.

Ahaziah the son of Ahab became king over Israel in Samaria in the seventeenth year of Jehoshaphat king of Judah, and reigned two years over Israel. He did evil in the sight of the LORD, and walked in the way of his father and in the way of his mother and in the way of Jeroboam the son of Nebat, who had made Israel sin; for he served Baal and worshiped him, and provoked the LORD God of Israel to anger, according to all that his father had done.

a. **He reigned two years over Israel**: Ahab reigned 22 years, but his son only reigned two years. Though his repentance was shallow, when Ahab repented after an announcement of judgment in 1 Kings 21, God relented from the immediate judgment and promised to bring judgment in the days of Ahab's son. Ahaziah's short reign was a fulfillment of this prophecy in 1 Kings 21:29.

i. "By comparing this verse with verse 41, it appears that Ahaziah was made king by his father, and reigned in conjunction with him, a year or two before Ahab's death." (Poole)

b. **He did evil in the sight of the LORD, and walked in the way of his father and in the way of his mother and in the way of Jeroboam**: Considering the sinful ways of Jeroboam, Ahab, and Jezebel, there is hardly anything worse that could be said of a king.

i. "It is a dark catalogue of iniquity, yet only what might be expected of the offspring of such a couple as Ahab and Jezebel." (Knapp)

ii. With this, the Book of 1 Kings ends on a low note. It began with the promise of the twilight of Israel's greatest king, David. It ends with the sad reign of one of the most wicked kings over one of the kingdoms coming from the divided tribes of Israel.

1 Kings – Bibliography

Clarke, Adam *The Holy Bible, Containing the Old and New Testaments, with A Commentary and Critical Notes, Volume II – Joshua to Esther* (New York: Eaton and Mains, 1827?)

Cook, F.C. (Editor) *The Bible Commentary, 1 Samuel – Esther* (Grand Rapids, Michigan: Baker Book House, 1974)

Dilday, Russell *Mastering the Old Testament Volume 9: 1, 2 Kings* (Dallas: Word Publishing, 1987)

Ginzberg, Louis *The Legends of the Jews, Volumes 1-7* (Philadelphia: The Jewish Publication Society of America, 1968)

Henry, Matthew *Matthew Henry's Concise Commentary on the Whole Bible* (Chicago: Moody Press, 1950)

Knapp, Christopher *The Kings of Judah and Israel* (New York: Loizeaux Brothers, 1956)

Maclaren, Alexander *Expostions of Holy Scripture, Volume 2* (Grand Rapids, Michigan: Baker Book House, 1984)

Meyer, F.B. *Our Daily Homily* (Westwood, New Jersey: Revell, 1966)

Meyer, F.B. *Elijah: And the Secret of His Power* (Fort Washington, Pennsylvania: Christian Literature Crusade, 1978)

Morgan, G. Campbell *Searchlights from the Word* (New York: Revell, 1926)

Patterson, Richard D. and Austel, Hermann J. "1, 2 Kings" *The Expositor's Bible Commentary, Volume 4* (Grand Rapids, Michigan: Zondervan, 1992)

Payne, David F. *Kingdoms of the Lord* (Grand Rapids, Michigan: Eerdmans, 1981)

Poole, Matthew *A Commentary on the Holy Bible, Volume 1* (London, Banner of Truth Trust, 1968)

Redpath, Alan *The Making of a Man of God* – Studies in the Life of David (Old Tappan, New Jersey: Revell, 1962)

Spurgeon, Charles Haddon *The New Park Street Pulpit, Volumes 1-6* and *The Metropolitan Tabernacle Pulpit, Volumes 7-63* (Pasadena, Texas: Pilgrim Publications, 1990)

Trapp, John *A Commentary on the Old and New Testaments, Volume 1 – Genesis to Second Chronicles* (Eureka, California: Tanski Publications, 1997)

Wiseman, Donald J. *1 and 2 Kings, An Introduction and Commentary* (Leicester, England: Inter-Varsity Press, 1993)

As the years pass I love the work of studying, learning, and teaching the Bible more and more than ever. I'm so grateful that God is faithful to meet me in His Word.

Thanks again to Debbie Pollaccia, my valued partner in so many books over so many years. Debbie, thanks for making another book better.

Because of the wonderful people at Blue Letter Bible, my Bible commentaries was available online in 1996. My first commentary went into print in 1998. After 20 years of using the same cover design, it was time to make a change. Thanks to Brian Procedo for the cover design and all the graphics work.

Most especially, thanks to my wife Inga-Lill. She is my loved and valued partner in life and service to God and His people.

David Guzik's Bible commentary is used and trusted by many thousands of regular users. Pastors, teachers, class leaders, and everyday Christians find his commentary helpful for their own understanding and explanation of the Bible. David and his wife Inga-Lill live in Santa Barbara, California.

You can email David at
david@enduringword.com

For more resources by David Guzik,
go to www.enduringword.com

9 781939 466402